Techniques of Group Psychotherapy

Techniques of Group Psychotherapy

Myron F. Weiner, M.D.

Department of Psychiatry
The University of Texas
Health Science Center at Dallas

American Psychiatric Press, Inc.

1400 K Street, N.W.
Washington, D.C.

Cover design by Sam Haltom
Text design by Tim Clancy and Richard E. Farkas
Typeset by Unicorn Graphics
Printed by R. R. Donnelly & Sons Co.

Library of Congress Cataloging in Publication Data

Weiner, Myron F.
Techniques of group psychotherapy.

Bibliography: p. 259
Includes index.
1. Group psychotherapy. I. Title. [DNLM:
1. Psychotherapy, Group—methods. WM 430 W423t]
RC488.W45 1984 616.89′152 84-16908
ISBN 0-88048-034-3

To Jeanette,
who is teaching me
patience and understanding

Contents

Preface

This is a beginner's text in basic group psychotherapy techniques. But even a beginning text requires the reader to have studied normal human cognitive and psychosexual development and to have a descriptive and psychodynamic knowledge of emotional disorders. Knowledge of coping and defense mechanisms, acquaintance with the concepts of fixation and regression, and primary and secondary gain are essential. So is an appreciation for the role of the unconscious in psychopathology and in the treatment process.

In spite of my own psychodynamic bias, I am heavily influenced by learning and behavior theorists, by interactional theories of psychopathology and psychotherapy, and by the fact that all of us must come to grips with our own finiteness.

In contrast to many other psychodynamic psychotherapists, I do not believe that insight into unconscious mental processes is the best and most efficacious means to treat the majority of emotionally troubled persons. I believe that a person's group therapy experiences should be tailored to fit his or her psychological set. Thus, persons who conceive of symptoms as symptoms can be given direct means to relieve their discomfort, usually through advice, suggestions, and other forms of support. Those who relate their difficulties to interpersonal issues can be treated with a focus on interpersonal relationships, and people who conceive of their problems as intrapsychic can be encouraged to introspect when they have adequate ego strength and environmental support to tolerate that type of probing. The above tripartite frame of reference is incorporated into my classification of psychotherapeutic techniques as repressive, ego-supportive, and evocative.

While it is tempting to view the evocative method as *the* psychodynamic technique, one discovers in practice that ego-supportive and repressive techniques are far more applicable and better tolerated by most patients. However, the latter techniques are applied with an appreciation of psychodynamic factors and in response to specific psychodynamic indications.

I have not tried to be encyclopedic. Instead, I have presented a body of established techniques and suggest when and how they are best applied. My own bias is now toward ego-supportive and repressive techniques, having spent much time attempting to use evocative techniques with patients who had previously been hospitalized or who required psychotropic medication in addition to psychological treatment.

I hope I have provided a useful frame of reference that will enable beginners to make good use of their direct supervision and their case conferences. I hope that advanced students will find food for thought and stimulation to seek answers to the many unanswered questions in group therapy.

Myron F. Weiner, M.D.

Acknowledgments

This book is a labor of love. It has taken more than 14 years to assume its final form, and it is a tribute to my teachers and colleagues in group therapy. My greatest debt is to John Gladfelter, Harold Winer, and Sterling Bell: the first faculty of the Dallas Group Psychotherapy Society's Training Program. I owe much to Juanita Kirby who has sustained that program and my teaching over the many years since she and I were members of the first training group.

The Dallas program was inspired by Manny Schwartz and Asya Kadis. Max Markowitz helped mold us into a cohesive group. I had the privilege of filling in for Asya Kadis as a coauthor of *Practicum of Group Psychotherapy* after her death, and Max Markowitz made himself available to me years later at a time of personal crisis.

The material for this book evolved slowly but gained impetus as I developed the conviction that a broadly based, up-to-date elementary text is badly needed. My wife, Jeanette, encouraged me to take the final plunge, and I assembled the first draft during an intense flurry of activity that culminated in June 1982. The final draft required another year of reflection and interaction with Gary Weiner, who helped unite much disjointed material into a more smoothly flowing whole. Ron

McMillen and Tim Clancy of the American Psychiatric Press helped with the final alterations of structure and content.

As with my last two published works, Jeanette listened to every word as I recited the text while pacing the kitchen floor or sprawled on the living room couch. Thanks, Jeanette. And thanks to you, Lisa Jackson, for pushing my material through the word processor so quickly that we nearly exhausted each other. And Bettye Culwell, whose patient proofing and careful indexing have contributed to the high quality of the finished product. Thanks also to my boss, Ken Altshuler, who allowed me to give reign to my demon.

Myron F. Weiner, M.D.

Techniques of Group Psychotherapy

1

Introduction to Group Psychotherapy

THE GROUP PSYCHOTHERAPIES are important and effective therapeutic modalities for psychotherapists working in varied settings (Meltzoff and Kornreich 1970). Since the founding of the American Group Psychotherapy Association in 1942, the entire field has changed its emphasis, widened its theoretical base, and broadened its applications so much that there are few types of patients and few clinical situations in which some form of group therapy has not been used.

Definition

Group therapies are diverse. Their chief common attributes are the meeting at stated intervals for specified periods of time of one or more designated leaders with three or more designated group members for the purpose of bringing about psychological change in the group members. Three or more group members are needed to establish the types of interaction that give psychotherapy groups their unique character and enable the operation of forces that differ in quality and quantity from individual psychotherapy (Yalom 1975).

Any group interaction can have a positive influence on the

lives of the people involved, and in that sense, any group can be therapeutic. Group psychotherapy, on the other hand, is a deliberate effort to alter the thinking, feelings, and behaviors of the group members. Clinical experience suggests that whether group leaders are untrained or are well-trained mental health professionals, having a designated leader is an essential aspect of a therapeutic group (Weiner 1983c).

Therapy groups are usually composed of people who do not have preexisting emotional ties to each other, but couples may become part of a group of unrelated persons or may join other couples in a group, just as groups of families may be treated. Group therapy may also be used in conjunction with individual therapy. *Combined therapy* is group and individual treatment with the same therapist. *Conjoint therapy* is individual and group therapy by different therapists (Kadis et al. 1974). Combined or conjoint group therapy may be adjunctive to individual therapy (Wong 1983), or may add a separate and equal dimension to therapy (Lipshutz 1957). A *homogeneous group* is a group of persons with the same presenting complaint, diagnosis, or life problem; a *heterogeneous group* has members with different presenting complaints, diagnoses, or life problems. *Closed groups* are closed to new members. *Open groups* replace members as they drop out or graduate.

Applications of Group Therapy

Group therapy can be the sole form of treatment or the primary treatment for many types of life problems and emotional disorders. Unfortunately, group therapy is not the answer to limited numbers of professional personnel or the limited financial resources of persons seeking help. Group therapy does not enable therapists to see more patients than individual therapy. Groups are usually less efficient than individual therapies that can be tailored to meet the needs of individual patients. Because groups are usually less efficient and because group members need individual sessions from time to time, the overall cost of group therapy to patients in open-ended, once-a-week groups is probably the same as once-a-week individual psychotherapy. However, Budman et al. (1981) report that short-term group therapy (16 sessions) is effective for persons who have had a previous positive experience with psychotherapy.

Persons with profound ego impairment can be treated in hospital groups (Kibel 1981), day hospital groups (Henisz 1984), and in post-hospital groups (Scher 1973). Persons with mild to moderate neurotic disorders and personality disorders can be treated in insight-oriented groups if they are psychologically minded (Weiner 1983b) or cognitive-behavioral groups if they are not (Beck et al. 1979).

Group therapy is not indicated as the sole treatment for persons who are acutely or severely psychotic, severely depressed, or acutely suicidal or homicidal, but may be helpful as part of an overall institutional treatment program in combination with drugs and milieu therapy. Ongoing heterogeneous groups are not suitable for treating acute situational crises, but crisis groups (Donovan et al. 1981) help people cope with a variety of life crises and traumas, including divorce (Granvold and Welch 1979) and physical violence, including rape (Sadock 1983).

Group therapy is now used in general hospitals to aid rehabilitation after myocardial infarction (Rahe et al. 1979), to deal with the psychological impact of terminal illness (Yalom and Greaves 1977), and to help staff cope with the stress of treating the seriously ill (Weiner and Caldwell 1981, 1983). Grobman (1981) has assembled a selected bibliography that indicates the many settings in which groups are used.

The rational use of group therapy requires a general knowledge of the advantages and disadvantages of groups in relation to other therapies.

Advantages

Groups have the advantage over individual therapies in that more people can be reached simultaneously by a single therapist. For techniques that rely heavily on active teaching, groups are an ideal medium for imparting the material to be learned and for its reinforcement through group discussion and individual or shared homework. Group therapists also have the advantage of viewing and interacting with patients in a broad interactional matrix instead of the limited interpersonal context of individual sessions (Wolf and Schwartz 1959).

Groups provide a good medium for learning and practicing social skills. Those skills can be taught in a positive, nondemeaning way by fellow group members, and can be practiced in the protected environment of the group until they are sufficiently well learned to be used in ordinary social relationships. The social risk of making social blunders is minimal, and the group applauds such efforts, even if inept or miscarried at first. Furthermore, the group supports the development of more adaptive behaviors through the period of time when important others in members' lives are still puzzled or disturbed by their new behaviors, and helps sustain positive changes even when temporarily opposed by members' friends or families.

Real friendships develop, based on knowing people as they really are, without social facade. The fact that people who really know each other still want to be friends is a strong boost to self-esteem. As members respond more healthily to others in a group, their positive behavior is reinforced and the process is kept in motion.

Because group therapy is an active medium in which people come and go and make active attempts to change their lives, there is a greater push to action in the group and outside of the group. Many therapists introduce the idea of a group to their patients as a transition from individual therapy to being on one's own, analogous to an adolescent's shift from primary dependency on parents to dependence on peers. Groups help counter the fantasy that change comes solely through reflective insight; they push members toward facing and acting on the real issues in their lives. In addition, they offer a slice of life. As members try out their insights in the group, they are helped to extinguish maladaptive behaviors and understand that others' needs must be considered before one acts.

Groups urging their members toward activity differ from individual therapists pushing their patients. Peer pressure is less infantilizing and less stimulating of negativistic regression because it is less transference-contaminated than individual patient-therapist relationships.

Certain ego-syntonic attitudes or defenses that do not emerge in one-to-one therapy manifest quickly in the group setting, where multiple interactions give a broader view of each group member's varied interpersonal reactions. Narcissism, clinging, defensive isolation, and many other character attributes, coping mechanisms, and defenses manifest in the interpersonal network of the group and become available for comment and therapeutic work (Wong 1980).

Commonly shared group experiences provide grist for the therapeutic mill. In addition to each member's behavior being available for comment, therapists can also inquire about reactions to their level of activity in therapy.

Groups focusing on the current interactions between their members prevent lengthy rumination about past experiences and rationalization of behavior by blaming early traumas. Groups can therefore be useful with people who seek to recapture their past to avoid taking action in the here and now. And, because group members react to and deal with real events that occur in the lives of group members and in the life of the group, therapy groups can help keep their members in reality and out of the fantasy whose strong regressive pull often works against therapy. Trying out new behaviors in the group is a type of reality testing, as is asking other group members their evaluation of each member's reactions to certain events. The process involves consensual validation and a growing awareness that there is no correct way to react to or deal with emotions or life events, but there are many constructive alternatives.

The opportunity for multiple partial identifications is an important aspect of group psychotherapy. For many people, identification with the therapist is the cornerstone of therapy (Weiner 1982b). Although group therapists are more exposed than individual psychotherapists because of their multiple interactions in the group, they are not highly exposed, and group members can still idealize them enough to reinforce their own sense of inadequacy. There is less tendency to over-idealize other group members, and identifications with them do not carry the intense superego-driven push toward perfection. As members accept the inevitable human flaws of the others, they become more self-accepting and can see clearly that their expectations of others are not the same as their self-expectations, highlighting the irrational operations of the superego.

Constructive identification with other group members may be easier than constructive identification with the leader for still another reason: the limitations imposed by the personality of the leader. Bandura (1971) has argued that the passive, reflective therapist is a poor identification model on which to build personality attributes of active coping. An outgoing, flamboyant leader with many intellectual interests may be a difficult identification model for an introverted group member without a wide educational background. Identification with another member who is successful in many ways, but whose personality attributes are not so different, may be easier, and in the long run, more constructive.

Groups also offer opportunities in relation to transference. Groups can diminish the transference resistance of overvaluing therapists that leads to patients attempting to please their therapists or feeling unable to please them. That transference resistance may stem from projection of the ego ideal or punitive superego introjects onto the therapist, and can immobilize patients in one-to-one psychotherapy. Because group members' communications to each other less often stimulate transferences, they are frequently more easily understood and accepted (Grunebaum and Kates 1977). Comments about maladaptive behaviors are seen less as condemnations when voiced by peers than by therapists, who are invested with parental authority and omniscience.

There is also the opportunity to work through in relation to other group members a greater number of transferences than would be available were the therapist the only transference object.

A final advantage of groups is their ability to help therapists deal with countertransferences. Mature groups can point out therapists' inappropriate countertransference reactions, thereby enabling therapists to reflect on the meaning of their own behavior, instead of stimulating or reinforcing pathological interactions between themselves and members of the group. Thus, the group as a whole can serve as an adjunct to (but not a replacement for) the therapist's ego.

Disadvantages

The greatest disadvantage of groups is that the therapist's attention is divided. Subtleties of the thought and behavior of group members can be readily missed, as can severe decompensations and acting out. It is difficult to focus on intrapsychic processes in a group that meets once a week, and it is also difficult to stay aware of each patient's level of coping and adaptation.

While groups are a good arena for learning and practicing social skills, the norms of a particular group may lead to acting out impulses instead of self-understanding, or intellectualization instead of constructive action. On entering a group, some persons are terrified by the expressiveness of the more experienced group members and withdraw from the group in fear that they are being pushed into an orgy or a lynch mob. Groups can also push their members to act in ways their ordinary environment cannot tolerate.

The tendency of groups to stimulate members' acting on their impulses instead of controlling and attempting to understand them may disrupt group members' lives. Encouraging group members to explore their own sexuality can culminate in extramarital affairs and in an overwhelming flood of guilt for real or fantasized sexual activity. Important sources of nurturance may be compromised by groups' stimulating members to express negative feelings toward those on whom they most heavily depend.

Patients who do not conform to group norms of intelligence, interests, or interaction frequently drop out. Common misfits are members who lack psychological sophistication and interpersonal sensitivity and who make extensive use of denial (Yalom 1966). Having failed to live up to their groups' norms, such patients may find themselves ostracized by other group members and traumatized by the group. Misapplication of group norms to daily living can be destructive, too. Group members who seek to apply the group norm of complete honesty in their daily lives may find that they have greatly compromised important relationships.

The real friendships that develop in group therapy can block emotional growth if they result in subgrouping and failure to communicate important information to the group for fear of angering new-found friends or endangering the flow of positive feelings from those friends. Therefore, every friendship has the potential for emotional blackmail. Friendships between group members can also result in judgment errors, such as helping a friend from the group obtain a job for which he or she is not qualified.

In the process of pointing out maladaptive behaviors, groups may persecute persons whose manner of presentation stimulates aggression. The group's aggression is rationalized as being for the member's own good, and the resultant flight from the group is seen as unwillingness to face issues, and not as the result of a massive attack on self-esteem.

The visibility of the human frailties of leaders and group members may lead to their devaluation and to discounting their observations and reactions, as if a person's flaws make his observations or actions less valid.

The active life of the group can engulf some persons, who substitute the group for their social life and live within the group instead of using the group to learn how to live in the world. While serving as a counterforce to intellectualization, groups can focus excessively on interaction in the here and now. Focusing on events in the group may discourage examination of events in daily life and consideration of dynamic and genetic factors that play important roles in present-day attitudes and behavior.

Opportunities for multiple identifications may cause confusion instead of growth. Members may attempt to identify with attributes of highly valued group members that are unattainable for them. They may become confused by the many coping mechanisms that they see employed and may be unable to find one that is right for them. Some patients require a one-to-one relationship to establish an identity stable enough to be placed in the flow of certain groups.

There are also important transference-countertransference difficulties in group therapy. Transferences may be obscured by the development of real relationships in the group and by the fact that the persons toward whom they develop closely resemble the original transference object. Thus, acting out of transference-based behavior may be stimulated. The greater availability of the therapist as a person may also impair the development of transference reactions toward him or her, and make their recognition more difficult.

Because the relationship with the therapist is diluted in group therapy, there may be inadequate cathexis of the therapist for transference development. Once developed, transferences may be uninterpretable because other events in group life call for the therapist's attention or distract therapist and group members alike. Other group members may not be able to tolerate the regression involved in the development of transference by one of their peers and can punish or ridicule a member for his or her transference feelings.

Therapists' countertransferences can be readily acted out because they seem to be reasonable responses to certain group members' provocative behavior. In addition, pressure on the therapist by a runaway group can lead therapists to act on their feelings instead of setting limits and pushing group members to reflect on their behavior (Ormont 1968).

At times, groups will not recognize the leader's countertransference-based behavior toward one member. If it is aggressive, group members fearing the leader's aggression or fearing possible desertion by the leader may form a gang and help the leader act out countertransference feelings.

Finally, group therapies are less flexible than individual therapy. It is much easier to change the direction and focus of individual psychotherapy than to alter the long-standing modus operandi of a group.

Summary

Group therapy techniques are as varied as individual therapy techniques, but there are differences between group and individual therapists and therapies. Group therapists must be more tolerant of uncertainty than individual therapists, because there is much in the group that they cannot discern or react to effectively. Therefore, there is greater potential for stimulating acting out through identification with group norms, or through the emotional contagion of the group.

Individual therapy is generally better than group therapy for resolving acute situational crises, and is safer for persons who require close professional monitoring. Group therapy may be more effective for teaching, for stimulating action, or for resolving certain ego-syntonic character resistances. It is also useful for persons for whom multiple partial identifications are an important part of the treatment.

Although qualitatively and quantitatively different, group and individual psychotherapies are not mutually exclusive, and group therapy can augment individual psychotherapy, hospital milieu therapy, and psychotropic medications.

A thorough understanding of the advantages and disadvantages of groups enables the psychotherapist to ascertain the suitability of a particular person for group therapy, or of group therapy for a particular person.

2

An Overview of Group Techniques

GROUP TECHNIQUES HAVE BEEN RECOGNIZED as powerful tools for influencing thinking and social behavior for thousands of years. They have been employed by medicine men, priest-healers (Mora 1967), religious orders (Johnson 1963), and physicians, including the infamous Anton Mesmer in the latter years of the eighteenth century (Zilboorg 1941).

New therapeutic techniques develop in many ways. Some begin as a theory of personality (Scheidlinger 1952), and some as the outgrowth of a theory of psychopathology (Bateson et al. 1956). Others derive from theories of societal and family structure and interaction (Beavers 1977). Many systems of psychotherapy are derived empirically from observing what works in psychotherapy. Rarely, a beginning system is developed methodically and subjected to rigorous scientific evaluation each step of the way toward becoming a system of practice. More commonly, the original investigator becomes an advocate of the technique or theory he has investigated. Usually, that person has substantial charisma and attracts students to his theory or technique. At that point, acceptance of the basic premises of the system becomes an article of faith rather than the subject of further investigation. The system is then expanded by its originator and his students. Finally, levels of competency and training standards are set up within the system. The system thus developed may have great internal consistency, but little general applicability.

The evolution of treatment techniques is not an orderly unfolding of more and more effective therapeutic instruments. It is a process in which there is an occasional new discovery and frequent rediscoveries of parts of older theories and methods of practice.

The group treatment approaches that have been employed in the last eighty years defy any simple system of classification. Some techniques treat individuals in the group, using the other members as auxiliary therapists. Some advocate dealing with the group as a whole. Many therapists focus on the relationship between the individual member and the therapy group. Some techniques attempt to bring unconscious processes to consciousness. Others retrain behavior without reference to the unconscious. There are techniques that relate here-and-now behavior to past patterns of behavior or unfulfilled childhood wishes. There are also ahistoric approaches, but most currently used techniques promote some type of self-understanding. There has been a general move away from viewing a person as a closed system toward viewing individual psychopathology as part of a complex interaction between the individual and himself, his peers, his family, and his larger social context. It is perhaps this latter view that is responsible for the tremendous growth of group psychotherapy.

In outline, the major group techniques are the following:

1. Didactic, inspirational, and suggestive methods
2. Group dynamic approaches
3. Behavior modification
4. Encounter
5. Transactional analysis
6. Psychoanalytic
7. Tavistock method
8. Psychodrama
9. Gestalt Therapy
10. Neo-catharsis
11. Interactional group psychotherapy
12. Cognitive therapy

Didactic, Inspirational, and Suggestive Methods

Joseph H. Pratt (1917), a Boston internist, noted that tubercular patients' emotional reactions, such as shame and discouragement, often interfered with self-care. After years of visiting patients at home, he conceived of meeting large numbers of patients at the hospital to discuss their attitudes, to report on their efforts at self-help, and to receive instruction. This "class treatment," started in 1905, helped patients understand the nature of their illness, taught them how to contribute to their own recovery, and inspired courage to sustain them in living with chronic illness. Pratt's talks included readings from secular writers and the Bible; they were designed to improve attitudes and inculcate an optimistic view of life. As many as 80 to 100 patients were seated auditorium-style, facing the speaker's platform. Those with the best attendance were moved to the front. "Star" patients sat facing the audience next to the doctor (Pratt 1922).

E. W. Lazell (1921) applied Pratt's group lecture method in the hospital treatment of mental disorders in 1919, and in 1921 began his group lecture method of treating chronic schizophrenics at St. Elizabeths Hospital. Lazell included discussions of the patient's dynamics interpreted along Freudian lines, but later used only exhortation, inspiration, and general supportive techniques.

Cody Marsh (1931) de-emphasized rational understanding and relied on inspiration and exhortation. He worked with psychotic patients and emphasized the "total push." He organized social groups, work groups, and committees, and used group activities to involve patients in the realities of living and in mutual assistance. His motto was: "By the crowd they have been broken; by the crowd they shall be healed" (Committee on History 1971).

Snowden's (1940) method consisted of eight weekly lectures, in which he discussed the causes of mental illnesses for 20 minutes. For the remainder of a three-hour period, patients discussed the lectures in relation to their own problems. During the discussion period, the therapist saw each patient individually for a few minutes to point out the relationship between the lecture and his individual problem. Klapman

(1946) used a method that emphasized group interviews rather than lectures and recitals.

Joshua Bierer (1942) began "situational treatment" in a psychiatric hospital: a living experience in a social club aimed at changing attitudes. Bierer believed that the social club helped to change patients from "objects" to "subjects." The activities of the club included entertainment, sports, writing, painting, and discussions. Of the 50 to 100 Runwell Club members, about 10 gathered weekly to discuss one member's problems in an impersonal way. Bierer thought it was best if group members did not know whose problems were being discussed. During the discussion periods, individual members identified and worked on their own problems privately.

In 1935, Robert H. Smith, a surgeon, and Bill Williams, a stockbroker, both alcoholics, founded Alcoholics Anonymous (Williams 1949). The AA pathway of 12 steps begins with the premise that one is helpless to deal with alcohol and must rely on a higher, spiritual power. At AA meetings, examples of recovery from alcoholism are given in a manner reminiscent of religious conversions. New members are assigned sponsors who are available 24 hours a day to help combat the urge to drink. AA emphasizes the need to commit wholeheartedly to the AA way of life.

Recovery, Inc. is a nonprofit self-help organization founded to offer former psychiatric inpatients after-care help in the hope of reducing incapacity and preventing relapses. Founded in 1939 by Dr. A. A. Low, the treatment method is the Recovery meeting, led by a lay person trained in Dr. Low's method. Members read in turn from Low's *Mental Health Through Will Training* (1952). Then, each group member gives an example of his application of Recovery techniques to a day-to-day difficulty. He gives the facts of the situation, tells how he reacted, indicates how he applied Recovery principles, and then tells how he would have handled himself before he learned the Recovery techniques. After this, the other group members "spot" the constructive aspects of his management of the situation according to Dr. Low's doctrine.

Synanon (Yablonsky 1967), an entirely lay-conceived organization for helping narcotics addicts, was founded in 1967. It has been succeeded by a number of self-help programs for addicts (Kaufman 1983). Alcoholics Anonymous relies heavily on testimonials and a concerned, interdependent fellowship. Recovery, Inc. relies strongly on the text written by Dr. Low. Groups for addicts frequently employ aggressive, demeaning confrontation and group pressure to force awareness of behavior. The original Synanon group, because of its vicious confrontations, was called the attack group.

Group Dynamic Approaches

The group dynamic approaches originated from Sherif's research in the psychology of groups (1936), which showed that each person entering a group has a "mental set" that influences his perceptions, and that this set can be altered by the group norm.

In 1935, Samuel Slavson (1964), an engineer turned educator, introduced a creative recreational program for small groups of socially maladjusted girls. He structured the activities of his groups so that the girls could use arts and crafts in a freely self-expressive way. The positive results were attributed by Slavson to group interactions and relations in a permissive environment and to the neutrality of the leaders. These activity groups eventually became coeducational, but were limited to eight- to 12-year-old children in groups of eight.

Kurt Lewin coined the term *group dynamics* in 1939 (Marrow 1969). He defined a group as a structure that emerges from individuals in constant dynamic interaction with one another. The individuals are interdependent parts of a larger whole, which is different from the sum of its parts (Lewin 1951). Forces unrelated to individual psychopathology act within the therapeutic group, at times enhancing the therapeutic process and at times obstructing it.

In 1946, Kurt Lewin was asked by the Connecticut Interracial Commission to help with the state's interracial problems. With three colleagues, he brought together black and white leaders to discuss their differences. He also appointed observers to meet later with the group leaders and discuss the flow of the meetings. The conferees insisted on being included in these subsequent sessions. These "feedback" sessions were more exciting than the conferences themselves and led to the establishment of the National Training Laboratories in Bethel, Maine, in 1947 (Benne 1964). In the 1950s, the National Training Laboratories established several regional branches, and by 1962 the notion of a "T" (for training) group as "group therapy for normals" had become established (Golembiewski and Blumberg 1970). T groups are learning laboratories that focus on how to learn through dealing with immediate ideas, feelings, and reactions (Bradford et al. 1964). The initiators of the T group movement believed that people are being pressured to change by technological advances, but are ill-prepared to handle the necessary changes in interpersonal relations. They hoped to promote greater individual integrity, greater effectiveness in self-change, and eventual change in the larger social environment.

Behavior Modification

Behavior therapy aims to modify symptoms directly, without regard for underlying dynamic factors. Behavior therapy utilizes procedures such as the systematic construction of hierarchies of anxiety-provoking situations, carefully graded training programs, and specific schedules of positive and negative reinforcement. Behavior therapy shares with other forms of psychotherapy the positive expectations of the patient, the therapist-patient relationship, suggestion, persuasion, and encouragement (McLean 1982). Lazarus (1975) finds desensitization in groups works best with patients who have had prior psychotherapy. In his groups, he shapes and models behavior through the leader or group members demonstrating constructive, adaptive behaviors.

Encounter

Carl Rogers' group work began with intensive training courses for Veterans Administration counselors in 1946. A week-long intensive workshop on psychotherapy that he led in 1950 profoundly affected Rogers. For a dozen years afterward, Rogers heard from group members about the impact of the six-day interaction. From those and similar experiences, he evolved the concept of the basic encounter group. Rogers described the basic encounter group as follows:

> In an intensive group, with much freedom and little structure, the individual will gradually feel safe enough to drop some of his defenses and facades; he will relate more directly on a feeling basis [come into a basic encounter] with other members of the group; he will come to understand himself and his relationship to others more accurately; he will change in his personal attitudes and behavior; and he will subsequently relate more effectively to others in his everyday life situation. (Rogers 1967)

Encounter-type groups led by facilitators (instead of therapists) have become widespread and have been used by a number of lay self-improvement organizations (Rhinehart 1976).

Transactional Analysis

Eric Berne, who originated Transactional Analysis as a group method (Berne 1958), was a strong adherent of the medical model of psychotherapy. A group of interacting patients made it easier to identify ego states and interpersonal "games." Berne spoke of curing patients and felt that the basic problems of people are caused by faulty parental programming. Employing a blackboard, Berne (1961) used his concept of ego states to establish a rapid alliance with the adult aspect of his patients. This was reinforced by his insistence on a clear therapeutic contract with each patient: the patient's statement of what he wished to be cured of, and the therapist's agreement to help cure him of it.

According to Berne (1966), a person experiences one of three different ego states (a term borrowed from Federn [1952]) at any given time. Those ego states are parent, adult, and child, and each is a way of thinking, feeling, and behaving. The parent ego state is an aggregate of parental permissions and injunctions. The adult is the rational aspect of a person. The child embodies one's spontaneity, creativity, and intuitive qualities. The ego states correspond roughly to the superego, observing ego, and id.

A transaction is defined as a stimulus by one person and a related response by another. Transactions between one person and another cause difficulty when there is an ulterior transaction, which is in turn part of a game. Games are an orderly series of transactions that include a gimmick (a way of concealing the ulterior transaction) and a payoff for the players (Dusay 1983). Payoffs are positive or negative strokes (psychological gratification). Games are based on early childhood decisions and can be unlearned (Goulding and Goulding 1978). The type of strokes one can accept is determined by one's script, or life plan, of which there are two basic varieties: winners and losers. However, banal scripts also exist. Structural analysis (diagnosis of current ego state), analysis of transactions, game analysis, and analysis of underlying scripts are the therapeutic procedures in Transactional Analysis. In addition, the transactional analyst often gives specific permission to ignore certain parental injunctions (Dusay 1968).

Psychoanalytic

Although Alfred Adler is said to have used a group approach in Vienna child guidance centers in 1921 (Dreikurs 1957), the first analyst to utilize psychoanalytic principles in actually treating groups of patients was probably Trigant Burrow (1927). Burrow introduced in 1920 what he first termed "group analysis" and later, "phyloanalysis." His groups were predominantly residential. Doctors and patients lived together and the tensions that arose were reacted to, analyzed, and discussed by the group. The terms "here and now" and "analysis of group tensions" were originated by Burrow.

His method was based on the theory that people are part of a society; that isolation of the individual in treatment may destroy his relatedness with his group or with society. Burrow felt that the group diminished resistance to treatment. As patients became aware that their problems were not unique, they became less secretive and isolated.

Paul Schilder (1939) applied psychoanalytic principles to the treatment of groups. He reported that patients' ideologies were developed from the self or body image. Psychotherapy enabled patients to see that their convictions had little basis in fact. Patients were asked how they came to accept their ideologies and how they gained influence over their actions. Because patients' ideas and convictions are part of their life in the community, it seemed logical to discuss individual ideologies in groups. Discussions started on a general level and led to individual experiences, reducing feelings of isolation and enabling other group members to work on their own related problems.

In 1938, Alexander Wolf (1949) started a group with 10 of his own analysands. He adhered closely to psychoanalytic principles, but added *alternate sessions* (formal sessions without the therapist). The alternate sessions made it easier for some patients to express themselves and allowed the group members to function as a group away from the leader. He revived Burrow's term, group psychoanalysis, and originated the method of "going around," in which each person in the group was encouraged to speak in turn about whatever bothered him. Wolf and his followers ordinarily meet with their groups once a week, and have one alternate session (Wolf et al. 1970).

Durkin (1964) thought that analysis of the transference could be achieved in a group setting. Other analysts, such as Mann (1955), make more modest claims and tend to deal primarily with the emotional interaction and behavior within the group at the moment, avoiding anamnestic material and dream analysis.

The findings of Kohut underscore what many group therapists have intuitively understood from their practice. Kohut (1971, 1977) advocates, in working with preoedipally fixed personalities, that therapists accept their patients' idealizing and mirroring transferences instead of analyzing them. He does so on the grounds that temporary gratification of such transferences is a necessary developmental step; that interpreting them only results in further fragmentation of the personality. He also recommends abandoning strict therapeutic neutrality and encourages analysts to be open about here-and-now feelings in relation to patients. The analyst, thus functioning as a self-object, is incorporated into patients' psychic economy and is used as a stepping stone toward more mature self-object relationships (Tolpin 1983).

Tavistock Method

From the work of Bion and Ezriel, a method of group psychotherapy evolved at the Tavistock Clinic that involves here-and-now interpretations of the unconscious group theme followed by comments on each individual group member's way of contributing to it. Therapeutic intervention is restricted to interpretation. Interpretations of group tensions are three-tiered and include a comment on the relationship the group members are attempting to make (required relationship) by way of avoiding expressions of something else (avoided relationship) for fear of what might happen if they did (calamitous relationship). The therapist points out the contribution of each member to this common group tension (Heath and Bacal 1968).

Psychodrama

J. L. Moreno (1959, 1971), who originated the technique of psychodrama in the 1920s, introduced the term "group psychotherapy" in 1932. Psychodrama is a technique in which one group member interacts with others, taking various roles: himself, parts of himself, and important others in his own life. Moreno believed that people are innately creative and spontaneous, but become ill if they cannot use their natural endowment. He used groups to help people recover their lost spontaneity. They act out their conflicts in spontaneous stage plays. Acting out leads to catharsis and diminution of the forces that impede creativity. The actor-patient is self-healing and a healing agent for other group members. There are four basic rules. The production that emerges during the session focuses on the present instead of the past. There is free action and interaction in addition to free association, and the three dimensional social space is used instead of simple verbal interaction.

Psychodrama encompasses many techniques (Moreno 1971). Almost all of the encounter techniques, except for the touching games, had been explored previously by Moreno. He introduced the concept of "warming up" to a group interaction. He also saw his psychodramatic sessions as a "rehearsal for life" and thereby antedated the behaviorists in using the concepts of shaping and modeling behavior.

Gestalt Therapy

Gestalt Therapy, originated by Frederick Perls (Perls et al. 1951), aims to unite a person within himself in the here and now and to eliminate repression so that a person can be at one with his unconscious processes. The unconscious is not to be feared. People are inherently good, and becoming aware of one's self enhances the possibility for actualizing the goodness in one's self. People are people, and not the sum of their physiology and psychology. Perls indicated that people need to be dealt with in terms of what is right with them and need to be focused on the process of becoming, not in a goal-setting way ("I must do this"), but in a free-flowing way that Carl Rogers (1961) calls "becoming process." Perls held that once emotion is understood to be not a threat to rational self-control, but a guide which furnishes the only basis on which human existence can be ordered rationally, then the way is open to cultivating continuous awareness of its positive aspects (Perls et al. 1951).

Perls treats individuals in a group. The group is a participant audience. One person occupies the "hot seat" and addresses an empty chair to help him become aware of his projections and, hence, his psychological introjects. The process of growth from an incomplete Gestalt (incomplete self-awareness and incomplete self-other awareness) to a state of more-or-less completeness is envisioned as peeling away layers. The first layer is that of cliché (Berne's rituals and pastimes). Next is roles and games; again, coinciding with Berne's games. Following that is impasse, one's point of psychological fixation, and behind that is the paralysis of opposing forces called "implosion." Following penetration of this area comes "explosion" into grief, anger, orgasm, or joy that connects finally with the authentic self (Perls 1969). Perls attempted to avoid explanations and speculation. He preferred that patients learn about themselves from emotional experiences in the here and now. Gestalt therapists help to stimulate the emergence of feelings and to encourage confrontation with feelings that have been avoided. Manifestations of transference behavior are not sought out, nor are they pointed out. Patients are simply encouraged to give up maladaptive behaviors (Fagan and Shepherd 1970) and to adopt more constructive behaviors.

Perls' work has been expanded by Polster and Polster (1973) and integrated with Transactional Analysis by Goulding and Goulding (1978).

Neo-Catharsis

A resurgence of emphasis on catharsis and the reliving of emotionally traumatic experiences occurred in the late 1960s. Casriel (1972), who treated narcotics addicts through the use of the therapeutic community, was greatly impressed by the intense feeling involvement created by the Synanon group (Yablonsky 1967) and helped form Daytop, a therapeutic community for addicts. Based on those experiences, he formulated a cathartic group therapy.

Janov's now-discredited Primal Therapy (1970) is an attempt at reliving early traumas and developing awareness of one's emotional difficulties as a reaction to those traumas. Patients were allegedly cured by reliving and making a part of themselves previously warded-off physical and psychological hurts. As less energy is used for repression and dissociation of affect, individuals become less tense, more relaxed, and have a greater sense of being in charge of themselves. During group sessions, attempts are made to replicate aspects of the patients' earlier lives so that they can relive what they repressed. Much physical contact is employed. One of the major traumas reenacted is the birth trauma, which many patients felt able to reexperience and work through.

Feeling-expressive therapy (Pierce et al. 1983) is the newest of the cathartic therapies. It is a combined individual therapy, group therapy, and peer counseling technique that emphasizes remembering with feeling and vigorously carrying out the physical actions that express those feelings. It is held to be useful because it helps people reevaluate early painful experiences and change maladaptive habits of emotional restraint.

Interactional Group Psychotherapy

Irvin Yalom, who originated Interactional Group Psychotherapy, holds that emotional symptoms originate and are expressed in disturbed interpersonal relations. An unstructured therapy group evolves into a miniature representation of each patient's social universe, a social microcosm. Through consensual validation and self-observation, group members become aware of the inappropriate perceptions and interpersonal behavior that call forth untoward reactions from others.

Those behaviors and misperceptions often result from negative group experiences which have led to the internalization of a derogatory self-image. Emotionally troubled people have not learned to distinguish objectionable aspects of their behavior from themselves as a whole, partly because of others' awareness of their sensitivity and also because of the normal rules governing social interaction. The accurate feedback of a therapy group facilitates such discrimination through a series of steps, beginning with the display of maladaptive behavior and followed by feedback and self-observation through which group members become aware of their behavior and appreciate its impact on the feelings of others, the opinion that others have of them, and the opinion they have of themselves. They become aware that to a large degree they are the author of their interpersonal world. They also become aware that they alone can change it. Those insights are thought to be effective in direct proportion to the emotion they arouse. As a result of awareness, one risks new behaviors and expressions of feeling if adequately motivated for change, if one has need for the acceptance and appreciation of other group members, and if one's character and interpersonal style have some degree of flexibility.

Changed behavior generates a new learning cycle through self-observation and the feedback of others. Patients learn, as a result of the new behavior, that their fear of a calamity (death, abandonment, derision, engulfment) was irrational. Eventually, behavior learned in the group extends into everyday life. In and out of the group, an *adaptive spiral* evolves. As interpersonal distortions diminish, group members are better able to form rewarding relationships. Social anxiety diminishes, self-esteem rises, and self-concealment diminishes. Others reward that behavior, facilitating further change (Yalom 1975).

Cognitive Therapy

Beck's Cognitive Therapy (1976) is a treatment technique that can be employed in groups for the alleviation of depression. It is based on the hypothesis that an organized system of negative beliefs or assumptions about oneself, one's world, and the future predispose to depression. Treatment is based on correcting these cognitive distortions by thought-stopping (interrupting negative cognitions) and substituting more positive alternative thoughts. Early cognitive therapy groups were short-term, but cognitive techniques have been applied to open-ended groups (Roth and Covi 1984).

Summary and Commentary

Group therapies continue to change and develop, more influenced by personal charisma and clinical lore than by formal research, but formal research, discussed in Chapter 15, is having greater impact.

The tendency to plunge into "new" techniques without adequate validation is a time-honored practice. The tendency to deride "traditional" methods is reminiscent of adolescents' differentiation from their parents and the Hegelian dialectic of thesis (the "traditional" view) and antithesis (the "revolutionary" view), followed by synthesis, the constructive integration of new and old. As scientists, we must beware of dogma. As humanists, we must have concern for the people to whom we offer our services. And, as scientific practitioners, we must remember that our field is still young.

By this brief exposure of the reader to a sampling of historically important group techniques, I hope to have underscored the multiplicity of factors and the variety of contexts that influence groups and their development, and to persuade the reader to evaluate carefully claims of dramatic cures and radical new insights. New methods need to be suggested and tested, not only for their general applicability but for their applicability by practitioners as individuals. Most group therapists settle on a single approach or combination of approaches that best suit their character, their philosophy of life, and their training. That leads to stability, but can also lead to stagnation. The learning group therapist needs to derive from the many systems available a basis from which to conceptualize and deal with groups that can be modified later through clinical experience. I hope the following chapters will provide such a usable base. The reader with a special interest in the history of group therapy is referred to Anthony (1971), Kadis et al. (1974), Whiteley and Gordon (1979), and Kaplan and Sadock (1983).

3

General Principles of Psychotherapeutic Intervention

THE BASIC THERAPEUTIC PROPERTIES of all psychotherapeutic interaction are discussed in this chapter, which deals with the factors that govern therapists' choice of intervention, modes of intervention, and levels of intervention. The personal needs of therapists as they affect therapist-patient relationships are also discussed.

Elements of Psychotherapy

Yalom (1975) divides the therapeutic or "curative" aspects of group therapy into 12 categories: interpersonal output, interpersonal input, catharsis, insight, existential factors, cohesiveness, guidance, altruism, identification, instillation of hope, universality, and family reenactment. Interpersonal output is risking new behaviors in a group. Interpersonal input is learning the reactions of others to one's own behavior. Catharsis is expressing formerly withheld feelings, and insight is discovering formerly unknown aspects of one's self. Existential factors are coming to grips with the realities of life, such as the need to assume responsibility for one's self. Cohesiveness refers to mutual acceptance and a sense of mutual belonging. Guidance is being offered suggestions. Altruism is doing for others without self-interest or a sense of obligation. Identification is acting like, or following the lead of others. Universality refers to being comforted by finding that others have the same problems. Family reenactment is reexperiencing aspects of one's own earlier life in the group.

Using Yalom's 12 categories, I compared patients' appraisal of the most important therapeutic factors in four groups; a group of eight patients preparing to enter long-term group therapy, a group of nine patients after a time-limited group of 10 sessions, Yalom's sample of 20 patients (75 sessions), and a group of 10 patients with more than two years of experience in a group (Weiner 1974a) (see Figure 1). Patients rated 11 of Yalom's 12 categories as important (family reenactment was not considered important by any group), but most important were interpersonal input (what they learned about their own behavior), interpersonal output (their risking new behaviors), catharsis, insight, existential factors (assuming responsibility for one's self), and group cohesion. Hope was only important

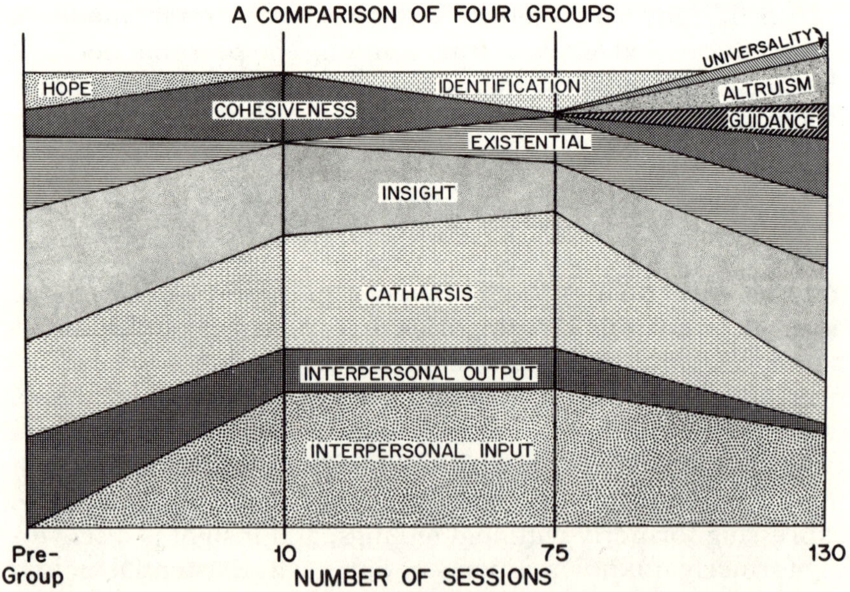

Figure 1. Curative Factors in Relation to Length of Psychotherapy: A Comparison of Four Groups. Adapted from Weiner (1974a).

before patients entered group therapy, and identification, universality, altruism, and guidance came into play in the longer-term groups, suggesting that the longer people are involved in a group, the more factors are involved in producing change.

Careful examination of Yalom's categories of curative factors and careful review of videotaped patient-therapist interactions suggest that Yalom's categories are too broad. With the help of Dr. Allan Shirks, I have been able to discern at least 20 therapeutic elements.

In the following discussion of therapeutic elements, existential factors are subsumed under insight, universality under identification, and guidance under suggestion.

The basic therapeutic elements of all psychotherapies are listed in Table 1. Those unique to groups are in Table 2. Each element is more or less useful at different times in therapy or in different therapies.

Interaction

Psychotherapy involves cognitive, emotional, and behavioral *interaction* between therapists and group members. The quality and quantity of interaction is determined by the group members' need for interaction, and the type of interaction that will be best tolerated. They are also determined by the unique blend of personalities that occurs in a group, and are influenced by a host of environmental, physiologic, psychological, and social factors.

There must be sufficient interaction for patients to feel involvement with other people, but enough sensitivity of therapists and group members to not traumatize persons for whom interaction threatens annihilation, engulfment, esteem-threatening competition, or seduction. The interaction must be sufficient to help members produce information, feelings, or behaviors that can be dealt with in the therapeutic situation, but not so great that patients are overwhelmed by their feelings and impulses, or that their thinking becomes disrupted. The *multiple interaction* that occurs in groups adds to their stimulating quality, but poses the danger of overstimulation unless the therapist actively monitors and regulates the overall intensity of group interaction, and encourages individual members

Table 1. Elements of Psychotherapy

1. Interaction
2. Stimulation of hope
3. Stimulation of cooperation
4. Suggestion
5. Education, including information-giving and role-playing
6. Encouraging the development of external support for new behaviors
7. Reframing
8. Command
9. Manipulation
10. Encouragement to face emotional issues
11. Facilitation of catharsis
12. Reinforcement
13. Desensitization
14. Feedback
15. Promotion of identification
16. Insight
17. Attribution of meaning
18. Testing of perceptions
19. Working through, including behavior rehearsal
20. Altruism

to interact more or less, according to their tolerance and need.

In evocative groups, multiple interactions lead to *reactive associations:* the associative responses of one or more other group members to a particular group member's associations. These multiple associations may provide important links for the person who first made the association and are particularly useful in working with dreams.

Hope

As noted earlier, *hope* is most important as a therapeutic element at the beginning of therapy. Hope can be actively stimulated by indicating the possibilities for change and by pointing out actual progress made in therapy. Hope is reinforced by therapists' credentials as helpers and by patients' positive experiences with being helped by others throughout their lives. Hope is also stimulated by watching and helping other group members make positive changes and eventually graduate from the group.

Table 2. Elements Unique to Group Psychotherapy

Element in Group Psychotherapy	Individual Therapy Analog
1. Multiple interaction	• Interaction
2. Observation of others' progress	• Instillation of hope • Education
3. Group pressure	• Suggestion • Manipulation • Reinforcement • Identification • Encouragement to face emotional issues • Facilitation of catharsis
4. Multiple feedback	• Feedback
5. Multiple identification	• Identification
6. Vicarious desensitization	• Desensitization
7. Multiple transference	• Transference
8. Reactive association	• Association
9. Carom	• None
10. Real friendship of group members	• Professional relationship with therapist
11. Support outside the therapeutic hour	• Recruitment of support
12. Altruism	• None

Cooperation

Cooperation is group members working within the framework provided by their group and therapists. Cooperation is based on the hope of change, and therapists reinforce that hope by their optimistic attitude and by offering a treatment approach group members can understand. Cooperation is partly based on transference from positive relationships with important persons earlier in life. Much-abused persons who have been rejected, abandoned, or exploited by the important persons in their early lives may be unable to trust enough to cooperate with group therapy.

Cooperation is an important group norm, without which the group cannot function. Not all of what transpires in groups will be directly useful to all group members. Group therapies, therefore, require that potential group members have the ability to cooperate for the sake of others.

Suggestion

The modern use of *suggestion* in groups began with Anton Mesmer (1734–1815), a physician who employed group methods to reinforce therapeutic suggestion (Ellenberger 1967). Mesmer constructed a baquet, a trough-like arrangement of mirrors and iron rods that could be manipulated in various directions. People surrounded the baquet and formed a closed chain by holding hands. Mesmer then appeared, magnetic wand in hand, and the treatment was carried out under his direction, the patients being touched, stroked, and closely opposed to the magnetizer in the initial stages of the séance (Zilboorg 1941). When the French Academie des Sciences examined Mesmer's work in 1784, they concluded that the effects of Mesmer's treatment were entirely due to excitement of the imagination and forbade further public exhibitions, but the use of suggestion to stimulate emotional contagion still continues. In 1971, a proponent of encounter conducted a demonstration in Dallas, Texas. A group of perhaps 500 participants in a large room had been divided into groups of six for the purpose of the demonstration. At the end, each participant was asked to cross his arms over his chest, grasp the hands of his neighbors, close his eyes, and feel the current flowing from right to left!

Suggestion, when employed constructively, is proposing mental or physical activities for group members to carry out during or outside the therapeutic session. Group members can be encouraged to engage in fantasy or to feel an emotion deeply. Therapists can suggest activities such as relaxation, increased socialization, or becoming more assertive (Kelley 1979). When therapists make suggestions, they acknowledge that group members are in control of their own behavior, but lend their special expertise in helping to determine a course of action. Suggestion also requires that therapists and individual patients develop a plan for implementation. Suggesting that group members be more active is not helpful unless they are encouraged to select specific activities and determine how they can be undertaken.

Planning includes mobilizing patients' assets and reducing

the effect of their liabilities on the planned course of action, and frequently involves *education* (Strupp 1969) and *encouraging development of external support for new behaviors.* For example, a socially inhibited woman who wishes to date, but who is fearful of men, can be encouraged to interact first with other women in her group and later with the men. The men help her to practice her social skills in a nonthreatening environment as she works through her inhibitions and eventually develops relationships with men outside the group. In addition, group members can supply support outside the therapeutic session, being available to help tide their peers over crises and actively join with them in positive endeavors, such as shared hobbies or sports.

In making suggestions, therapists avoid telling group members what they *should* or *ought to* do, and point out that there are few absolutes in human relationships. Therapists also avoid those terms to keep from reinforcing guilt ("Why don't I do as I should?") instead of conscious choice as a means of self-regulation, and aim instead to increase group members' self-awareness and their repertoire of constructive behaviors. In making suggestions, therapists take into account the individual group members' ability to follow suggestions and the group's tolerance for the therapist making suggestions. Suggestions made by one group member to another are also an important part of group therapy.

Education

Education, the mainstay of many forms of psychotherapy, is imparting new information or, more commonly, a different view of information patients already possess. All educational techniques can be useful at times, including written material (Klapman 1946), a blackboard (Berne 1966), and lectures about psychodynamics (Wender 1936). Patients may also be educated through interacting with therapists and other group members. Meek patients can be taught that failing to communicate their needs directly prevents others from recognizing and meeting those needs. The same patients can be allowed to experience the impact of their nonassertiveness through the report of other group members or through experiences in which they role-play themselves and then reverse roles with others in the group whom they feel are more assertive.

The educational process teaches the cognitive skill of focusing: attending to one aspect of one's thinking or behavior as a means to better understand or control it. Teaching patients to focus requires that the therapist track the statements or actions of group members, to note when and why they leave that track, and to find means to keep patients on important tracks for discussion. That can be done by summarizing a group or a patient's verbalizations or activities or by suggesting a central theme that is being developed, that is being avoided, or that would be profitable to follow.

In the following example, the patient was taught to recognize his symptoms of depression.

> Mr. Q. suffered recurrent episodes of depression and was contemplating suicide when he started group therapy. He obtained relief from his depression by taking an antidepressant medication. He achieved greater self-esteem through group therapy and had become a more effective manager and employee through his increased ability to assert himself. Nevertheless, he still experienced episodes of depression that could not be attributed to work, family, or intrapsychic pressures. Part of Mr. Q.'s group treatment was teaching him to recognize depression and to differentiate it from actual failure on the job or in his interpersonal relationships, thus enabling him to turn more quickly to antidepressant medication instead of suffering for months and being at risk of suicide.

Reframing

Reframing, or relabeling, is an important aspect of education. It is looking at the same information from a different point of view, viewing symptoms in positive ways that allow constructive activity or provide relief from inappropriate superego demands (Haley 1973). At first, overly self-critical group members see their problems as personal failures. Therapists reframe the situation, and present them as problems of self-acceptance and of setting realistic standards. For example:

> A group member's goal for himself was to earn as much money as possible. The therapist pointed out that he had set himself up for a life of self-torture because if he pursued that goal, he would always have to strive for a larger income, no matter how great his income became. The problem was reframed as one of needing to develop attainable goals.

Command

In rare instances, group leaders can *command* group members to do or not to do something, but commands are usually ineffective unless therapists have some physical or emotional control over their patients, or take their patients by surprise. A therapist can command a teenage group member to talk to the group instead of hiding behind a pillow and teasing the person next to her, or command a psychiatric inpatient group member to stop agitating a fellow patient. In the first case, the control over the patient may stem from the force of the therapist's personality; in the latter case, from the strength of the institution in which the patient is confined. Although useful in overcoming some forms of negativism, commands are seldom used in outpatient group psychotherapy because of therapists' insufficient control of their patients and because a command sets therapists over patients and in opposition to them. Both positions can preclude the development of cooperation.

Manipulation

A *manipulation* is an indirect means to enable or stimulate patients to act or think in a certain way. In contrast to suggestion, manipulation does not require a cooperative relationship with patients, and in contrast to a command, it does not openly set therapists against their patients.

A common manipulation involves therapists temporarily accepting group members' attitudes or behaviors that they would ordinarily oppose. At one level, that type of manipulation avoids a power struggle with patients who may resist giving up a symptom (Modzierz et al. 1976). At another level, it makes patients' symptomatic behavior into a form of cooperation with the therapy (Adler 1956). It may also allow a needed period of regression for an overstressed ego, and may help modify inappropriate superego demands. For example:

> A teenage group member with a school avoidance problem was told that her education was in her hands and that neither the leaders nor the group could force her to go to school. In that way, the situation was reframed as an educational issue, her potency in resisting was affirmed, and the group leader and members were not set against her.

Another type of manipulation is *paradoxical intervention:* actively encouraging group members to perform acts that they consciously want to avoid repeating, but have strongly resisted giving up (Weeks and L'Abate 1982). This technique is receiving wide attention as a means to deal with people who resist ongoing therapy (Stanton 1981). As an example, a group member who complains of submerging her own personality to meet the needs of others can be encouraged to be agreeable to everyone in the group, and can be instructed in behaving agreeably. That type of intervention frequently results in the behavior changing in the opposite direction. The mechanism is not fully understood, but it may result from placing patients in situations that they cannot escape without developing ways of dealing with themselves previously outside their repertoire of responses—what Watzlawick et al. (1974) described as a second order change. Equally well described as cutting the Gordian knot,* it is changing patients' entire frame of reference so that they can act constructively.

Manipulations, like commands, are of limited use because patients soon learn that they are being manipulated and come to mistrust their therapists. Therefore, manipulation tends to be most useful in emergencies, short-term treatment, or as a last resort.

---

*The knot tied by Gordius, King of Phrygia, who prophesied that the person who undid the knot was destined to rule all Asia. Alexander the Great examined the knot and solved the problem by cutting the knot with his sword.

Encouragement to Face Emotional Issues

Group therapists assess what issues their patients have motivation and strength enough to face, which are relevant, and then decide how to encourage patients to face them. All that is done in the context of each group's ability to deal with the same issue and to support the concerned group members.

Patients in repressive groups are encouraged to face real issues in their daily lives: applying for a job, concentrating on getting each day's work done, or seeking help from fellow employees when they do not understand how to perform a task that has been assigned. Members of ego-supportive groups are encouraged to face their anger toward the leader and other group members, their jealousy when a fellow group member seems special to the leader, and their sense of loss when members leave the group. In evocative groups, the issues faced are the unconscious processes underlying their thoughts, feelings, and behavior that are brought to light by members openly revealing their associations, fantasies, and dreams.

Catharsis

Catharsis is the expression of formerly suppressed or repressed thoughts and their accompanying feelings (Weiner 1977). The person(s) who receive this communication react with understanding and acceptance instead of counter-ideas or counter-affect. Catharsis is a highly valued part of the treatment process for many patients, largely because it feels good. The good feeling may stem from a symbolic purgation of unwanted aspects of one's self (Ellenberger 1970), from a sense of acceptance by the listener, or from an expected magical transformation after offering up part of one's self. Pierce et al. (1983) explain the positive affect of catharsis as the completion of emotionally incomplete acts; finishing unfinished emotional business.

Catharsis is the treatment of choice in emotional disorders that result from temporary overwhelming of the ego by massive psychological trauma (Fenichel 1945). Catharsis drains off dammed-up emotions, and gives immediate and dramatic relief. The cathartic process is initiated by establishing an atmosphere of acceptance and by then encouraging group members to relive traumatic events in as much detail and with as much feeling and immediacy as possible. Caution must be exercised to not overwhelm an already compromised ego.

Catharsis in groups frequently occurs as part of a carom or as part of a mutually reinforcing buildup of group emotional tension called group contagion (Kadis et al. 1974).

Reinforcement

Group members' behavior during and outside of therapeutic sessions is partly determined by their therapists and their groups' positive and negative reinforcement.

Positive reinforcement encourages certain behavior by group members. It may be freely expressing feelings during a therapy session or focusing attention on the interaction between group members, depending on the group norm. Positive reinforcement is accomplished by therapists communicating approval and interest in what group members are saying or doing. Leaders can extinguish behaviors by failing to provide positive reinforcement. The leader frowning, actively changing the subject, or telling group members that they are dwelling on an unproductive topic are all forms of *negative reinforcement.*

Desensitization

When group members discuss their fears and wishes, there is usually an element of *desensitization.* The fear-producing ability of a thought, experience, or feeling is decreased through repeated verbalization. A woman who is frightened by her sexual feelings may be desensitized by talking about them in the group and by finding that talking about sexual feelings does not mean that she will act on them or that she will be sexually approached. Another person in the same group who is frightened of sexual feelings may also be desensitized indirectly.

Feedback

Feedback is an important aspect of ego-supportive group therapy that entails leaders or fellow group members informing other members of the effect of their here-and-now behavior on the leader or other members. It helps develop an observing aspect of the ego (Greenson 1967), and helps to make ego-syntonic behaviors ego-alien. It often involves disclosure of feelings, such as therapists telling patients of their anger in reaction to certain of the patient's behaviors (Weiner 1983a), or other group members telling their similar feelings to persons who experience their own feelings as strange or inappropriate. Discovery through feedback that one is not basically different from persons in the group who are competent and highly valued does much to restore self-esteem. The *multiple feedback* of groups reinforces the observations of the therapist or other group members. It also allows for the expression of different points of view.

Identification

Identification is a cornerstone of normal maturation. Identification with valued others occurs throughout life, and may be the primary therapeutic vehicle for many group members (Weiner 1982b). It begins with introjection, taking into the self part of the external world. Identification then makes the self similar to the introjected object. Identification may begin with conscious imitation, but is unconsciously mediated (Greenson 1954). Freud (1921) proposed that group members project certain of their ego functions onto their leader. They attribute qualities to the group leader that the group members take in, enabling them to discard old values and to replace them with new values based on their identification with the leader, repeating the process of superego formation in which parental values are introjected positively or negatively, and form the nucleus of the child's adult value system.

A transient, partial identification with therapists and other group members is necessary for the individuation of patients and their separation from therapist and group. Its great importance for some persons may be based on the past unavailability of suitable objects for identification or an impairment of a person's ability to make the necessary identification at the appropriate point in psychosexual development (Jacobson 1954).

Identification with the therapist's acceptance and inquiring attitude and with the willingness of others to be similarly deprived allows patients to tolerate the deprivation of evocative therapies and, together with positive transference, forms the therapeutic alliance (Greenson 1965).

By noting with whom in the group a particular member identifies, the leader may come to understand that person's wishes and fears. Group members often identify with some physical aspect of feared persons, with their aggression (by becoming aggressive), or with their role in the group, recapitulating the identification with the aggressor that is an important step in the superego formation of children (Freud 1946).

Another positive aspect of identification is universalization, a sense of similarity to others that reduces the alienation frequently felt by people with emotional problems. It can also reduce group morale by engendering a feeling of hopelessness ("If there are so many of us, it must be impossible to change") or promoting acting out. In these latter situations, therapists deal with identification as a resistance to constructive work.

Insight

There are many types of *insight*. Insight in the psychoanalytic sense means becoming aware of the unconscious meaning of thoughts, feelings, or behavior (Greenson 1967).

The term insight also includes becoming aware of patterns of thought or behavior of which one was formerly unaware. An important aspect of insight is *attribution of meaning*; explaining a hitherto unexplainable symptom, feeling, or behavior. When therapists or other group members attribute meaning to thoughts or behavior that are incomprehensible to a group member, that person often experiences relief at being understood. Every patient's self-understanding comes about in different ways at different points in therapy. At times, insight is adopting the view of the therapist or other group members. At other times, it is learning from one's interactions with others, and for a few patients it is coming to understand the unconscious forces in their own minds. The level of insight for which one strives with a given patient at a given time in a particular group depends on many variables, but primarily on the ego strength of the individual patient and the anxiety tolerance of the group as a whole. The less the patient's ego strength and the group's anxiety tolerance, the more the therapist relies on active teaching. People with adequate coping skills can acquire insight through examining their interactions in ego-supportive groups, and people with better-than-average coping skills can become aware of their unconscious mental processes in evocative groups through the medium of interpretation.

Working Through

Whether change in behavior is preceded by insight into unconscious mental processes, or only the conscious wish to rid oneself of a troublesome behavior, the process of changing that behavior by repeated application of insight or repeated attempts at new behavior is called *working through*. Working through is facilitated by *behavior rehearsal*. Members practice being more cooperative, assertive, or sexual in the therapeutic sessions.

Altruism

Opportunities for enhancing self-esteem through altruistic behavior toward therapists are rare in one-to-one psychotherapy, but they do occur when patients offer comfort to their therapists during times when the therapist is in personal distress. For those patients able to respond with empathy and altruistic intent, if not acts, there is at times an increased sense of potency and self-worth (Givelber and Simon 1981; Rodman 1977; Singer 1970).

Although not rated highly by group members as a curative factor, the opportunity for altruistic behavior presents itself frequently in long-term groups, in the form of opportunities to advise, to comfort, or to perform concrete acts such as providing transportation to a meeting or refreshments at an alternate meeting. It seems logical that in the context of a group, people may become more willing to do for others in a way that is neither self-serving nor self-destructive and that contributes to the overall welfare of the group. If, as Vaillant (1977) suggests, altruism is an important attribute of a mature person, the greater opportunity to engage in altruistic behavior may be an important advantage of group therapy over individual therapy.

Factors Governing Choice of Intervention

Therapies must be structured properly to function effectively. The most difficult part of psychotherapy for therapists is learning when and how to apply the therapeutic elements and learning when and how they can be mixed. Dosage, timing, and mixture must be considered in terms of the type of therapy, the real therapist-patient relationship, individual group members' ego strength, the psychological relationship or alliance between therapist and individual group members, individual group members' feelings about therapists, therapists' feelings about individual group members, and groups as a whole.

Type of Therapy

Without doing them great violence, most of the techniques described in Chapter 2 can he subsumed under one of three categories; repressive, ego-supportive, and evocative. Table 3 shows which of the basic elements of psychotherapy are most commonly used in each type.

Each of the three types of psychotherapy is dynamic in the sense that underlying dynamics are always considered by the therapist, whether or not they are brought to the conscious awareness of group members.

Repressive. Repressive group therapies are highly structured and reinforce the repression of unconscious material. They utilize direct teaching, foster identification with the therapist's values, and focus on coping with one's own feelings and interpersonal relationships and developing interpersonal skills (Kadis et al. 1974). Regression is discouraged because of its potential for arousing material from the unconscious. Patients are encouraged to adopt slogans such as "think positively" or "move your muscles," which help them toward positive behaviors. Psychological assets and basic emotional health or goodness are stressed, and attention is diverted from the unconscious toward problems of daily living.

Table 3. Types and Elements of Psychotherapy

Type	Elements
Repressive	Stimulation of hope Attribution of meaning Reframing Command Suggestion Education Desensitization Reinforcement External support Manipulation Testing of perceptions Behavior rehearsal Altruism
Ego-Supportive	Stimulation of hope Interaction Attribution of meaning Reframing Feedback Identification Suggestion Education Desensitization Reinforcement Catharsis Facing emotional issues Testing of perceptions Working through Altruism
Evocative	Stimulation of hope Interaction Attribution of meaning Reframing Catharsis Facing emotional issues Interpretation Insight Desensitization Identification Testing of perceptions Working through Altruism

A repressive approach is used with persons who have little capacity, need, or motivation for insight or self-awareness. It is indicated for acute situational crises and for persons of low ego strength whose daily functioning would be compromised by having to deal with unconscious material. Repressive measures are appropriate in the early stages of all types of group psychotherapy. They facilitate cooperation with the treatment and minimize anxiety until a bond is established between each patient, the therapist, and other group members.

Ego-Supportive. Most once-a-week groups operate on an ego-supportive level. Its focus is interpersonal. Ego-supportive therapy is indicated for persons with greater capacity and motivation for self-understanding than those for whom a repressive approach is indicated. Candidates for repressive therapy may need hospitalization or medication in addition to their group experience. The best candidates for ego-supportive therapy are able to function adequately on a day-to-day basis.

Ego-supportive therapies require less structure than repressive therapies. They encourage the development of less crippling ego defenses and continued repression of thoughts and feelings that are too overwhelming. Therapists confront group members with their denial, projection, and rationalization. They are encouraged to take responsibility for their feelings but are not encouraged to explore the unconscious roots of their feelings or perceptions. Perceptual distortions are corrected in the here and now. Regression is discouraged. Patients are encouraged to think for themselves and to become aware of their behavior toward others and their reactions to the behavior of others.

Evocative. Evocative techniques enable emergence of unconscious thoughts and feelings. Evocative groups stimulate partial ego regression through an unstructured session, a lack of interpersonal cues, free association, and frustration of the group members' object needs. Ego regression results in the members experiencing their drives, infantile conflicts, and fixations as though they were part of the current group interaction (Wolf 1949). Group members rework their defenses against their instinctual drives and work toward resolving their infantile conflicts and overcoming their fixations. This type of approach requires a stable life adjustment, intact reality testing, and a capacity for a nondestructive partial ego regression.

Group members must be able to reverse their ego regression at the end of each session and become aware of their feelings instead of acting them out. Self-observation comes about through a "split" of the ego, one side caught up in the transference, the other observing itself in the transference relationship. The ego must also have sufficient strength to cope with the superego, so that it can observe its own defensive operations objectively and not become destructively self-critical.

Evocative group therapy is, in a sense, a process of deprivation. Group members are deprived of infantile gratification through interpretation ("It looks like you're trying to make us into an all-giving mother") to free them to pursue adult gratifications.

Many group techniques have been developed to break rapidly through the ego's defenses in the hope of speeding up and deepening the therapeutic process. They include Gestalt Therapy (Perls, Hefferline, and Goodman 1951) and psychotherapy through imagery (Schorr 1974). In those approaches, therapists actively prescribe verbal and nonverbal exercises to elicit repressed or avoided thoughts and feelings.

Evocative methods have no place in the treatment of persons with markedly impaired reality testing or impulse control, except under controlled circumstances in an institution.

The Real Therapist-Patient Relationship

The real (nontransference) patient-therapist relationship refers to the context of their initial contact, the purpose of their relationship, and their working conditions. There are two issues concerning the context of the initial patient-therapist contact: Does the prospective group member think he has a problem, and is he motivated to deal with the problem? If the prospective patient does not perceive a problem, or lacks motivation to deal with the problem as perceived by the therapist or the referral source, the prospective patient is not a candidate for group therapy. If, on the other hand, a prospective patient expresses concern over another problem that the therapist deems treatable in a group, he or she may enter a group to deal with that complaint. In many instances, the problem for which a person is referred is not the problem for which help is wanted. It is not useful to enroll in a group a person who is unmotivated or feels he has no problem, in the hope that he will eventually acknowledge the problem or become motivated to deal with it. If prospective patient and therapist agree to work together, they establish a contract, as detailed in Chapter 5.

In addition, therapists need to be aware of the general impact of their personality on others. Taciturn therapists need to be aware of their tendency toward withholding; effusive therapists, their tendency to invade others' space. Their self-awareness helps them distinguish between transference-based reactions and reality-based reactions. They must also be aware that correct observations by patients can be transference-based.

The Group Members' Ego Strength

Before attempting to impart information to group members, therapists assess their ego strength, which is their capacity for coping with reality and their thoughts and feelings. Ego strength also involves the ability to distinguish observations from fantasy, feelings from fact. All of those factors influence one's capacity to receive and integrate new information. Evidence of ego strength can be gathered from group members' history of impulse control, self-reliance, constructive interpersonal relationships, job and school performance, and from observing their behavior in the group.

The Nature of the Alliance

The ideal therapist-group member alliance is between the rational, health-seeking part of the group members and the rational, objectively observing aspect of their therapists. Other types of alliance are possible. Some group members hope to continue acting on their impulses instead of dealing with them and therefore seek acting-out groups. A person who wishes to reinforce the harsh aspects of his own conscience may seek punitive, judgmental reactions from other group members. A person who wishes to enhance his intellectual defenses may seek out a group that promotes rationalization. The quality of the therapist-patient alliance is also greatly affected by transference and countertransference.

Group Members' Feelings About Therapists

Therapists take into account group members' expressed feelings toward them, as well as their probable unconscious feelings.

Transference is the unconscious attempt of patients to relive or master some aspect of their past life in the therapeutic hour. Instead of remembering the conflicts they have repressed, patients act out the residues of unresolved infantile conflicts in the therapeutic session (Ezriel 1950).

Much of what patients present in psychotherapy is transference-determined. Initially useful in establishing a cooperative relationship and in determining patients' conflicts and defenses, transference may become a resistance to cooperation or self-awareness.

All group members have some transference feelings. Other feelings stem from the real situation—anger, for example, if the therapist keeps the group waiting or obviously favors one group member over others. Still other feelings are based on nontransference expectations, such as the reasonable assumption that members will find some acceptance by the group and the therapist.

In repressive groups, positive feelings toward the therapist are accepted and not examined. Therapists attempt to dispel negative feelings toward themselves by apologizing for or explaining away behavior that angers group members. Negative transference feelings are also explained away. Therapists may reveal negative feelings of their own that developed under similar circumstances to promote patients' identification with them and to indicate the essential normality of the patients' feelings.

Ego-supportive groups explore the current factors and habitual aspects of members' reactions to therapists and fellow group members. Because patients in an ego-supportive group have enough ego strength to experience and express their negative feelings without being disruptive or acting in a self-destructive way, awareness and expression of both positive and negative feelings are encouraged.

In evocative therapies, therapists consider dynamic and genetic factors as they explore group members' feelings toward them and toward each other. In repressive and ego-supportive groups, therapists begin correcting transference distortions as soon as they arise to prevent them from obstructing therapy. In evocative groups, transferences are allowed to become obstructions and are then dealt with by appropriate interpretations.

Therapists' Feelings About Group Members

The impact of therapeutic interventions depends on the quality of the therapist-patient relationship. Cooperation can be blocked by therapists' or patients' fears or unrealistic expectations and by emotional reactions in the therapist-patient relationship. Carl Rogers' triad of therapist-offered conditions (1957)—accurate empathy, nonpossessive warmth, and genuineness—were at one time held forth as the sine qua non of successful psychotherapy (Truax and Mitchell 1971). Based on a more recent appraisal by Mitchell et al. (1977), it seems reasonable to conclude that therapists who are perceived as understanding, who are personally warm without being intrusive, and who do not appear phony or manipulative are more effective than therapists who do not seem to understand, who appear uncaring, and who deal with their patients as objects to be manipulated.

Therapists develop different feelings about different group members. Sometimes their feelings enable them to do better work; at other times they impair the therapeutic relationship. Therapists also take into account their feelings about the group members before they intervene. They try not to belittle patients whom they dislike or to enhance themselves in the eyes of patients from whom they wish admiration.

Therapists' unconscious feelings and reactions to group members are of even greater importance than their conscious attitudes. To effectively deal with their own unconsciously determined reactions, therapists begin by observing their group members and themselves. Not all unconscious reactions of therapists to group members are countertransference. Often, therapists react to their anxiety about their own feelings or impulse control.

Therapists' object needs are a consideration in their interventions with group members. At times, therapists' object needs are great because of important losses. They need sufficient self-awareness to know if their interventions are motivated by group members' therapeutic needs, by their own object need, or by their countertransference.

Countertransference is often defined as all of the therapist's personal reactions to the patient, including neurotic reactions to the patient and the patient's transference (Racker 1957). However, it is more precise to label the reactions of the therapist that stem directly from patients' behavior or therapists' personal needs simply as the feelings of therapists toward patients.

A repeated urge to interact in a specific way with particular group members suggests the operation of countertransference. The nature of the intervention that therapists wish to make can also give some clue to the nature of the countertransference. For example, pointing out a group member's sexual enticingness may not only confirm the member's attractiveness but may also act out a wish to seduce the patient into a sexualized relationship.

Effective therapists are attuned to transference and countertransference, regardless of the type of therapy they employ.

Transference- and countertransference-based behaviors are often difficult to recognize in group therapy. A group member may correctly detect the leader's hostility. He may also have a strong transference need to focus on that aspect of the leader. The leader's confirmation of the patient's hypothesis about him may reinforce the transference as a resistance to exploring the patient's feelings about the leader. The leader's strong urge to confirm may be partly based on the patient's urgent need for information, but it may also result from the leader's attempt to block awareness of his own unconscious conflicts. Transference and countertransference can be suspected from the urgency with which therapists or patients are impelled to share a thought or act on a feeling. The greater the urgency felt, the more likely transference or countertransference is operative. In general, the more intense the feeling and the less it relates to the immediate leader-member interaction, the greater the likelihood of transference or countertransference contamination. Therapists' most effective means to detect transference and countertransference is awareness of their own and group members' past and present-day relationships and interactions, especially as they affect each other's known psychological vulnerabilities. Therapists can bring that knowledge into play by stepping back emotionally from the group and allowing themselves time to reflect before acting or reacting.

The Group as a Whole

Groups are more than collections of individuals. Every group develops a personality of its own, partly shaped by the unique blend of members and partly by its interaction with the therapist. The relationship of groups as a whole to the therapist greatly influences the type of work that can be done, especially if the real relationship between group and therapist is antagonistic, as occurs in prisons and with involuntarily hospitalized patients. If the ego strength of a group as a whole precludes a working alliance, if the leader-group alliance is with the tendency of group members to act out instead of understand themselves, and if there is a climate of mistrust between therapist and group members, there may be much destructive activity and little therapeutic work. The group leader must consider at all times whether the group as a whole is a workable therapeutic vehicle or if it needs to be changed to increase its positive impact or decrease its potential for destructiveness to individual group members or to outsiders. For example, an adolescent group led by a permissive therapist in a general hospital outpatient clinic rapidly became a gang and had to be disbanded because of protests from the clinic administration. In other cases, subtracting a member with poor impulse control or adding members with adequate impulse control establishes a more positive balance when the situation cannot be managed by the therapist's verbal interventions alone.

Modes of Intervention

Group therapists take action in response to the behavior or verbalization of group members. Before actively employing one of the elements of psychotherapy, they ask themselves, "To what end?" Do they wish to *accept, suppress, facilitate,* or *explore* the material that has been offered? These four modes of intervention supply the momentary context in which the therapist operates. Is the therapist gently splinting a fragile emotional structure, trying to reduce the intensity of a feeling, stimulating its expression, or moving toward an understanding of the factors that underlie manifest behavior, thoughts, or feelings?

Acceptance

Acceptance is the empathic, nonjudgmental acknowledgment of verbal or behavioral communication that is important in all types of group therapy. Acceptance can be conveyed in many ways. The following vignette illustrates a therapist's acceptance of a patient's urge to express anger and was facilitated by his willingness to serve as a symbolic lightning rod.

> A group member was discussing the impending death of a friend, the earlier death of his own father, and the closeness he experienced with his father during the latter's terminal illness. Mrs. U., whose father had died violently and unexpectedly when she was a teenager, began to cry. She said that the words, "The Lord giveth and the Lord taketh away," had come to mind, and that she had the urge to blaspheme. The therapist encouraged her to say what she felt to God. He said that if she were afraid of being struck by lightning, he'd be her lightning rod, and touched her lightly on the wrist. She vented her anger and, as the therapist terminated the session, thanked him for having been her lightning rod.

Empathy is the ability to partially identify with some aspect of each group member. The information from that partial identification can be used by therapists to determine the timing, dosage, and content of later interventions. It is difficult to conduct insight-oriented therapy without empathic awareness because interpretation requires therapists to partially identify with patients' point of view and way of thinking, not only to recognize latent content but to phrase interventions in a manner the patient can understand.

Expression of uncensored and empathically aroused emotional responses to group members is quite another matter. It is an exposure of the therapist's primary process thought unmodified by his ego. There is a place for directly expressing the therapist's empathy, but the therapist, with rare and specific exceptions, needs to deal rationally with patients and to maintain a professional relationship (Wolf and Schwartz 1959).

Suppression

Suppressive interventions aim to inhibit a thought, feeling, or act and are commonly employed in repressive therapies. Thoughts may be suppressed by therapists changing the subject or encouraging patients to interact with the group instead of being caught up in thinking. Therapists must directly suppress physical violence. Therapists may request reconsideration of a contemplated behavior, warn that the behavior will not be allowed, or physically restrain a group member (Weiner 1970).

In the presence of physical danger, safety takes precedence and dictates the form of intervention. In an evocative therapy, therapists may wish to suppress other forms of activity, such as casual person-to-person conversation, after explaining that therapy progresses best if they stick to business (Ormont 1969). In repressive or ego-supportive groups, therapists may encourage social interchange to ease emotional pressures during the therapeutic session.

Facilitation

Facilitative interventions bring material to awareness or make material available for discussion. They include asking patients to talk, confrontation, clarification, and interpretation. A confrontation establishes that something is being avoided; for example, "There is a different tone to your voice today. Do you feel different?" A clarification aims to establish a sharp focus on a particular psychological event. One might say, "You've also been talking abstractly about anger today. Maybe that's what I hear. Perhaps you're angry now." Confrontation and clarification refer not only to content but also to the direction of communication. For example, "You discount me as a person when you look at other group members while talking to me." Confrontation and clarification are utilized in repressive, ego-supportive, and evocative groups.

Interpretation is usually reserved for the middle and end stages of ego-supportive and evocative treatment. An interpretation made early to defuse a rapidly-building transference ("You're reacting to us as though we were as critical and rejecting as your father") does not make unconscious material conscious. It reframes the patient's reaction as appropriate behavior out of context. Calling it inappropriate would reinforce the patient's view of the therapist as punitive and judgmental (like the critical aspect of the father) and his view of himself as defective (like a bumbling child).

Exploration

Explorative interventions help establish new links between thoughts, feelings, and behavior. In repressive groups, new links are made by offering explanations and suggesting alternatives to a given behavior. For example, if the question of nail-biting is raised by a group member, the therapist may respond, "Nail-biting is often a sign of needing to do something active. If I were you, I might become physically or mentally active each time I felt the urge to bite my nails." Or, the therapist might ask others for their suggestions about useful types of physical or mental activity.

Seeking the meaning of thoughts and behavior is valuable in ego-supportive groups, or when any group must be dealt with at an ego-supportive level. In dealing with a new group member who is frightened of the others' displays of anger during his first few sessions, the therapist can comment that they are showing off their ability to be verbally aggressive. Thus, therapists indicate that others' behavior is meaningful and that patients can also come to understand the meaning of their own behavior. In evocative groups, members explore themselves through their own associations and their associations in reaction to other group members. Therapists can also stimulate their self-exploration by encouraging the expression of fantasy, or by offering fantasies of their own that emerge during the hour (Schorr 1974).

Areas of Focus

Focusing is the means by which therapists shape group members' conceptualization of their problems and capture their attention. The three general areas of focus are day-to-day reality, the emotional forces currently operating within individual group members, and the relationship of group members' past thoughts, feelings, and experiences to their present perceptions of and reactions to their interpersonal and intrapsychic worlds. They can be designated as *here and now, dynamic,* and *genetic* (Weiner 1970).

Here and Now

Here and now focuses on present symptoms, thoughts, or behavior, without reference to antecedents. Focusing on the here and now is appropriate in repressive, ego-supportive, and evocative groups. For example, "Joan has been angry with John today," or "Joan, are you angry with John?"

Dynamic

A dynamic focus suggests psychological cause and effect, and is useful in supportive and evocative groups. A dynamic focus leads to awareness of reactions to specific thoughts, feelings, and events, and helps increase patients' ability to observe themselves objectively. After Joan acknowledges her anger with John, she can be asked what angered her, if she is usually angered by the same actions of other people, or if her anger with John is displaced from something else in her current life.

Genetic

A genetic focus emphasizes psychologically important historical events and is used with individuals who can constructively observe themselves. It is most effective in evocative groups. Bringing affective material from the past into the here and now permits emotional reworking of a feeling or thought pattern. Joan might be asked if John's behavior or John as a person reminds her of someone from her past, or to whom in the past she has reacted in the same way she reacts to John.

The genetic focus is often considered the deepest level of work, in the sense that it deals with unconscious psychological material. Depth is often equated with curative power based on the presumption that rearranging patients' unconscious thoughts and feelings will cure their symptoms. A more reasonable attitude is that for some people, dealing with unconscious factors brings about the type of self-understanding that promotes change. Others, particularly those with little ego strength or psychological sophistication, find it a disruptive experience. The experienced therapist learns how deeply to probe without causing unnecessary pain or damage.

Meeting Therapists' Needs

Therapists are entitled to meet some of their own needs in the therapeutic setting, as long as they do not compromise their patients. Therapists can allow themselves the gratification of being recognized as a person by group members, but they should not insist upon it. Group members who are interpersonally aware and relatively mature are often able to recognize their therapist as a person. On the other hand, many patients begrudge their therapist personal recognition; others are incapable of it. If withholding personal recognition from the therapist is a resolvable, relevant aspect of patients' emotional problems, it needs to be explored. With group members who would be compromised by acknowledging the therapist as a person, the issue need not be pressed.

Events in therapists' outside lives, as well as in group sessions, affect their need to be accepted as a person by their patients. The more therapists' object needs are frustrated in outside relationships, the more likely they are to press for real involvement with group members (Dahlberg 1969). It may be detrimental to both patients and therapists if therapists seek in their groups gratification that is denied to them, or that they are unable to allow themselves in their lives outside the office.

Summary

This chapter has dealt with the elements of psychotherapy, the factors governing the dosage and timing of psychotherapeutic interventions, modes of intervention, areas of focus, and the needs of therapists.

In considering any intervention, therapists begin by exploring its transference and countertransference implications and by determining if it facilitates one of the therapeutic elements listed in Tables 1 and 2. It is then evaluated in terms of the type and goal of treatment, the context of the therapeutic relationship, individual group members' ego strength, the nature of the therapeutic alliance with individuals and the group, and the feelings of therapists and group members toward each other. Finally, therapists select therapeutic mode and area of focus.

The personal needs of therapists are an important aspect of the treatment relationship. Therapists are entitled to be treated as persons, remaining cognizant that they cannot demand or extract personal recognition in a manner that violates patients' personal integrity or detracts from therapy.

4

The Group Process

GROUP PROCESS refers to the ongoing life of groups. Although Lacoursiere (1980) and Bion (1959) hold that all groups have a common basic course, the process of every group differs because of the combination of particular therapists with specific group members. There are, however, universal phenomena called G-responses that are unique to therapy groups (Kadis et al. 1974).

In repressive groups, the leader works against the development of group process and instead tries to establish a stable milieu that will allow effective didactic teaching. That differs from ego-supportive and evocative groups, in which the group is allowed to develop its own life for the sake of stimulating interpersonal and intrapsychic processes that can be observed, commented on, and changed.

G-Responses

G-responses, or group responses, are recurring, ubiquitous phenomena that differentiate group therapy from individual psychotherapy. Some G-responses are attempts to maintain group stability in the face of psychological threats. Other

G-responses are nodal points (Weiner 1982a) at which groups can be modified in significant ways, or at which particular members of groups become more available for therapeutic work. G-responses are also points of increased vulnerability for group members.

Knowledge of G-responses helps to structure different kinds of therapy groups. In repressive and ego-supportive groups, therapists can use their knowledge of G-responses to direct and limit the group interaction and the depth of self-exploration. In evocative groups, therapists use G-responses to stimulate fantasy instead of limiting the group's sphere of interest to the realities of daily living.

Homeostasis

The need of the group members for structure, predictability, and security leads to mechanisms for reducing group members' anxiety, much as every individual strives to maintain his anxiety at a tolerable level and to maintain psychological intactness. Group homeostasis results from an empathic consensus between group members that establishes the least anxiety-provoking manner in which they can operate together. The leader allows homeostasis to develop when group tensions run too high. It is challenged by the therapist when homeostasis brings the group's work to a halt.

Plateauing

Plateauing is the tendency of groups to work effectively and then stall for a period of time. As in individual therapy, advances are frequently followed by an increase of resistance as the next level of therapy or new problem is approached. Plateauing during individual therapy probably results from the establishment of a new dynamic balance between ego, id, and superego that must be overcome before dealing with the next challenges to the ego. In groups, these increases of individual resistance are intensified by the resistance of the group to changes in mutually rewarding relationships between group members. For example, group members may discourage a member's relinquishing a nurturing role toward others in the group because of the comfort they derive from that nurturance.

Group Climate

Group climate refers to the type of homeostasis at which the group arrives. Bion (1959) has described three basic types of group climate, based on the behavior of group members: the dependent group in which members cling to the leader, the flight-fight group in which members attempt to preserve themselves by fighting with each other or fleeing, and the pairing group in which bonding develops between group members. These types of group climate are not normal developmental stages of therapeutic groups. They are types of homeostasis that develop if the group is not actively directed by the leader.

A group of psychologically sophisticated persons can also develop an intellectualizing climate in which members sort out and diagnose each other's problems. Other groups easily enter highly emotional interchanges. The group climate can be friendly or hostile, changing in relation to the leader's interventions and the material with which the group members are dealing.

Each member exerts pressure on the group to meet his own needs, but not every group member's growth needs or needs for support can be met by the group at any given moment. Group members who are comfortable with the status quo resist changes in group climate. Others push for change to better meet their needs. Part of therapy groups' climate is the tension between the members' resistance to change and the countervailing desire for change. The group climate is modified by therapists in the direction they feel most helpful for their groups. Their means of changing the group climate include changing the subject of the group's discussion, focusing on the problems or behavior of individual group members, or focusing on events in the life of the group. If, for example, a group responds to a member's impending departure from the group by intellectualizing about the comparative merits of group and individual therapy, the leader can turn to individual members and ask their reaction to losing the departing member. That will usually stimulate emotions in one or more of the members in the group, and will start the group toward dealing with reactions to separation and loss. If, on the other hand, the leader is certain that the members will be overwhelmed by their emotional reaction to loss, he can turn the discussion toward the positive aspects of the departing member leaving the group and the positive plans that he or she has made.

Cohesion

Cohesion refers to group members' sense of belonging, their loyalty to one another, and their willingness to work together and assume responsibility for one another as they pursue common goals (B. J. Sadock 1980). A therapy group that has achieved a satisfactory homeostasis is likely to be cohesive.

Group cohesion can facilitate or block change. Group members can unite to facilitate change, to defy or to cling to the leader and each other. Cohesion between group members may be based on shared antagonism toward others or on positive mutual attraction.

The group leader stimulates sufficient cohesion to promote interchange among the group members, and works to break down patterns of cohesion that interfere with the progress of the group, such as group members banding together as a rigidly structured social group instead of a medium for self-evaluation and for risking new behaviors.

Group Contagion

Group contagion occurs when group members' acts or expressions of feelings stimulate the conscious or unconscious wishes or feelings of other members. Once the common theme arises, some group members may be so powerfully stimulated that they can no longer avoid acting on their feelings or expressing themselves.

Group contagion is a form of stimulation through identification that can rapidly change the climate and cohesiveness of a group. It occurs commonly in relation to certain events in the life of a group, such as the therapist's absence. At that time, group members may reinforce each other's anger over abandonment and stimulate flight from the group.

Displacement of Aggression

Displacement of aggression onto the therapist or individual group members is common in groups (Weinstock 1979). Teenagers frequently attack the physical environment, abusing furniture and slamming doors. Displacement of aggression occurs because of group members' fear of harming or being harmed (for example, by loss of affection) by a person in the group or the group as a whole. The aggression is often displaced onto group members who are relatively passive, less valued, or negatively cathected. Displacements must be differentiated from justifiable expressions of anger and frustration, but many justifiable behaviors also contain an element of displacement. For example, a group's vigorous confrontation of a member's passivity may be a displacement of the group's wish to confront its overly passive leader.

Attacking the Therapist

Attacking the therapist is easier in a group than in individual treatment because group members provide mutual support. Additionally, the exposed position of the leader and the multiple negative transferences directed toward him make him a tempting target, as in the following vignette.

> When two members of a group became sexually involved, the leader indicated that one or the other might need to leave the group. Mr. U., another group member, said angrily to the therapist that he was punishing them instead of understanding them. As Mr. U.'s reaction was explored, the transference basis of his anger became clear. His father had never understood the worth of anything he had ever been involved in, and once his father made up his mind, he would never be influenced to think differently.

As the above vignette illustrates, an attack on the therapist provides an excellent opportunity to examine the attacker. Problems in dealing with authority and peer relationships often manifest as an attack on the leader. Other group members may criticize the leader for spending too much time with one person or insufficient time with another. In either case, the reason for the attack is important. At times, it is a form of sibling rivalry. At other times, the group is focusing on a specific vulnerability of the therapist.

Attacking a Group Member

Group members attack each other for many reasons. They often counterattack when they feel unfairly criticized by others in the group. Counterattacking is a favorite defense of persons who discount the observations of others in the group by pointing out that they, too, have similar flaws. Group members will also initiate attacks when they sense an impending attack, as a means of warding off the anticipated injury. This is a common gambit of paranoid group members.

Attacking other group members can result from defensive identification with the critical aspect of the group leader, or from reality-based or transference-based anger. Reality-based anger is often directed toward monopolizers and provocateurs. Transference-based anger may stem from situations in the group that resemble earlier parent-child or sibling relationships. For example, a woman who had been the youngest child of a large family became angry at an older woman in the group who became close to the leader. The younger woman felt left out, much as she had felt in her original family.

Events in the Group's Life

A therapy group develops a life of its own, and the many events in the group's life form part of the group process. Among the group's life events are changes in status of group members and the addition and loss of members.

Introduction of New Members

The leader bears the primary responsibility for integrating new members into the group and for helping to avoid premature termination.

To minimize dropouts, patients need to be carefully selected for their personal compatibility with other group members and for the compatibility of their treatment needs and goals with the needs and goals of the group, and individual support should be available during their period of introduction into the group. In some cases, it is useful to introduce two new members at once to reduce their sense of isolation. Other new group members will require a number of individual sessions to help them acculturate.

Therapists should allow their groups time to reintegrate following periods of crisis and should avoid introducing new members at times of high group tension. If that cannot be avoided, it may be useful to orient potential new members to the problems in the group before they enter the group.

Change in Status of Group Members

A member's marriage, divorce, bereavement, birth of a child, graduation from school, or change in job status all affect the homeostasis and climate of the group.

A divorcing man or woman becomes more emotionally and sexually available in fact and in fantasy and may stimulate a change in group climate from intellectualization to acting out. The subgrouping that occurs when two group members become lovers can also seriously affect the functioning of the group and make it impossible to deal with the behavior of either one.

> Mr. R. and Mrs. A.O., a divorcée, became lovers after Mr. R. decided to divorce his wife. That seemed an ideal opportunity to explore each one's behavior in an intimate relationship, but they became a subgroup, making their behavior impossible to deal with in the group. No resolution would be possible until after they left the group. A crisis then arose, and the therapist was able to make a split in their joint defense by working with one member of the couple and referring the other to a former therapist.

Other couples, after having established romantic ties and having secured mutual support, leave their groups to avoid further confrontation with emotional issues.

Changes in status that are valued by other group members stimulate envy, competitive feelings, and hope. Losses in status through being fired or laid off arouse other members' fear of similar losses and may temporarily create a climate of hopelessness and helplessness in the group.

Separation and Loss

Groups offer multiple opportunities to deal with other separations and losses in addition to the eventual loss of the therapist. Anxiety over separation at vacation time or other absences of the therapist occurs in groups as in individual therapy, but the anxiety is cushioned by other group members' availability during that time. Separation anxiety is usually most marked at the time of leaders' first scheduled absence from their groups.

If disruptive tension arises in a group from anticipating its first vacation from the leader, the leader can reduce the tension by explaining to the members that their uneasiness is a normal result of memories and feelings associated with important losses that everyone has experienced. If the group is able to tolerate the tensions generated, the leader can ask group members to discuss their feelings about the impending separation and their past experiences with separations, and can ask group members to project themselves into the future and imagine themselves during the period of time when the therapist will be gone and the group adjourned.

A group's ability to deal with a loss depends on the significance of the loss to the group as a whole and to individual members of the group, and the ability of each member and the leader to face and deal with loss. The manner of dealing with the loss depends on the norms established by the group.

Loss of group members can be an important emotional learning experience or a traumatic event. The loss of a member, whether expected or unexpected, has wide repercussions in a group. If a member graduates, envy is stimulated, as is fear of discharge from the group before sufficient independence has been achieved. If a member leaves without having made much progress, group members question the therapist's potency. Because there is a tendency to avoid issues raised by the loss of the member who quits prematurely, it is imperative that group leaders deal with such losses by helping members focus at an appropriate level on their own thoughts about staying or leaving.

The most traumatic losses are due to death, especially death of a group member by suicide. A group reported by Kibel (1973) was shocked at first and tried to defend against the impact of a suicide by analyzing the motivation of the deceased member. Two of the seven remaining members quit the group. Others felt guilty over not having done more and were frightened about the outlook for themselves. As a result of his experience, Kibel suggests that the therapist deal with this type of crisis by sharing his grief, by increased activity, by structuring the group more highly, and by offering individual sessions as needed. Cohen (1976), following the accidental death of a group member, found the group resistant to accepting new members. The next three new members of the group terminated prematurely after being unable to gain a foothold. He suggested that a period of mourning is necessary before the group members become able to invest themselves in a new relationship.

The suicide of a group member was a major trauma for the members of one of the groups I worked with.

> Mrs. A.G., a manic-depressive woman who had previously been hospitalized several times, overdosed with her antidepressant and an oral antidiabetic agent. She lingered in a coma for several weeks before she died as the result of prolonged hypoglycemia. During the time her prognosis was in doubt and until shortly after her death, the four remaining group members became closer and offered each other support. They soon recoiled from that intimacy and two members fled the group, both expressing doubts about the efficacy of group therapy. The remaining two were unable to function as a group, and the leader placed them in other groups instead of adding new members to join the discouraged pair.
>
> In the new groups, the two remaining members were able to work through their feelings about the suicide of the former group member.

There are so few reports in the literature on group reactions to the death of a group leader that they cannot be generalized. Rosenthal (1947) analyzed the reactions of 27 patients who were in Paul Schilder's groups at the time of his death and concluded that each reacted according to his level of development. He questioned that a group could distract a neurotic from his private concerns for purposes other than the expression of hostility toward the leader. Dumont (1966), who took over a group of schizophrenic patients after its leader's suicide, found that they were only able to deal with their leader's suicide by intellectualized displacement onto the assassination of President Kennedy.

Calendar-Based Events

Holidays are frequently important events in the life of the group, and need to be considered as sources of tension in the group. Holidays often have different significance for different members of the group, depending on their religious and cultural heritage. Of especial importance in the United States are the secular holidays of Thanksgiving and the New Year and the religious holiday of Christmas.

Themes of alienation and depression are especially common at Thanksgiving, Christmas, and at the New Year. Persons who are physically and emotionally distant from family life are affected, as are the persons for whom holiday family gatherings consist of much thankless hard work and hypocritical pleasantness toward family members whom they dislike, but feel obligated to entertain. The New Year holiday has the additional burden of reflecting on the past year and looking forward to the coming year.

> In one session of an ego-supportive group, there was much talk about the impending arrival of Christmas, and how one ought to have a loving relationship with one's family. The theme then changed to one member's complaining about the fee for the group, and another complaining about the therapist's unresponsiveness. As the group's anger toward the therapist increased, several of the group members acknowledged that they wanted the therapist to be the loving, responsive person that they wished their parents had been.

The feelings that are aggravated in group members at the time of important calendar events can best be dealt with if the leader actively notes the coming holiday to the group and asks the group's reaction. In repressive groups, the leader helps to stimulate positive plans to avoid loneliness; in ego-supportive groups, obstacles to intimacy are explored; and in evocative groups, the emotional significance of the holiday is explored.

Dealing with Resistances

A resistance is any intrapsychic or interpersonal activity that slows or subverts therapeutic progress. In addition to intrapsychic resistances, resistances specific to therapeutic groups are *group silence, social conversation, advice-giving* and *labeling, subgrouping,* and *problem behaviors.* Resistances shared in common with individual therapy are *transference* and *acting out.*

Group Silences

Group silences are best managed by therapists asking direct questions of individual group members and then asking other group members to respond to the answers given. In that way, leaders encourage group members to interact. Comments made to groups as a whole usually reinforce silences and raise emotional tension instead of dispelling it. When leaders begin questioning group members during a period of silence, they may choose to begin with relatively neutral topics, such as an account of recent events in a member's life, or they may ask directly how he or she reacts to the silence in the group. Leaders may then press harder to find out what individual members are withholding and why.

Social Conversations

Social conversations in a group can be managed by changing the subject. With cohesive groups of psychologically intact patients, leaders can point out that group silences and social conversations occur at times of high emotional tension, and can indicate events in the life of the group that are being avoided. Or, leaders may push individual members to deal with issues without commenting on the resistance as such.

Advice-Giving and Labeling

Advice-giving and labeling certain behaviors as games with payoffs (Berne 1964) are useful aspects of group treatment that can also become resistances to penetrating more deeply into intrapsychic and interpersonal issues. In the following example, the defensiveness of the group manifested itself in mutual advice-giving and eventually led into a circle.

> *MRS. X:* I had a nasty turn last week. I was standing in a queue waiting for my turn to go to the cinema when I felt ever so queer. Really, I thought I should faint or something.
>
> *MRS. Y:* You're lucky to have been going to a cinema. If I thought I could go to a cinema I should feel I had nothing to complain of at all.
>
> *MRS. Z:* I know what Mrs. X means. I feel just like that myself, only I should have had to leave the queue.
>
> *MR. A:* Have you tried stooping down? That makes the blood come back to your head. I expect you were feeling faint.
>
> *MRS. X:* It's not really faint.
>
> *MRS. Y:* I always find it does a lot of good to try exercises. I don't know if that's what Mr. A means.
>
> *MRS. Z:* I think you have to use your willpower. That's what worries me—I haven't got any.
>
> *MR. B:* I had something similar happen to me last week, only I wasn't even standing in a queue. I was just sitting at home quietly when. . . .
>
> *MR. C:* You were lucky to be sitting at home quietly. If I was able to do that I shouldn't consider I had anything to grumble about.
>
> *MRS. Z:* I can sit at home quietly all right, but it's never being able to get out anywhere that bothers me. If you can't sit at home why don't you go to a cinema or something? (Bion 1959, p. 51)

In the vignette above, Mrs. X. made a complaint. Mrs. Y. told Mrs. X. to stop complaining. Mr. A. then responded with concrete advice that Mrs. X. rejected. The group members made no further effort to deal with Mrs. X.'s complaint and began telling each other to stop complaining. Members seemed to be telling each other to meet their needs for advice and support elsewhere; they were too busy with their own concerns.

The leader had at least three options: investigating Mrs. X.'s complaint further so that better advice could be given, noting individual group members' turning away from her, or wondering aloud how it felt to Mrs. X. to be essentially ignored by the group. The first option would fit with a repressive mode, the second with an ego-supportive focus, and the third could have led to her dealing with feelings of being ignored at other times in her life.

Advice-giving and labeling were more effective in the following situation.

> Mrs. K., who had previously been hospitalized for a psychotic episode, had been a group member for only a few weeks when she became quite agitated at home, at work, and in the group. The therapist advised that she resume an antipsychotic agent to help her calm down, and wrote her a prescription. When she stormed out of the next group session feeling that she had been unjustly criticized, the therapist indicated to the other members that she was emotionally ill, and suggested that she was projecting her own angry feeling onto the group.

The therapist's advice that Mrs. K. resume her medication (and her taking the medication prescribed) helped to make her less defensive, and his labeling her as ill helped group members to be tolerant of her temporary outburst of unreasonable anger.

When advice-giving or labeling become resistances, the leader points out that the group members can deal best with emotional issues by allowing themselves to react emotionally to what is happening in the group instead of giving advice or deciphering each other's patterns of behavior (Flowers 1979). A further departure from advice-giving and labeling can be made by encouraging group members to associate to events in the group or to fantasize about other group members (Schorr 1974).

Subgrouping

Subgrouping is the formation of a tie between several of the group members that is stronger than their tie to the therapist or the group as a whole. It often involves an agreement between the subgroup members to avoid exposing their special relationship. It may be a subtle resistance, and the group leader may not become aware of a subgroup until after it has become deeply entrenched. Subgrouping is disruptive to the therapy group because the relationship between several members goes on out of the view of the group as a whole, and therefore cannot be examined, understood, or even commented on.

Subgrouping is dealt with by identifying the special relationship between the involved group members and urging them to discuss it in the group. Whether or not a special tie is acknowledged, the subgroup members are reminded of the group rule that all communication between group members outside the group is important, and needs to be brought up in the group. When the subgrouping is a form of resistance, one member of a subgroup usually binds the others to secrecy because something he or she has confided is too embarrassing to raise in the group as a whole. After members of the subgroup deal with their guilt over betraying their fellow and their anger when they realize they have been manipulated, the subgroup loses its power as a resistance.

Problem Behaviors

Certain problem behaviors arise in nearly all ongoing therapy groups. They are the assistant therapist, the silent member, the provocateur, and the scapegoat. They may result from character problems of individual patients, transference reactions toward the therapist or other group members, or a particular configuration of forces within the group. Provocateurs are frequently quarrelsome persons who project their aggressive impulses onto others. Scapegoats are persons who are willing to offer themselves for the group's abuse. Assistant therapists cope by identifying with the therapist's role and frequently attempt to displace him. Silent members attend regularly but find verbal communication with other group members blocked. The job of the group leader is to ensure participation in the group by all members, in amounts and at a level useful for each.

Assistant Therapist. The assistant therapist role is frequently taken by persons who are attempting to stabilize their identity by making gross incorporations of the therapist. Frequently, the group member who starts out by massively identifying with the therapist role has the least ego integration and the least capacity for dealing with the group's reaction. It is usually to his or her advantage to be gently nudged out of the leadership role without interpretation by the therapist.

The assistant therapist role is often assumed by persons with paranoid and narcissistic trends who seek to protect themselves from attack and to maintain their grandiose self-images by placing themselves above other group members.

While it is advantageous for group members to assume leadership and develop their ability to understand and help others, therapists must understand their motivation for assuming this role. Therapists may be tempted to take a back seat, but if they do, group members may feel that they have abdicated their authority to the assistant therapist. That can undermine therapists' authority and reduce the therapeutic value of their contributions to their groups.

Silent Member. If silence is a reaction to the strangeness of the group situation, other members' encouragement to speak usually resolves it. If, however, silence defends against anticipated attack, an approach by other group members may prolong the silence or precipitate a member's flight from the group. Some group members use silence to defend against anxiety; others are silent because they lack contact with reality. There are, however, some members who remain silent and yet are quite involved with the group. Those persons, although silent, occasionally gain from identification with other members, and may vicariously work through some conflicts or maturational tasks.

As group members feel less threatened, they usually participate more actively. Periodic silences may be observed and related to specific anxiety-producing activities and topics. Once the group is aware of those anxiety-arousing situations, it may work toward overcoming the threat the group member experiences by supporting the silent member through statements such as, "We know you get scared when we start talking about sex. That's okay. A lot of people do. Maybe after a while it won't be so scary for you, and you can tell us your thoughts on the subject, and even some of your experiences if you like."

Provocateur. Provocateurs are members who use the group to discharge their aggressive impulses under the guise of ventilation or stimulating group interaction. Depending on the level at which the group operates, group leaders may attempt to redirect provocateurs' aggression into more constructive channels, actively interrupt their provocations, or guide provocateurs toward understanding their behavior. In many instances, provocateurs are attempting to prove personal potency, but the raw aggression in their interactions with other group members often stimulates counteraggression that can rapidly develop into a fist fight if leaders do not intervene quickly.

In repressive groups, provocateurs are discouraged from provoking without calling attention to their behavior as provocative. Their provocations are gently interrupted, and they can be asked to go easy for the sake of the person they are provoking. Provocateurs in ego-supportive groups can often be made aware of their behavior through role-playing in which other group members act toward provocateurs as they act toward others. In evocative groups, other group members are encouraged to tell their associations to the provocative behavior.

Scapegoat. Group members who feel threatened by something they dislike in themselves project it onto another person in the group, whom they attempt to expel, thus eliminating the person who now bears the bad quality (Kadis et al. 1974). The scapegoat in a group is a less-esteemed member who usually occupies the position of scapegoat until the group leader actively intervenes. The role of scapegoat is reinforced by leaders who wish to escape the hostility of the group, and by the scapegoat's willingness to be abused. Scapegoats ordinarily recapitulate in the group their masochistic position in other interpersonal relationships. Group scapegoats can often defend their submission to the verbal lashing of others as something done for their own good or as the inevitable consequence of expressing feelings freely. It is at times useful to point out the parallels between the scapegoat's role in the group and past or present outside relationships, but it is generally more useful to alter group interaction to diminish the group's acting out against the scapegoat.

In repressive groups, leaders redirect the group's attention or tell the group that attacking one of its members is counterproductive. In ego-supportive groups, attention is called to the persecutor and victim roles of the provocateur and scapegoat, and attempts are made to reshape the relationship into one in which dependent needs are gratified without the scapegoat having to suffer in payment and in which the scapegoat's aggression is expressed actively instead of passively. The persecutor is helped to express his aggression in nondemeaning ways. In evocative groups, the relationship between persecutor and victim is allowed to develop sufficiently so that it is apparent to all, enabling other group members to share fantasies about the interaction and enabling the participants to deal with the meaning of the behavior in terms of their character structure and transference.

Transference

Transference is a source of resistance in groups as well as individual therapy (Gladfelter 1974). Depending on their approach, group leaders may reinforce, circumvent, explain, interpret, or ignore transferences. Generally speaking, transferences are left alone as long as they facilitate progress. Thus, the transference expectation that therapists will help and the transference-based perception of therapists as accepting and understanding are usually uninterpreted. When the transference leads group members to expect that the group and the therapist will accept any kind of behavior, it must be dealt with. In repressive therapies, therapists reinforce transferences that facilitate positive coping and minimize transferences that impair coping. In ego-supportive therapies, therapists encourage minimal expression of potentially disruptive transferences, and leaders of evocative groups deal openly with the entire range of transferences. Transferences occur to the leader and to the other members of groups, with varying degrees of intensity. Leaders have available the same tools for dealing with transferences as in one-to-one therapy. They can confront, clarify, or interpret (Greenson 1967). They have an additional therapeutic tool in group therapy: feedback from the other group members who can perceive and deal with distorted perceptions and overdetermined emotional reactions.

Acting Out

Acting out is compulsive, repetitive behavior based on transference, patients' character, and impulses stirred up in treatment (Langs 1973). Each of the problem behaviors discussed earlier can be a form of acting out in the group. There is great potential for acting out in group therapy because of emotional contagion, because of multiple transferences and identifications with other group members, and because members of a therapeutic group are not under as close scrutiny as patients seen individually. Acting out differs from taking advantage of a group as a social or sexual outlet. Acting out, while it may take a social or sexual form, is an unconsciously determined resistance. As such, it cannot be dealt with through establishing a therapeutic contract forbidding certain kinds of behavior. Acting out can be dealt with by psychological means only if group members have sufficient ego strength and impulse control to integrate the relevant information. Unless the therapist actively provokes the development of transferences and acting out, the rapidity with which they develop are important clues about group members' ego strength. The more rapidly they develop, the less strong the group members' egos. However, sexual activity between therapist and patient is more often a function of therapists' personal need than patients' difficulty with impulse control (Dahlberg 1969).

Acting out in group sessions (often termed "acting in") may be disguised as ordinary social interaction or peer support. Acting out should be suspected when group members' behavior together is unreported, concealed, or violates some aspect of the group contract. Strong emotional ties between members of a group allow acting upon certain feelings instead of understanding them. Group therapy has the potential for naive collusion by other group members with highly manipulative persons who seek self-indulgence instead of self-understanding or self-control. The group leader must therefore select his members with the needs and psychological sophistication of other group members in mind (Rosenbaum 1976).

When leaders detect antitherapeutic activity in repressive groups, they explain that it is antitherapeutic and curtail it if possible. In ego-supportive groups, its compulsive quality and interpersonal significance are pointed out and dealt with. In an evocative group, the behavior is dealt with through clarification, confrontation, and finally by interpretation of its genetic significance.

Using the Unique Mechanisms of Groups

Certain group processes give group therapists extra leverage in dealing with patients. They are *group pressure, multiple interaction and feedback, multiple identifications and transferences, reactive associations, caroms, reality testing,* and *facilitation of working through.*

Group Pressure

Group pressure strongly affects group members' behavior and judgment, depending on the attractiveness of group members to one another, the extent to which they value each other's approval, and the other pressures the group members can bring to bear. Group norms alter the intensity and frequency of certain behaviors (Asch 1952). Therapists can bring group pressure to bear by simply encouraging the interaction of group members. When working in schools, prisons, or psychiatric hospitals, therapists must be aware that certain group norms will interfere with the progress of groups, and they may have to develop a core of group members whose norms differ markedly from the prevailing norms in the institution before treatment can be effective.

Multiple Interaction and Feedback

Multiple interaction brings aspects of each member's characteristic interpersonal behaviors into the group. As each member becomes himself in a social sense, there is opportunity for feedback from other group members about the effect of his or her behavior on the others in the group. Promoting that type of awareness is extremely important in dealing with character pathology and the secondary gain of neurotic symptoms. Group members often try to avoid direct moment-to-moment interpersonal feedback by labeling a fellow group member as hostile or dependent, or as a game player, but groups whose members have varied levels of ego strength can deal with the impact of each member on the others if interventions are carefully timed and dosed.

Multiple Identifications and Transferences

As a consequence of multiple interaction, multiple identifications and multiple transferences develop. Group therapy has the advantage of offering multiple objects for identification and transference development in the therapeutic situation, thus broadening the opportunity for emotional growth and for conflict resolution (Gladfelter 1974).

Reactive Associations

Reactive associations occur spontaneously, or the leader may press for reactive associations when emotionally loaded subjects arise in groups. The reactive associations of other group members illuminate the problems of all members of the group, as well as the protagonist of the moment. When emotionally important subjects arise, leaders ask each member's reactions at a level appropriate for that group at that point in time.

Caroms

Leaders must also stay alert for caroms, in which interactions between persons in the group have an impact on a member who was not part of the interaction. Caroms often occur when leaders make remarks to any one group member. Addressing one group member's passivity may cause another to wonder if the therapist is speaking to his problem as well. A vicarious harmful experience may be undetected unless the leader pays careful attention to the nonverbal behavior of group members, including posture, facial expression, and alterations of the seating arrangement (Kadis et al. 1974). Patients who feel hurt may begin to look dejected and move physically to the outside of the group or near the door. Some caroms do not come to the therapists' attention until a much later time.

> Mrs. H. had been in a group in which a fellow member, Mrs. A.G., had committed suicide. She recalled the therapist noting before the other woman's suicide that both of Mrs. A.G.'s parents had died by suicide and remembered her feeling that her own fate was probably sealed as well.

Reality Testing

The group offers an opportunity for reality testing through comparing perceptions. As one group member describes his perception of an event in his life outside the group or in the group, others tell their view of the same situation. Anticipated reactions can also be discussed in response to questions such as, "Will my boss get angry and fire me if I ask for a raise, or if I make a suggestion as to how the work could be done better?" In the group, members can ask other members, "Did you get angry when I asked for advice, or was it my imagination?" Even when a negative response occurs, it may not occur for the reason a group member surmises. For example, "No, I didn't get angry about you asking for advice. I was angry because you think so little of your own judgment, even though you're usually right on target."

Facilitation of Working Through

In addition to behavioral rehearsal, the group facilitates working through by repeated positive and negative reinforcement from group members. Group members can role-play spouses, employers, parents, or children to help develop necessary interpersonal skills and to facilitate the transition to more adaptive behavior. In that way, the pressure toward action in groups can be harnessed constructively. The following example shows correction of reality testing and part of the working through process.

> Mr. P. came gloomily to a group session one day and said he had been severely chastised in a letter from his company president. He was encouraged to read the letter to the group,

> whose members responded by telling him that he had totally misread it, that it was highly complimentary. He disbelieved the group at first. Later, he was chagrined, and finally, pleased. He had earlier dealt at length with his father's critical attitude toward him, but the group clarifying his boss's letter helped him recognize his distorted perceptions. Many similar incidents of his inability to recognize praise were corrected by the group until he became able to accept praise when he received it.

Summary

A group is more than the sum of its parts. Working together, people in a group can provide each other with a powerful impetus for growth or can seek a level of mutual comfort that results in a prolonged stalemate or destructive acting out. Familiarity with the common attributes and tensions in small groups allows leaders to shape their groups in the best direction for all of their members. G-responses and events in the lives of groups all have the potential for blocking or stimulating therapeutic progress.

Group leaders need to know the resistances unique to groups and the unique therapeutic mechanisms of groups and to have objective information about their own operations as people and in relation to patients. Self-aware group leaders with a knowledge of group process are equipped to deal with or use the group process as needed to work with group members at the most helpful level.

5

Conducting Groups

THERAPEUTIC GROUPS HAVE THE ADVANTAGE over preexisting interpersonal systems (such as families) in that the group leader, within certain limits, can compose the group and conduct the group interaction to produce different types of interaction and different therapeutic effects.

The type of therapeutic group employed and the conduct of that group depend on many variables, including the potential group members, the setting, and the length of time group members will be available for treatment. A group in a short-term psychiatric inpatient facility may be ongoing, but may involve each group member for only a short period of time and deal with a very narrow range of issues. Groups on college campuses often begin shortly after the school year starts, focus on school-related problems, and conclude after a finite number of sessions—typically, at the end of the school year when the students leave campus. In a private practice setting, groups may be ongoing, may encourage membership for several years, and may cover a wide range of interpersonal and intrapsychic issues.

Leaders begin structuring their groups long before they actually convene. They make tentative decisions about goals for the group, the therapeutic means they will employ, the optimal style of group leadership, the best type and number of group members, and the group rules.

They consider whether projected groups are best conducted as open or closed groups, whether the groups will include patients in combined or conjoint psychotherapy, and whether they will encourage coordinated meetings or use methods such as marathon sessions or encounter techniques to stimulate interaction or break through resistances. Group therapists may decide that time-limited groups are most appropriate for their patients, or may even choose not to designate group members as patients, but instead as groups of persons facing common environmental or physical stresses.

When a group is convened, the leader shares his goals and the means by which he proposes to attain them. The leader and the group members decide together (during a single session or over many sessions) whether the goals or the means toward those goals should be modified.

The Basic Structure

The basic structure of a therapeutic group depends on the leader's goal and the method of treatment, and includes the following:

1. The group's focus
2. The relationship of the leader to the group
3. The leader's interventions
4. Intermember relationships
5. Frequency and length of meetings
6. Duration of the group
7. Group size
8. Provisions for adding new members
9. Coordinated meetings
10. Combined or conjoint therapies

By properly designing the structural arrangements listed above, the therapist can construct any of the three general types of group therapy (repressive, ego-supportive, or evocative) that will be described next. Although described separately, there is much overlap between these basic approaches. They are separated to clarify certain fundamental aspects of group structure and leader intervention. Repressive interventions are often used in ego-supportive and evocative groups when anxiety levels run too high or the overall ego strength of group members is too low. Evocative techniques may be used occasionally in repressive groups to demonstrate the existence of unconscious mental processes. Of most importance is that the therapist's techniques meet the treatment needs of the group members.

Repressive Groups

The techniques of repressive group therapy are the most widely applicable of the three types of groups. Because these groups have a concrete focus, patients usually come away from each session with a sense of having gained something: a technique for coping better, an explanation of their symptoms, or a catch-word or catch-phrase that enables them to be more tolerant of the ups and downs of daily living.

Leaders of repressive groups teach means to deal with conscious attitudes and concrete reality problems, give advice, and encourage group members to advise one another. Encouragement of advice-giving emphasizes that group members have something of value to offer and stimulates peer interaction.

An agenda or formal plan is often used to provide structure for meetings. That agenda may be established by the leader or by the leader and the group members together. It may be decided at the beginning of a session, or may be formulated at the end of the preceding session. Active discussion can be encouraged, but the group may also be conducted as a class with limited discussion and interaction between group members.

Group sessions focus on problems of daily living. If patients are living in a hospital or residential treatment facility, discussion may be limited to events occurring in that setting. Generally, the focus is not on the life of the group itself. Active structuring of the group by the leader minimizes interpersonal tensions. When conflicts arise between group members, they are dealt with as misunderstandings or as the result of differing points of view. Transference and childhood antecedents are referred to in a didactic way. Statements such as "many people act toward their therapists as if the therapist were a parent" or "many of our present-day ways of seeing and reacting to others are determined by our experiences in childhood" are used to explain transference-based behavior and attitudes linked to childhood experience.

Group members are encouraged to accept and identify with one another instead of identifying each person's maladaptive patterns of behavior. They are encouraged to support others' positive behaviors and ways of thinking. Universalization is promoted by discussing individual problems and connecting them to those of other group members.

In order for repressive groups to function effectively, members are taught means to reduce rapidly the tensions that would otherwise hamper group discussion. Anxiety is treated as an unpleasant emotional state that cannot always be avoided, but that can be reduced by engaging in mental or physical activity that focuses attention away from feelings. As in all groups, excessive levels of anxiety are signaled by individual absences, group silences, and the inability of the group to focus on any one subject. Those signals in a repressive group indicate that the leader needs to provide more input or more structure. Anxiety is also kept low by helping group members avoid developing intense feelings toward one another, or by circumscribing expression of intense negative feelings to specified short periods of time (Yalom 1983).

Focusing on the members' potency and avoiding despair and other intense negative feelings also helps to promote camaraderie and avoids challenging members' control of their emotions. When angry feelings arise in the group, they are explained as a normal reaction to frustration and effort is made to discover what real event in the group or the group member's present life situation stimulated them. If no source is discovered, groups generally accept the leader's comment that everyone has bad days. When part of a repressive group's goal is acceptance of angry feelings in one's self and others, group members can be praised for feeling anger and then challenged or helped to find useful and acceptable channels for discharging that anger.

The prototype of a repressive group is Pratt's (1917) "class treatment" of tuberculous patients. Cognitive Therapy (Beck 1976), Reality Therapy (Glasser 1963), and Rational-Emotive Therapy (Ellis 1975) are repressive therapies.

Repressive groups are also used to orient patients to psychiatric hospitals, to deal with the problems of being a psychiatric inpatient, to improve reality testing (Betcher et al. 1982), to increase social skills (Yalom 1983), and to help work out tensions related to hospital discharge. Lonergan (1982) has reported on the use of repressive groups with medical/surgical clinic patients and inpatients in a general hospital.

1. The Group's Focus

The focus of the group is on living in reality, learning to work for what one wants instead of wishing for it, and assuming reasonable responsibility for one's self. Therapists help group members maintain repression of unconscious wishes and fears. They do so by explaining, not interpreting. Dreams are explained in terms of here-and-now problems. Behavior in the here-and-now is explained by reference to patterns of behavior learned in childhood, but patients are not encouraged to delve into dreams or to relive traumatic events from childhood that have been partially repressed. Instead, they are encouraged to assume responsibility for changing their behavior.

2. Leader-Group Relationship

The group is usually leader-oriented, with the leader frequently choosing the activities or focus of each session.

3. The Leader's Interventions

The principal therapeutic interventions in repressive groups are listed in Table 3 on page 41. The primary therapeutic intervention in repressive group psychotherapy is direct education. For example, persons who require psychotropic medications can be told why their medication is important, how to take it, and what side effects they can expect. Direct education is useful in dealing with persons who have brittle psychological defenses and in dealing with persons for whom psychological probing in a particular area is of no avail.

An example from a cognitive therapy group shows the use of a highly structured format with a specific agenda aimed at teaching cognitive skills.

Therapist: Okay. Let's set our agenda for today; Ed, anything to put on?

Ed: Well, not specifically. Things have been maybe a little better.

T: We'll want to be sure to go over the self-monitoring you did. Marilyn?

Marilyn: I've got that party coming up Friday. . . . I just don't know how I'm going to be able to manage it.

T: That's the party you talked about two weeks ago?

M: Yes, one of us, one of the cousins, has it every year. . . . It's my turn this year. . . . I just don't think I can do it.

Ken: Why is that, Marilyn?

M: It's too much, I just can't do it. . . . I have trouble getting dinners on the table, I have trouble getting out of bed in the morning, I even have trouble getting here to group. . . . How can I give a party for a group?

K: What exactly do you have to do?

M: Everything. . . . I've got to clean the house, do the shopping, cook the meal, everything. . . .

T: Sounds like you're feeling overwhelmed. Ed, if you were Marilyn, how would you try to go about organizing for the party?

E: For the party? I don't know. . . .

T: I'm thinking about the way you went about getting your apartment cleaned up last week. . . .

E: Oh, you mean breaking it up?

T: Yes. You're something of an expert now in chopping big jobs down to size. What kind of steps might be helpful for Marilyn, do you think?

E: Well, it was helpful to me to make a list of what I needed to do, then check the things off as I finished them.

T: You mean actually write things down.

E: Yeah, write out a list. When we did that last time, I just took the list home and went through it.

K: I always try to start with something easy first; that seems to make it easier to get started. . . .

T: Marilyn, you look upset; what's going on for you?

M: It just all seems like so much, I'll never be able to do it.

> *T:* That's a good example of an automatic thought, isn't it? Why don't we try listing the things you'll need to do; then we'll see whether or not some of Ed's and Ken's suggestions might not help make it easier.
> *M:* It just seems like too much.
> *E:* It did for me, too. I know just how you feel, like it's all too much. But breaking it up seems to really help.
> *T:* If nothing else, it will give us some good practice both in terms of breaking up big tasks into manageable units, and helping generate some good examples of automatic negative thoughts to practice with—like the one you just had. Ken, will you be the "scribe" here for Marilyn? Ed, what would you want to know from Marilyn about what she needs to do? . . . (Hollon and Shaw 1979, pp. 348–349)

The therapist used Ed's experience in chopping big things down to size to reinforce his sense of competence and to teach Marilyn the coping technique he had learned.

4. Intermember Relationships

Therapists actively limit and control group members' interaction. Cohesion is fostered through universalization and the encouragement of mutual identification. Therapists build positive ties with group members and try to minimize or avert intense affective interchanges that might polarize group members. Positive interactions are reinforced. Leaders deal with potentially disruptive interactions by changing the subject, by labeling them as potentially destructive and directly suppressing them, or by helping members to find a positive way to state the same feelings or point of view.

Usually, extragroup contacts are encouraged in repressive groups. Members are encouraged to support each other in real ways (such as providing transportation) and to become friends, thus reinforcing a view of the world as basically friendly and helpful instead of hostile and uncaring.

Group members are encouraged to practice the skills that they learn in their groups and to use their groups as a place to rehearse positive ways of thinking and behaving. Patient government, a form of repressive group therapy employed in long-term inpatient settings, stimulates coping skills such as cooperation and sharing of responsibility (Jones 1953).

5. Frequency and Length of Meetings

The frequency with which repressive groups meet depends on the setting and the group task. Ward groups in psychiatric inpatient facilities can meet five days a week (Yalom 1983). Such groups can meet for periods of time ranging from 30 minutes to an hour depending on the length of the group's agenda.

Outpatient repressive groups, such as former hospital patients being maintained on medication, can meet as infrequently as once a month for a 60- to 90-minute session. Other outpatient repressive groups, such as cognitive therapy groups, meet once or twice a week for one or two hours (Hollon and Shaw 1979).

6. Duration of the Group

Hospital ward groups continue indefinitely; the length of group members' stay is dictated by the length of their stay on the ward. Inpatient repressive groups may be established to deal with certain tasks and may be time-limited, such as four-session predischarge groups.

Cognitive Therapy groups for treating depressed outpatients are usually established on a time-limited basis (Rush and Giles 1982). Outpatient groups that provide long-term support for former hospital patients may continue indefinitely.

7. Group Size

The maximum size of a repressive group is dictated by the group leader's ability to capture members' attention and to control the group interaction. Thus, it might be possible to deal with a group of 15 cooperative patients, but a much smaller group would be necessary if some group members required substantial individual attention or limit-setting.

8. Provisions for Adding New Members

Unless the group is time-limited and has a specific agenda, new members can readily be added to repressive groups. New members frequently stimulate discussion and seldom impede the function of large groups. The addition of new members is often not discussed in advance, as the focus of the group is on coping with specific problems or with daily living and not on events in the group's life. Often, new members are assigned to inpatient groups without preparation, and experienced members can be assigned to acquaint the new members with the group's rules and style of operation.

9. Coordinated Meetings

Formal group meetings without the leader may be encouraged or discouraged, depending on the task at hand. If the goal of the group is to help develop social skills, planned social meetings without the therapist may be indicated. Repressive groups may have premeetings to plan the day's agenda or postmeetings to practice cognitive skills introduced during the regular sessions. If the group members have little capacity for self-regulation, group meetings without the leader may be detrimental.

10. Combined or Conjoint Therapies

Repressive groups are often part of broader treatment programs that include antipsychotic or antidepressant medication, hospital or day treatment center milieu, and individual psychotherapy. The need to take medication is stressed, and members advise each other on detecting and dealing with side effects of medication. Dealing with issues of dosage is usually left to the treating physician. The content of individual therapy sessions is often excluded from repressive groups because of their sharp focus on dealing with day-to-day living.

Ego-Supportive Groups

Ego-supportive techniques are probably the techniques most commonly employed by trained group therapists. They are more comfortable for therapists than repressive techniques because they require less intense activity by the group leader and involve a give and take that is more personally stimulating than the one-way interaction of repressive group leaders with their group members.

Ego-supportive group psychotherapy is synonymous with counseling (Kadis et al. 1974) or interactional (Yalom 1975) group psychotherapy. Ego-supportive groups cultivate an awareness that interpersonal events cause feelings that in turn stimulate behavior. They help modify pathological interpersonal and ego defenses, and develop sensitivity to interpersonal actions and reactions in the group and in daily life.

A formal agenda is not commonly employed. Active discussion of relationships and interactions with other group members is encouraged. Conflicts that arise between group members are explored and not suppressed or explained away. Ties to the past are established to understand behavior in the group and to work through attitudes or transferences that interfere with interpersonal relationships. Anxiety is viewed as a signal of potentially resolvable intrapsychic conflict; tensions in the group are viewed as signs of potentially resolvable interpersonal conflict.

When group members have sufficient ego strength, attempts can be made to deal with certain maladaptive ego defense mechanisms. However, leaders avoid directly challenging group members' most important pathological defense mechanisms until they are certain that the group will support them through a period of deprivation.

Most once-a-week outpatient groups, whether designated as psychoanalytic group psychotherapy, Transactional Analysis, or Gestalt Therapy, operate at an ego-supportive level.

1. The Group's Focus

The group focuses on interpersonal relationships. Group members learn about themselves through their interaction with other group members and through connecting their feelings and behavior in the group to the interpersonal events of their present and earlier life. As each member's characteristic patterns of relatedness emerge within the group, they become available for reflection and for support or discouragement by other group members and the leader. Group members are encouraged to become aware of their feelings about others in the group and to express those feelings in words. That includes the entire gamut of feelings, and therefore requires that group members tolerate the expression of tender, sexual, and aggressive feelings toward one another. As feelings are expressed, reality-based feelings are sorted out from feelings rooted in childhood experience and feelings displaced from conflicts in present-day life.

In contrast to repressive groups, advice-giving is discouraged. Members are urged to share their feelings and perceptions with one another instead of offering alternative courses of action. As a result, the level of tension and anxiety is higher in an ego-supportive group than in a repressive group, and ego-supportive groups are more likely to stimulate acting out by persons with little impulse control.

As groups become able to tolerate emotional tension, individual members are encouraged to recognize their unique attributes, values, and conflicts. This emphasis on differentiation works against group cohesiveness and can polarize groups into persons with similar or complementary attributes, values, and conflicts.

2. Leader-Group Relationship

Leaders are no less active in ego-supportive groups than repressive groups, but they are active in a different way. The leader initiates the group by stimulating enough cohesion so that the group members interact and form meaningful relationships with one another. While still the central person in the group, the leader does less teaching and more encouraging of members to interact. Leaders withhold advice and turn group members' attempts at mutual advice-giving into mutual exploration, asking group members why they seek advice from the others, and also asking why others feel impelled to give advice. Thus, leaders turn the discussion away from behavior to motivation, and explore the interpersonal "why" of behavior instead of confining themselves to the "what."

Leaders' structuring of ego-supportive groups is more subtle than their structuring of repressive groups. In order to stimulate interaction, they may need to "go around" the group, asking group members in turn for their reactions to events in the group.

Leaders do not supply more structure as tension builds. Instead, they call attention to individual group members' increasing level of tension and encourage them to explore the interpersonal sources of that tension.

3. The Leader's Interventions

The principal interventions employed in ego-supportive groups are listed in Table 3 (p. 41). Using a variety of techniques, including direct feedback and modeling, therapists encourage group members to face emotional issues instead of seeking means to directly alleviate emotional discomfort. In the following example, the therapist manipulated the therapeutic situation to help a patient change a long-standing behavior pattern. The patient was also helped to change through her identification with other group members' acceptance of their angry feelings.

> Mrs. A.N. had sought therapy because she felt she had no personality of her own. She was out of touch with her own needs and desires. Because she did not know what she wanted for herself, she felt like a puppet that others manipulated.
>
> She was at first quiet and inhibited in the group, a problem compounded by her crying each time she touched on an emotionally significant issue. As therapy progressed, she told how she and her father had been emotionally crushed by her mother. She, for example, was a gifted musician, but had meekly followed her mother's profession of nursing.
>
> After a period of time, the group noticed a difference between her behavior in regular sessions and in alternate sessions. At the alternate sessions, she expressed herself well, interacted well, and did not cry. It was evident that she had transferred aspects of her relationship with her mother to the therapist, but was unable to alter her behavior toward him in spite of understanding it.
>
> The therapist dealt with her by gently playing out the uncaring aspect of her mother. He stopped responding to her occasional requests for advice and, instead, turned them back on her, sometimes shrugging his shoulders and saying that he didn't know what to do either. The other group members understood the therapist's tactic, but were angered

by his failure to respond to her requests. As the other group members expressed their anger on her behalf, supported the expression of her anger, and praised her when she began demanding what she felt entitled to, her behavior changed. At first troubled by her "bitchiness," she later took pride in developing definite likes and dislikes, in becoming aware of her needs and in seeking their satisfaction in appropriate ways. (Weiner 1983c)

Through the therapist's judicious role-playing of an uncaring mother, the patient was able to deal with and change a crippling interpersonal pattern. Thus, transference-related feelings are dealt with if they obstruct therapy or contribute to patients' problems in living, and accepted if they facilitate or do not block self-exploration.

4. Intermember Relationships

The members focus on their perceptions of each other and their feelings about each other. Group members recognize their differences, attempt to understand them, and work toward a mutually supportive interaction. Members are encouraged to report and discuss extragroup contact. Extragroup contact between individual group members may be supported when helpful and discouraged when viewed as destructive by the leader. Emphasis is placed on the differentiation of patients as individuals instead of on the cohesiveness of the group. Real friendships may develop between group members. They may socialize outside the group and call on each other in times of need, as in other relationships in real life. Incompatibilities develop, and usually can be resolved. At times they are not, and an incompatible group member may need referral to another group or to individual therapy.

Intimacy beyond friendship may also develop. In that case, the leader, the group, and the intimate persons decide if the intimate parties can work effectively in the group. It is often useful to transfer one of the intimately involved parties to another therapist or another form of therapy as a means to break up the resistance that might develop through subgrouping. At times, however, the couple can remain in the group as a couple.

5. Frequency and Length of Meetings

Ego-supportive groups ordinarily meet once a week. It is difficult to sustain interpersonal involvement when meetings are less frequent. An hour and a half has been empirically established as an adequately long group session; it is difficult for interpersonal issues to develop or be dealt with in less than 90 minutes. Some therapists initiate their groups with a marathon session or intersperse marathon sessions into ongoing group treatment to resolve stalemates with an individual or the group as a whole (Rachman 1969). (Also see Marathon Group Therapy.)

6. Duration of the Group

Ego-supportive groups are usually open-ended and have an indefinite life.

7. Group Size

The usual range of ego-supportive group membership is five to 12 persons. With fewer than five persons, there is too much opportunity to stir up unconscious material, and absences threaten the stability of the group. Issues such as separation and death can be dealt with in an ego-supportive group, but the loss of one or two members of a too-small group may provoke immobilizing anxiety. More than 12 members may result in loss of a controlled interaction and result in a shift toward a leader-centered repressive approach or toward a social group.

8. Provisions for Adding New Members

Group members are told that new members will be added periodically. New members are added at the leader's discretion, but advance notice to the group is useful. It allows group members to deal with the fact that change is both a source of stress and a potentially positive experience. Discussion of sibling rivalry can be encouraged, but more commonly the theme of competing for the advice and attention of the leader is discussed and related to events in daily living. Termination or group members dropping out is also discussed within the framework of the group's reaction to loss.

9. Coordinated Meetings

The primary purpose of coordinated meetings is to help work through group members' dependence on the leader. That in turn develops leadership within the group and fosters interaction and cohesiveness between group members. Alternate sessions may be considered for an ego-supportive group when a positive working relationship has been established between members. If the meetings are held in the group's usual meeting place, the symbolic presence of the leader helps to reduce group members' anxiety and to reduce the possibility of acting out. If group members are sufficiently mature to operate without the symbolic presence of the therapist, meetings may be held at group members' homes or offices.

10. Combined or Conjoint Therapies

Ego-supportive groups can augment or be augmented by antianxiety or antidepressant medication or individual psychotherapy. Discussion of medications can be carried on as part of the group, as can discussion of individual therapy sessions.

Evocative Groups

Evocative techniques are the most frustrating for therapists and group members alike. Because they call for a high level of ego function and frustration tolerance on the part of group members, they are applicable to only a small number of patients, usually highly functioning outpatients or groups of professionals.

Evocative group psychotherapy is similar in principle to psychoanalysis in groups (Wolf et al. 1970) and is synonymous with analytic group psychotherapy (Slavson 1964) and reconstructive group psychotherapy.

Evocative groups aim to rework unconscious patterns of thought and unconsciously determined patterns of behavior by stimulating emergence of material from the unconscious, and may involve developing and resolving transferences and working through resistances by interpretation. The resulting insight leads to change in perception and self-concept through retesting reality and working through. Tensions that arise within the group are actively discussed in terms of current interpersonal factors, childhood experiences, repetition-compulsion, transference, and resistance. Active discussion is part of the therapeutic contract.

Acceptance of and identification with other group members are important only in the early stages of working with the group, or treating an individual in the group. There is little emphasis on cohesion after the initial stages of group formation. Instead, each member is encouraged to see himself as a person with individual needs and an individual life-style. Anxiety is allowed to become intense enough to stimulate exploration of its origins. Individual patterns of defense against anxiety are clarified, and efforts are directed toward understanding their unconscious roots. Vigorous attempts are made to deal with characterologic defenses by clarification, confrontation, and interpretation.

Using role-playing or physical contact to soften ego defenses rapidly may be termed a provocative technique. The value of such techniques has yet to be determined, but they are widely employed (Pierce et al. 1983).

1. The Group's Focus

The group focuses on understanding the role of unconscious mental activity in daily living and on working through unconscious fears and wishes that obstruct mature functioning. The group therefore deals with thoughts, feelings, and acts that occur in the group as well as the events of daily life, material from childhood, and members' dreams and fantasies. The associations of one group member to another's dreams or behavior in the group are of particular value in understanding the unconscious mental processes of both persons.

2. The Leader-Group Relationship

Although the leader interacts with group members, the bulk of the work of self-exploration is left to the group members. The leader's relative passivity is usually a powerful transference stimulator. However, group members who have been traumatized by the emotional indifference of their parents may react with defensive indifference, and may need the leader to become more actively involved to break through their defense.

3. The Leader's Interventions

The leader's main interventions are listed in Table 3 (p. 41). Leaders use many repressive and ego-supportive interventions, but they emphasize confrontation, clarification, interpretation, and attempts to tie each member's behavior to his primary object relations.

In the following example, the leader's confrontation paved the way for later interpretation of the patient's dreams and for changing his attitude toward his father.

> Mr. B. was a manufacturer in his late twenties. He was a chronic stutterer and had been an academic failure at college. In addition, he had great difficulty making sales calls or business trips because of anxiety-provoked diarrhea. Mr. B. had made significant headway in reducing his symptoms through group therapy. His stuttering had diminished markedly. He had returned to college and was doing well, and his nervous diarrhea was abating.
>
> He stormed into group angrily one day, after having been severely chastised by his father, who officed in the same building with him and periodically dropped in to give unsolicited, unwanted advice. Mr. B. announced angrily that he was going to quit his job and let his father run the business. The therapist reminded him that the business was his, not his father's, and that if he quit there would be no business. He was startled and pleased by the therapist's remark, and it became his first positive step toward separation from his father. He had previously tried to separate in negative ways, such as failing in college and refusing to work in his father's business.
>
> Later, after working on material from dreams of shooting

policemen and being held captive by strangers, Mr. B. was also able to deal with his wish to be dominated by his father and his need to pay the price of humiliation.

As in all groups, evocative leaders are responsible for initiating and maintaining the therapeutic process. They do that by minimizing group structure and encouraging free verbal interaction among group members. They intervene when the group turns toward social conversation instead of self-understanding, but otherwise tend to avoid persuasion, exhortation, and direct suggestion. Therapists call attention to group members' irrational attitudes and behaviors toward them as a means to deal with transferences. They allow the regression necessary for the development of these transferences, but carefully monitor the group's level of regression to avoid stimulating acting out.

4. Intermember Relationships

In contrast to repressive and ego-supportive groups, evocative group members interact primarily to develop self-understanding and secondarily to develop social supports or to acquire and practice social skills. The relatively unstructured interchange allows the development and recognition of transferences between group members. Transferences frequently cause intense feelings that polarize and fragment the group, undermining the cohesion needed for working together. As much as possible, group leaders leave it to the group members to resolve these tensions, reserving their interpretations until a tension has developed that the group cannot resolve.

Mutual advice-giving is discouraged because it leads to action and premature closure instead of reflection. Members are therefore encouraged to associate to other group members' verbalizations instead of offering concrete solutions to problems. They are encouraged to share fantasies that are stimulated, and to bring forward those aspects of their own problems that are relevant to the group discussion. Extragroup contacts are examined as possible resistances, but need not be actively discouraged (Wolf 1983). Instead, members are encouraged to report such interactions when they occur so that they can be explored.

5. Frequency and Length of Meetings

Meetings are held from one to three times a week. Generally speaking, more frequent meetings stimulate the development of stronger transferences and other emotional tensions. Sessions are usually 90 minutes long. Some therapists prefer two- or three-hour sessions or sessions of flexible length, depending on the needs of group members. At the moment, there are no data to suggest the superiority of a longer or shorter session, but Wolf (1983) suggests sessions of 90 minutes to two and a half hours.

6. Duration of the Group

As in ego-supportive groups, the life of the evocative group is indefinite. Its open-ended membership enables members to deal with birth themes, sibling rivalry, and separation as members enter, change, and leave the group.

7. Group Size

Groups range in size from five to 10 members. More than eight members tends to favor the monopolizers, makes transference and countertransference difficult to untangle, and may prevent adequately exploring individual absences, silences, or group themes. Fewer than five members makes it difficult to keep the group interaction alive and tends to shift the group from intermember interaction to therapist-member interaction.

8. Provisions for Adding New Members

New members are added from time to time as old members graduate. That temporarily slows the group's progress and adds to the number of dynamic issues that must be dealt with. The group may be notified in advance when addition of new members is planned, to stimulate and deal with the unconscious material provoked by a prospective new arrival. Some therapists prefer to bring in new members without prior notice, thereby not allowing group members time to defend against the feelings stimulated by a new person's arrival.

9. Coordinated Meetings

Coordinated meetings are commonly employed in evocative groups (Wolf et al. 1970). In addition to diminishing leader dependence and fostering peer dependence, alternate meetings allow each member to contrast his feelings and behavior in the group during the leader's presence and absence. That allows transferences to be more readily identified and also enables inhibited patients to gain support in recognizing and expressing feelings toward the therapist that are suppressed in his or her presence.

Leaders must exercise care in initiating alternate sessions. Specifically, alternate sessions must await the establishment of trust and cohesion in the group and must be timed to coincide with a period during which there is not strong pressure in the group to act out.

10. Combined or Conjoint Therapies

Evocative groups are frequently integrated into an ongoing individual therapy. They may be used to stimulate individual therapy, to provide opportunity for self-observation, or to make a transition from self-preoccupation to interrelationships with others. Ordinarily, candidates for evocative groups do not require medication, but when antianxiety or antidepressant drugs are used, they may be discussed in the group.

Coordinated Meetings

Kadis suggested the term *coordinated meetings* to designate the three types of regularly scheduled group meetings that exclude participation by the therapist: alternate meetings, premeetings, and postmeetings (Kadis et al. 1974).

Alternate meetings were introduced by Wolf (1949) to bring into therapeutic focus the spontaneous gatherings that often occur after regular group sessions. Because those get-togethers allowed members to explore their feelings and lessened group tensions, he decided to integrate them formally into the group's life.

Kosseff (1975) suggests that the group is a transitional object in its members' ego development. The alternate meeting can also be experienced as a step away from one's early objects, leaving behind the therapist parent-surrogate.

Alternate meetings usually take place in members' homes, offices, or in the therapist's office. When the meeting place is group members' homes, the site is usually rotated to share responsibility among group members. All members are required to participate in alternate sessions to reduce subgrouping and fragmentation of the group. Members often arrange for light refreshments. Alcoholic beverages are usually suggested by one or more of the group members, and the group as a whole will often indulge once or twice. As they find that alcohol makes it difficult to get down to business, group members usually discontinue alcoholic beverages. When there is continued use of alcohol, it is often a form of acting out or a means to facilitate acting out.

Postmeetings, which immediately follow regular sessions, are held in therapists' offices in their absence, at members' homes, or at other convenient meeting places. The spontaneous development of postmeetings is a sign that the group may be able to tolerate alternate sessions.

Premeetings can be a valuable warmup before regular meetings (Kadis et al. 1974). It is therefore useful if therapists can provide a place for group members who arrive early to interact. Scheduled premeetings can serve as a test of whether group members can interact constructively in the leader's absence. In the regular group meeting that follows, leaders can observe the impact of the premeeting on group members to see how well they tolerate a small amount of unsupervised interaction. A premeeting is the most desirable form of coordinated meeting for patients with little ego strength or impulse control, and can even be employed on inpatient units. At the premeeting, group members can work up the agenda for the regular meeting by reviewing the previous meeting or bringing up an event that has transpired since the last group session.

Coordinated meetings should not be undertaken until the group has weathered many ups and downs during regular sessions with the therapist, or until the ego strength of the members is sufficient to restrain destructive forms of acting out.

When spontaneous social gatherings of two or more members occur, therapists have a good opportunity to raise the possibility of regularly scheduled coordinated meetings in which everyone participates.

While many group members probe for and reveal previously suppressed feelings without the therapist, others feel safer and communicate more when the therapist is present. The latter are likely to avoid attending coordinated meetings.

Beginning coordinated meetings involves several steps, and starts with the therapist deciding that the group is ready for coordinated sessions and will benefit from them, and that he can relinquish that much control over the group's activity. The therapist then introduces the idea to the group, offers a rationale for coordinated meetings, and observes and deals with the group's reaction at a level fitting the type of group treatment.

The therapist can emphasize that coordinated sessions are a step in group members' development of self-reliance. That helps to reassure patients who feel helpless, frightened of their object needs, and mistrustful of their own judgment. There is almost always fear that sexual or aggressive behavior will get out of control, and themes of anticipated rape or murder are common in groups dealing with prospective coordinated sessions.

The first coordinated meeting requires careful planning and a certain amount of enticement or coercion of reluctant members. A few rules governing the duration and subject matter of the meeting will help the meeting stay on course, as will the therapist's request that the alternate session be discussed during the regular meeting. The alternate meeting is usually the same length as the therapist-led meeting, and its content the thoughts, feelings, and behavior of its members.

Leadership emerges and changes quickly in coordinated meetings. Those who customarily lean on others rely increasingly on their own resources. Self-reliant members learn to accept support. Coordinated meetings also foster shifts in perception, meaningful personal experiences, and tolerance for others' feelings.

Acting out usually occurs during the course of alternate sessions (Wolf 1954; Durkin et al. 1958), and it is important that the therapist be apprised of it because the acting out can harm the individuals concerned and the group as a whole. Group members' agreement to discuss the alternate sessions in leader-led sessions is a help. Even when group members do not report directly about acting out, there are often tell-tale signs of guilt or anxiety when the alternate session is discussed.

If the group decides to withhold information from the therapist, one of the members usually makes it clear that the group has a secret. That reporting, which often occurs as a slip of the tongue, may be prompted by the patient's wish to help the therapy, to reduce his own guilt, or to ingratiate himself with the therapist. Such disclosures often reveal much about the revealer. It is important to make members aware of the importance of bringing all material for consideration by the group. To interconnect the two kinds of sessions, the therapist may start the regular session by asking if anyone would like to discuss thoughts and feelings stimulated by the alternate meeting.

Therapists need to examine their attitudes and feelings about groups meeting on their own. Can they relinquish control of the group and be nonjudgmental about the acting out that will inevitably occur? Some therapists are uncomfortable being excluded from the group's activities.

> One therapist had proposed alternate sessions to his group, and had suggested that they use his office for them. He told the group members that he would leave his waiting room door unlocked on the designated evening, but when the group arrived they found it locked. At the next group session, the therapist said with embarrassment that he had forgotten, but the following week the door was again locked. After reflection, the therapist concluded that he had mixed feelings about his exclusion from the group, dealt with his ambivalence, and the door was unlocked as promised the following week.

Coordinated meetings should not be initiated by a therapist who believes that his own authority is all important; that the group structure, with himself as focus, is immutable; or that any acting out is irreversibly destructive and must be suppressed, and that complete control is needed at all times.

Closed and Open Groups

Whether groups are closed or open to new members depends on the setting and the goals of the group. Closed groups are useful when patient contact is limited by time, such as college students' school terms, or the financial coverage provided for mental health care by health maintenance organizations or other third-party payers. In these situations, introducing new members would make dealing with events in the group life impossible, because no common frame of reference could be established. Closed groups are also useful in training mental health professionals, to give experience with the patient role, to develop their sensitivity to group process, to increase self-awareness and to promote the development of support networks.

Open-ended groups can be used in many ways. They can provide a long-term repressive experience, or can be an effective vehicle for ego-supportive or evocative therapies. Having an open group ensures that the group's membership can be kept at an optimal number and allows the therapist to change the mix of the group members to positively influence the quality and quantity of group interaction.

Closed Groups

Potential members of closed groups are asked to join for the life of the group. Closed groups can be of indefinite duration, but they usually function best if they are time-limited or addressed to a specific task, such as helping parents deal with adolescent children or helping medically ill persons deal with problems of convalescence.

Closed groups have the advantage that everyone is at the same point in the group process and is likely to be dealing with some of the same problems in relation to the group—getting acquainted and developing trust, working cooperatively, and saying goodbye. Members of closed groups need not relinquish each other as friends at the conclusion of their group experience, but they deal with separation from the leader and the group as a whole.

A closed group should start with the maximum number of participants compatible with the therapy to be employed. Dropouts always occur, and it is best to compensate by starting with enough people so that losing a few members does not destroy the group.

Closed groups have the disadvantage that the patient mix is fixed, and the group may develop a homeostasis that keeps anxiety at a minimum and prevents psychological work. Should that occur, the leader has the option of terminating the group or opening it up to provide greater stimulation and more productive interaction.

Open Groups

Open groups continue as long as potential new members are available and as long as the group is an effective treatment medium. Members who complete their treatment or leave for other reasons are replaced. Therefore, changes can be made to achieve a composition that will facilitate therapeutic movement. Patients may be added or transferred elsewhere at therapists' discretion after taking appropriate measures with the group as a whole.

Open groups can be initiated with as few as three members, but are more likely to succeed if therapists start with five or more, including some of their own individual therapy patients who are doing well. When new members enter an established group, feelings related to the birth of a sibling or the entry of a stepparent or grandparent into the home may be stimulated. The unconscious wish to eliminate that intruder may be acted out symbolically by the group. Therapists stay alert to the possibility that the group may attempt to eject a new member.

A newcomer's entry must be carefully timed because of its possible disruptiveness. An increase of group tension always occurs, and that is usually reflected in the content of group sessions. A newcomer can stimulate a stagnant group, but it is unwise to add a new member if the group is in a resistant phase that requires a period of working through. Different group climates produce different reactions to new members, but in most instances, the emergence of unconscious material and underlying conflicts is impeded by a stranger, regardless of the stage of treatment.

Individual group members have varied reactions to newcomers. Some ignore them; others try to actively exclude them. Some are friendly to the new members, but attack the therapist for having foisted new siblings on them.

The reactions of new members to a cold or even hostile reception depend on their need for acceptance. In order to be accepted by the group, they usually accept and conform to its norms unquestioningly. Usually, veteran members help new members integrate into the group after they work through their feelings about their new sibling.

After the group has experienced the entry of several new members, there is less sibling rivalry because alliances have been established with the group leader and other group members. Experienced group members who still react strongly to the entry of a new member may be indicating that they feel insufficient ties with the leader and other group members. They may also be experiencing specific reactions related to intrapsychic issues or problems in the group.

Death and separation themes occur frequently as members drop out or graduate from open groups. Members may seek to avoid dealing with feelings in several ways. They may ignore the real or impending loss, or they may cling to departing members or insist that they are not yet ready to leave the group.

The disadvantage of open groups is that members come and go. Therefore, new members need to be indoctrinated and worked into the group, and departing members need to be mourned. The comings and goings of group members in an open group can greatly detract from individuals' therapy by involving them in the life of the group to the point that they are distracted from intrapsychic events or events in their own lives.

Combined or Conjoint Therapy

There are no precise indications for combined or conjoint therapy. Both are useful when a person is making a transition from individual therapy to group therapy with his own or another therapist. They provide a continuing stable relationship and a familiar frame of reference, thereby easing separation anxiety and helping to minimize the stranger anxiety of a person entering a new group (Knobloch and Knobloch 1979).

Ongoing combined or conjoint therapy can also be useful (Brende 1981). Individual sessions can focus partly on the content of group sessions and partly on intrapsychic processes. Combined therapy may be useful for persons who produce little material spontaneously. The shared experience with the therapist can stimulate much discussion and can be especially useful in dealing with those aspects of the patient's personality that manifest interpersonally, but out of conscious awareness. The addition of group sessions to individual psychotherapy can also help provide an interpersonal, interactional focus to the therapy.

Conjoint therapy may help provide patients a different frame of reference, reduce dependence on the individual therapist, and help work through separation issues with the individual therapist. Combined or conjoint therapy can be a regular part of separating from the individual therapist and moving toward peer group support—an analogue of normal maturation.

Continuing other forms of therapy generally eases members' transition into a group and may help prevent premature dropping out (Stone and Rutan 1984), but can be a source of resistance if group therapy is introduced as a minor element in the overall therapy program.

Special Group Techniques

Many specialized group techniques have been developed. In this section, we will briefly describe video confrontations, marathon sessions, encounter techniques, short-term groups, and support groups.

Video Confrontation

Videotape recordings can help group members develop the capacity for self-observation and can stimulate further thoughts and fantasies about their verbal and nonverbal behavior (McCarty 1975). They enable group members to be confronted by patterns of interaction and modes of self-presentation without the judgmental quality that often accompanies the therapist's or other group member's confrontations (Wachtel 1983; Rosen and Spitz 1979).

Videotapes can be replayed during the course of a session, at its end, or at alternate sessions. It is important, however, that the group does not become distracted from its main purpose of interacting together by becoming overly involved in viewing tapes of the sessions.

Marathon Sessions

Rachman (1969) suggests using marathon sessions to begin a therapy group, to resolve a stalemate or a crisis in a group, to intensify the emotional involvement of group members, and to consolidate and test out insights and emotional gains. Mintz (1971) augments the marathon experience with interpersonal exercises that involve structured interaction.

Stoller and Bach (Bach 1968), who developed extended group sessions for patients in ongoing psychotherapy, suggest that eight to 14 (or more) participants meet over a weekend for a total therapy time of 12 to 48 hours. The atmosphere is informal; food and nonalcoholic beverages are provided. Complete freedom of verbal expression with immediate dropping of facades, psychological defenses, and interpersonal maneuvers is stressed; defensive maneuvering is immediately challenged. There is direct pressure for change during the group session. Participants are given advice and are directed toward new solutions. They suggest that the group operate with an ahistoric focus, emphasizing the responsibility of each person for his own fate and each participant's potential instead of his liabilities.

Marathon sessions have important drawbacks. The leader, handicapped by fatigue and the high intensity interaction, often falls back on his impulses, which may be counterproductive for the group (Weiner 1969). Postencounter "highs" may damage group members' marital relationships or block their ongoing therapy (Saretsky 1972). Episodes of psychosis have also been related to marathon group experiences (Jaffe and Scherl 1969) (Kane et al. 1971).

Encounter Techniques

Rogers' original basic encounter groups employed only the technique of confrontation over a prolonged period of time (Rogers 1967). Since then, many verbal and nonverbal techniques have been developed by encounter group leaders to break down intrapsychic and interpersonal barriers; for example, group members are asked to close their eyes and touch the faces of other group members or communicate messages with eyes and facial expressions (Schutz 1967). Asking the group to form a tight circle and inviting a person to break in dramatically illustrates the feelings of a newcomer in a group. Having group members fall backward into the arms of others or be suspended and cradled in the arms of six or more people arouses issues of trust and often produces feelings of security. Arm wrestling or growling at one another can stimulate discussion of aggression and its consequences.

Judiciously applied encounter techniques can facilitate self-awareness and communication between group members. Schutz (1967) and Mintz (1971) have catalogued many of those techniques, but they offer little beyond what the therapist can do by persistently dealing with individual resistances to positive action or productive reflection. Therapists who feel strongly drawn to crashing through group members' resistance may be caught in a transference-countertransference interaction that they unconsciously escalate by trying to find more and more powerful means to dislodge the symptoms that, to the group members, may symbolize their last vestiges of power.

The study of encounter groups by Lieberman et al. (1973) showed that the experience damaged 8 percent of the participants, and that emotional learning requires cognitive integration by the leader in addition to interpersonal feedback. They found that sustained levels of anger are unproductive. Staying with the "here and now" is not enough; present-day experiences need a tie to other life events, and group processes make a difference in personal learning. Furthermore, structured exercises were generally less effective than unstructured strategies that flexibly meet individual members' needs.

Short-Term Groups

Short-term groups operate as repressive groups or as ego-supportive groups with a limited focus. They embody therapeutic optimism and the development of a sharply defined, intensively explored treatment focus, and require the therapist to skillfully formulate psychological issues and treatment goals (Budman et al. 1980).

Donovan et al. (1981) have developed short-term crisis groups of six to eight members who meet for eight twice-weekly sessions over a four-week period. Group sessions are 90 minutes in length. Groups focus on the present. The therapists are directive and actively clarify and explain the patients' feelings and behavior. They discourage regression and encourage ego-oriented problem solving. Support and feedback from peers is stressed, and after-meetings are part of the helping process.

Support Groups

Mental health professionals with skills in leading groups have been asked to deal with the problems of workers in high-stress environments (Caldwell and Weiner 1981). Many have responded by organizing support groups—regularly scheduled on-the-job meetings conducted by mental health professionals to help workers deal with work-related problems. These groups operate as repressive groups. They do not directly reduce the stresses of the job itself, but diminish the interpersonal stresses that compound job stress. They have the advantage over therapy groups in that the members are not identified as ill, and the group is not designated as treatment.

The nurse support group is a prototype. It frequently begins as a conference to discuss cases that cause nurses personal distress or that they feel psychologically ill-equipped to manage (Simon and Whiteley 1977). The conference often progresses to regularly scheduled meetings focusing on problems of communication in the nurse group and between the nurse group and others.

These groups require active leadership. An agenda is often needed at first, including concrete suggestions for managing distressed parents or for managing personal distress in dealing with dying patients. As the group members come to trust the leaders, they express their personal concerns more directly, but need the leader to keep a tight rein on the expression of hostility in the group, which is often seen as very destructive (Weiner and Caldwell 1983).

The subject matter of the group is the here and now work situation. It helps if the group leaders are familiar with the work setting and discuss cases from time to time. Group sessions are generally held for an hour once a week, but may also be scheduled on an as-needed basis (Weiner and Caldwell 1981).

As with brief therapy groups, the aim of support groups is the mutual support of coworkers without prolonged dependence on the group leader. Support groups do not seem to fare well unless actively sought by the workers involved (Weiner et al. 1983).

Summary

The three different types of groups—repressive, ego-supportive, and evocative—each require a different structure, but the three techniques can be profitably blended at times. The focus of the group, the relationship of the leader to the group, the leader's interventions, the relationship between group members, and other factors are tailored to fit the type of group treatment employed.

Groups may be combined in various ways with individual therapy, and there can be great variation in duration of sessions and duration of the group. Sessions range in length from one hour to many hours, and in duration from eight sessions to hundreds of sessions.

New techniques and new applications for group techniques continue to be developed. Such techniques include video confrontation, short-term group psychotherapy, and support groups for persons working in high-stress environments. Knowledge of the general principles of structuring groups can enable the creative therapist to develop many other special applications.

6

Selecting Group Members

THE CHIEF FACTOR IN PATIENT SELECTION is the quality of the interaction anticipated between the prospective group member, the therapist, and the intended group. The group leader composes his or her group so that a maximum of growth-promoting interaction will occur (Samuels 1964). Thus, every person who enters a group should be specifically evaluated for that group, even if the person is presently in individual treatment with the group leader or if the person is referred by an esteemed colleague. Many patients are referred inappropriately for group therapy, at an inopportune time in their treatment, or at a time when the group is dealing with issues or functioning in a way that might damage a new member.

Initial impressions are often misleading. Therefore, an evaluation is best accomplished through a series of interviews over a period of time. During the evaluation period, therapists attempt to arrive at a working diagnosis of ego strengths and deficits.

Therapists need to have a basically positive feeling toward each group member, and should avoid negative placement: referring an unwanted patient to a group so he will not feel rejected and so the therapist can avoid dealing with his own negative feelings.

Indications

Because group therapy is no single type of treatment, and because different types of groups better suit some persons than others, there are no broad indications for group treatment.

Lack of funds for individual treatment or unavailability of individual treatment are not positive indications for placement of a patient in a group.

Contraindications

There is no absolute contraindication to group psychotherapy, and when contraindicating factors can be altered or removed, group psychotherapy may become feasible. Certain patients' aggressive or sexual behavior in the group will almost certainly force a group to eject them. Such patients may be better tolerated in inpatient groups because of the restraining effect of the institution. The same is true of persons undergoing rapid psychological decompensation. Although a rapidly decompensating member would bring an outpatient group to a standstill, an inpatient group can direct its energy toward helping members cope on a day-to-day basis.

The person who cannot trust or be trusted is unsuited for group psychotherapy. In addition, a person must have enough ability to conceptualize and verbalize to meet the level of psychological functioning of the group. The person who does not consider psychological cause and effect is certainly not a candidate for an insight-oriented group. The individual who is primarily seeking pleasurable gratification instead of personal growth or self-examination is also not a candidate for therapy. Other considerations are the propensity of a given person to act on his impulses and the likelihood of destructive psychological regression.

Generally speaking, it is unwise to place patients involved in criminal activities in groups of noncriminals. If group members become aware of those activities, they may become subject to subpoena and the discomfort and possible danger of testifying against one of their fellow group members.

Selection of a Group

When considering patients for placement in a group, the therapist must envision the needs and level of functioning of prospective group members and the group into which the therapist hopes to introduce them.

Repressive Groups

A repressive group can accommodate patients with a wide range of ego strength, anxiety tolerance, and impulse control because it does not threaten patients' defenses. Because it deals with "real" problems, such as physical or mental illness or delinquent children, it is most applicable to people who conceive of their problems as real, external, and manageable by learning concrete behaviors or attitudes. Little preparation of group members is necessary, and little psychological sophistication is required.

Psychiatric inpatient groups may be heterogeneous for age, sex, nature, and psychopathology. With outpatient groups, a more homogeneous group is desirable, but a broad range of patients can nevertheless be encompassed.

Ego-Supportive Groups

An ego-supportive group is effective for better-compensated psychiatric inpatients and for most outpatients with good reality testing, moderate anxiety tolerance, and good impulse control. Because a group often operates at the level of its weakest member, a suicidal, overtly psychotic, or marginally coping person in an ego-supportive group will all but eliminate its ability to deal with emotionally charged material.

Because there is more disclosure of sensitive psychological issues in ego-supportive groups than in repressive groups, the question of trustworthiness is more important than in repressive groups. Can prospective members be trusted with knowledge of and access to the vulnerable aspects of the other group members that are exposed in an ego-supportive group? Can they be trusted to express feelings verbally instead of involving themselves or others in physical expression of sexual, aggressive, or suicidal urges?

Varied age, sex, education, and marital status are often helpful in ego-supportive groups. Varied psychopathology and patterns of interpersonal behavior are also helpful. An occasional borderline or schizophrenic patient may profitably add his or her sensitivity to unconscious processes to the group.

Evocative Groups

The minimal requirements for an evocative group are psychological mindedness, capacity for understanding psychological cause and effect, intact reality testing, high tolerance for anxiety, and a high level of impulse control. There needs to be a positive relationship with the therapist, based on present experience, past positive therapeutic experience, or positive transference. Otherwise, negative transferences will be acted upon and not worked through. Prospective patients must be able to see other group members as potential helpers. Persons whose experiences in life have led them to expect destructive derision must delay their entrance into an evocative group until that can be partially worked through.

Finally, a candidate for an evocative group must be willing to talk about the violations of the group contract that invariably occur. Treatment of this sort must be entirely voluntary, because it requires full cooperation and may harm ego-impaired persons if they are not allowed an easy exit.

Homogeneous Versus Heterogeneous Groups

There is no absolute homogeneity in any group because of the wide range of psychodynamics, social status, cultural and economic backgrounds, interests, age, race, religion, education, etc. in any patient population. In a heterogeneous group, those differences may generate tension and friction (Furst 1960). However, the stimulation of contrasting personalities, pathologies, and problems may facilitate group movement (Glatzer 1956).

It is often desirable to combine patients with different educational levels, occupations, and social sophistication. Communication may be facilitated by a patient with little formal education who insists on keeping the language at a level understandable to all. Experience suggests that a 20-year age range is feasible when group members are over 20 years of age. Adolescents are best placed with other adolescents, but at times late adolescents can integrate constructively with a young adult group.

Specialized Techniques and Groups

Criteria for the many specialized groups and techniques now available have not been well worked out. Tentative criteria are listed below.

Video Confrontation

Video confrontation can be useful for patients with moderate to good ego strength, but would probably be disruptive to persons with poor reality testing and low anxiety tolerance.

Marathon Sessions

Extended sessions require a high level of ego integration. The intense stimulation of these groups has much potential for damage, as indicated earlier.

Encounter Techniques

These techniques require consideration of group members' ability to trust, to tolerate closeness, and to refrain from acting out. Along with marathon sessions, encounter techniques have the greatest potential for stimulating acting out by patients and therapists.

Support Groups

These groups usually are self-selected. Unless there is considerable peer pressure to remain in these groups, vulnerable persons usually drop out promptly, but even so, may be traumatized (Weiner and Caldwell 1983).

Short-Term Groups

The attributes needed for short-term group members are psychological mindedness, a capacity to see others as potentially helpful, good interpersonal skills, and problems of short duration.

Donovan et al. (1981) suggest that the best candidate for their short-term group psychotherapy is not psychotic, suicidal, or homicidal, and has experienced an acute onset of symptoms such as sleeplessness or inability to work that is connected with a definable precipitating event or stress.

Budman et al. (1981) have divided short-term groups (20 or fewer sessions) into young adult groups (early 20s through early 30s), midlife groups (ages 30 through 50), and later midlife groups (ages 50 through 70). They find that suspicious persons lacking peer relations and interpersonal skills do poorly in the young adult group. Persons who do poorly in the midlife groups externalize; are preoccupied with their physical or emotional symptoms; are in an actual state of crisis; have major psychopathology, including schizophrenia and antisocial personalities; or are substance abusers. They list no contraindications to the later midlife age group.

Adolescent Groups

Early adolescents (ages 12 through 14) are difficult to deal with in groups, and readily form alliances against the therapist when disturbing themes arise. Their primary relationships with adults still involve issues of control. They are apt to deal with sexual issues by giggling, squirming, or defensive denial. At this age, group therapy is primarily a repressive adjunctive treatment to facilitate interaction with peers. Same-sex groups are easier for early adolescents to tolerate than mixed-sex groups.

Mid-adolescent boys and girls (ages 14 through 16) can be grouped together if precautions are taken to balance those who express feelings by action with those who tend to intellectualize.

Repressive or ego-supportive groups are useful adjuncts to individual psychotherapy of the adolescent in the 16- to 18-year age range. It can be a primary treatment modality in that age range, but if elected as the sole treatment, it usually requires active involvement with the parents. Too much can be concealed in group sessions to relinquish all other sources of information.

Members whose ages are in the 16- to 18-year range work well together because they have several developmental problems in common without too great a disparity between members' levels of maturity. The age range usually covers grades 10, 11, and 12: the beginning of dating and romantic attachments, the consolidation of masculine-feminine identity, and the movement toward separation from the parents at the end of high school.

Repressive or ego-supportive groups can be used as the sole therapeutic medium for well-functioning late adolescents. Such groups help with the homesickness felt on entering college and facilitate independent decision-making and integration into college life. Instead of regressing, the late adolescent establishes himself in a new peer group that encourages him to operate at a higher level.

Therapists commonly overestimate the ego strength of adolescents. Failure in school combined with failure to assume minimal responsibility or to accept minimal controls at home point to marked ego impairment if the parents are relatively intact. Referral to an outpatient group must await some degree of stabilization in the adolescent's life and some willingness to assume responsibility for himself or herself.

Habituated drug users are best excluded from outpatient groups. Therapists tend to be readily "conned" by the habituated adolescent who believes he can control his habit. Many of these children have severe ego defects. Adolescents whose sensorium or school work is impaired by drug use are probably best referred for inpatient care to detoxify them and engage them in treatment in a drug-free setting.

Selecting adolescent patients for groups also involves parent selection. If parents are unable to support a child's participation in the group or cannot establish adequate rapport with the therapist, the likelihood of the child continuing in therapy is doubtful, unless the child is an older adolescent who can come to treatment alone.

Summary

The chief indications for group therapy are the likelihood that a person will profit from group teaching, from interpersonal interaction, or from communicating in depth with peers. While there are no absolute contraindications to group therapy, there are a number of relative contraindications for different types of groups, such as intactness of reality testing and ability to verbalize, to trust, to tolerate anxiety, and to control discharge of impulses.

A mix of personalities often enriches the group interaction in homogeneous and heterogeneous groups. No criteria have been established for special groups such as women's groups or support groups, but short-term groups seem to work best for persons who have circumscribed symptoms of recent onset. Because of their great differences in maturity that occur with small age differences, groups of adolescents function best if their members are close in age (Kraft 1980).

In the final analysis, the best means of selection when no criteria fit the patient well is a diagnostic trial of group therapy.

7

Preparing Therapist, Setting, and Patient

BEFORE BEGINNING A GROUP, therapists make preparations that include themselves, the institutional setting, the physical environment for the group, and arrangements for recording and observing the group.

The Therapist

Therapists actively evaluate their own suitability for leading a group (Liff 1975). If they have misgivings about conducting a group or how they may react to certain patients, it is best to evaluate and clarify those reactions by discussions with colleagues or supervisors before selecting members for a group. Above all, therapists need to become comfortable in dealing with groups.

Beginning group therapists are often as resistant to starting groups as their prospective patients. It is easier to introduce therapists in training to group therapy through coleading existing groups than through having them organize and initiate groups, although initiating a group is an important training experience. Learning how to propose group therapy to patients helps therapists learn how to introduce new ideas and to deal actively with patients. It also provides an opportunity to deal with resistance to the therapist's suggestions, and so forces therapists and patients to confront each other as real people.

The prospect of directing and observing the activity of a group of patients frightens many therapists. Therapists who cannot tolerate their inability to control a group might best be introduced to group therapy through coleadership. Group leaders also face many of the same concerns as prospective group members: that their personal and professional ineptness will be evident, and that they may be attacked by a mob.

The Institutional and Physical Setting

In institutions, group therapy must have administrative approval and there must be institutional commitment to facilitating group meetings and group therapy. Because of attrition and the need to add new members to bring the group to optimal strength, the therapist must have access to a pool of potential members who can attend meetings.

The physical requirements for group therapy are a well-illuminated, well-ventilated, quiet, moderately soundproof room with enough comfortable furniture to seat all group members. If the sessions are to be videotaped, the chairs in the room may need to be specially arranged. There is probably little lost by allowing smoking and eating in the group unless those activities disrupt the group interaction.

It is useful to have the furniture arranged roughly in a circle to promote easy visibility of all group members. Couches that seat more than two people may impede the flow of conversation between the people on the couch. Otherwise, the only requirement for the furniture is that it be conducive to group members staying awake. Also useful is a waiting area of sufficient size and with furniture arranged so that the group members can begin to interact before the actual group session.

Record-Keeping

Group leaders need to keep a record of the group for the benefit and protection of the group members and themselves.

A written record helps therapists to guide groups and to keep track of individual group members' progress. It also can include therapists' rationale for their treatment of the group as a whole or their treatment of individual members.

Ideally, group leaders record observations about each member and the group as a whole at each session, and may include a note about the leaders' own reactions. The record contains sufficient information to orient the therapist at the next group session, but not so much that it is burdensome. Some therapists take notes during group sessions. Most prefer to record their observations and reflections after the group. Writing notes after the group session is preferable because the leader can reflect on the session as a whole and is not distracted from interacting with the group by note-taking.

Audiotapes or videotapes are not useful for record-keeping because they do not compress the group interaction or extract themes. If the group leader plans to audiotape or videotape group sessions, that should be part of the group contract and should be explicitly recorded by the therapist.

It can be useful to have a group member serve as a recorder and circulate a summary of the meeting to be discussed at the next meeting (Yalom 1975). Nongroup members can also serve as recorders in therapy groups. Usually they are trainees learning group process by attempting to summarize and relate it to the group leader.

Observers

Observers can much more readily be accommodated in group therapy than individual therapy. Trainees frequently begin their experience in groups as observers or recorders. Observers can be a permanent part of the group structure or may be introduced from time to time with adequate preparation of the group. Repressive groups are usually told that a visitor is coming or is present. Ego-supportive and evocative group members are given a chance to express their feelings and fantasies about a visitor. A good means for a group therapist to obtain consultation is to have a consultant join his groups from time to time as an active participant or an observer. Groups are generally less threatened by an active participant than a passive observer, but activity on the part of the observer may stimulate competition with the group's therapist or may intimidate the therapist if the observer is a consultant or supervisor.

For teaching purposes, it is best if the observer is in the group or views the group on videotape instead of through a one-way mirror. An observer in the group experiences the immediacy of the group interaction. Observing through a one-way mirror lacks immediacy and tends to be boring. Videotapes have the advantage that they can be interrupted or replayed and are therefore extremely valuable as teaching tools.

Preparing Patients

Starting a new group or introducing a new member into an established group begins when therapist or patient raises the question of group therapy. Potential group members require different amounts and types of preparation to facilitate their entry into group therapy and to keep their apprehensions at tolerable levels.

The way in which prospective group members are prepared depends on the setting in which the group takes place, their life experiences, psychodynamics, previous experience with therapy, and whether they will continue in other forms of therapy after starting with a group (Ormont 1968). Persons who have been abandoned may require a long transition between individual and group therapy, and may require a period of combined treatment. The same is true of persons who regard placement in a group as a form of devaluation or an expression of negative feelings by the therapist.

All potential group members require some orientation to their therapy. Candidates for repressive groups can be told that the group provides an opportunity to learn from others coping with the same problem. Potential ego-supportive group members may be told that the group is a unique opportunity to study and understand their actions and reactions to others, while potential evocative group members can be told that the group is a helpful means to stimulate fantasy and to thereby gain access to unconscious intrapsychic processes.

It is generally more desirable to lower than to raise a prospective group member's concerns about entering a group, unless the therapist is testing their motivation, as in Synanon groups (Yablonsky 1967), or is assessing the ability of persons with ego-syntonic disorders to tolerate tension. If a prospective group member's level of tension is allowed to rise too high, he may fail to appear for the first group session or drop out prematurely from the group.

Prospective group members often ask the group leader what will happen if the group is not a positive experience. After exploring a prospective group member's concerns, the leader can reassure him or her that in the event of a negative outcome, the two of them will reassess the situation and attempt to work out a suitable alternative.

After explaining the potential benefits of group therapy, the therapist indicates the place, frequency, and duration of meetings; the group rules; and the fee. When appropriate, the therapist should also specifically discuss the legal limits of confidentiality. The therapist also deals with those persons in the patient's environment who are involved in the treatment process, and finally deals with the patient's own resistances.

Before discussing other specifics of patient preparation, the process of contract-making requires further elaboration.

Contract-Making

Many persons begin therapy with no idea of what to expect of the therapist or what the therapist expects of them (Berne 1966). Contract-making is psychologically important because it establishes a therapeutic direction, a mutual frame of reference, and a benchmark for progress.

A contract between a psychotherapist and a potential group member is an explicit, noncoercive, mutually agreed-upon statement of the tasks each is to perform and the ends to which those tasks are a means (Weiner 1981a). The contract may be written, but is usually verbal, and is recorded by the therapist in his notes. The therapist's record of the patient's agreement to the contract documents his having obtained the potential group member's informed consent to the treatment (Cohen 1979).

Through contract-making, group members begin to learn cooperation and mutuality instead of negativism, passive aggression, or manipulation as a means to deal with others. Contract-making acknowledges patients' influence in the therapeutic process, encourages the group members to assume part of the responsibility for the treatment, and also allows for changes in methods and goals of treatment based on periodic reevaluation of its progress by group leader and members alike. That affirmation of group members' potency and the therapist's willingness to share the direction of the therapy help to consolidate group members' self-esteem and their sense of ability to deal with the world, paralleling the experiences of persons growing up in healthy families (Lewis et al. 1976).

Specific Contractual Issues

A therapeutic contract may include a description of the group and its members (without breaking confidences), and may also include an orientation to the issues with which the group is currently dealing. It always includes the group rules. Most leaders of outpatient groups indicate that information arising within the group will be held in confidence by all of its members. It is at times important to indicate the actual legal status of privileged communication in the state in which the therapist practices.

Some therapists forbid extragroup contact because they fear it will stimulate acting out or will turn the group into a social group instead of a therapy group. Most leaders of outpatient groups suggest only that group members discuss outside contacts with other group members during regular sessions. In repressive groups, outside contact and mutual support between group members is frequently encouraged.

Also included in the group contract are the time and place of group meetings, the fee arrangement, and fees for missed sessions. The contract also calls for each group member to use his share of the group's time.

The therapist's failure to indicate the time, place, and rules of the group may indicate important problems in the therapist-patient relationship. In the following example, an unclear contract produced an impasse because of the therapist's reluctance to tell the referring physician and the patient that he felt group therapy was not an appropriate treatment.

> Miss K. was referred for group therapy. She had been hospitalized for a psychotic illness 10 years before, but had made a good recovery and was on no medication. At the time of referral, she was mildly depressed, felt isolated, and wanted help improving her few remote interpersonal relationships. She sought therapy with her former physician, who referred her for group treatment to help her establish and maintain social relationships.
>
> Miss K. grudgingly agreed to a reassessment before entering group therapy. During the evaluation sessions, it became evident that the bitter, quarrelsome interpersonal style that endangered her job and her social relationships also reflected a very brittle defensive system. In the third session, in spite of poor rapport, the group therapist told her that they were both adequately prepared for her to enter a group. When he then told her the time of day that the session was held, she became very upset. She worked across town, had only 15 minutes to make the 30-minute drive, and could not get off work early. She would not consider coming to the group a few minutes late, nor would she consider referral to another therapist's group. She decided to seek out a self-help group at a junior college and stormed out of the office. (Weiner 1982a)

During the evaluation, this woman's characterologic rigidity emerged, an alliance did not develop, and she self-selected out of the group. The therapist was relieved at not having to deal with her in his group. She had little latitude for change, and almost no tolerance for another point of view. Failing to tell her the group meeting time may have partly been the therapist's acting out of anger toward the referring physician. He had referred a number of similarly unsuitable candidates for group therapy who had been treated individually by the group therapist or referred back for continuing individual psychotherapy. While it was fortunate for the group that she was unable to attend, Miss K.'s difficulty with trust was reinforced.

Proscribing physical contact or violence between group members is part of the contract with groups of patients with poor impulse control, such as institutionalized delinquents or adults who have committed violent acts.

Because premature termination is a frequent form of acting out, it may also be useful to build an agreement about premature termination into the therapeutic contract. For example, the leader may explain that group therapy is often uncomfortable at first and that new members often think strongly about quitting during the first few months. The leader may ask each potential group member to discuss a decision to leave in a certain number of group sessions (usually two to four) before actually quitting.

Alternate sessions also need to be discussed if patients are to enter a group in which alternate sessions have begun. They are generally explained as a means to implement what has been learned in regular sessions and as a step toward independence from the leader.

Physical Contact

Groups tend to stimulate physical contact more than individual therapy, especially if strong feelings arise between group members. Physical contact occurs most commonly when the therapist establishes it as a desirable activity or as a group norm. Adult or adolescent inpatients may need to be told not to touch as a means to reinforce impulse control and to prevent flooding of the ego by unacceptable aggressive or sexual feelings.

Group therapists are tempted to proscribe sexual intimacy between members. That type of rule is less valuable than the general rule that all outside contact is to be reported. It is less useful to forbid a particular behavior between members of outpatient groups than it is to encourage talking about all kinds of interchange between members. Secrets between group members may be important forms of resistance, but emphasizing one type of behavior more than others may stimulate that behavior as a form of acting out.

Confidentiality

Confidentiality is an important consideration in preparing many patients. Some persons will not enter therapy groups because they fear a breach of their confidence. Although most states have privilege statutes, none guarantees complete confidentiality of communication between therapist and client or patient (Shuman and Weiner 1982). Therefore, group therapists can promise confidentiality only to the extent that the law allows in their state.

Group members often violate the confidentiality of their group by talking about fellow members to spouses and friends. That type of violation of the group contract gives therapists a chance to deal with issues of trust and trustworthiness, with members' responsibility toward each other, and with the reason for disclosure of confidential information. In rare cases, it may be necessary to expel group members who do not keep confidences. See Chapter 14 for a more detailed consideration of the legal aspects of confidentiality.

Contracting in Different Types of Groups

Group therapy contracts are made according to the type of group the patient is to enter: repressive, ego-supportive, or evocative. In repressive groups, the contract is to learn certain skills together with peers experiencing the same problems. In ego-supportive groups, the contract involves freely reacting to the others in the group, coming to understand the impact of one's behavior on others, and making use of the group's support to modify one's own behavior. In evocative groups, the contract includes sharing dreams and fantasies, and each patient associates to the others' productions. Contracts for all three levels of therapy involve active participation by the therapist and patient at levels commensurate with the goal of the therapy and the desirability of the patient entering a contractual relationship.

Repressive Groups. Contract-making is seldom carried out with severely decompensated persons in psychiatric hospitals. Ordinarily, these patients are told that they will be included in a group that meets at a particular time and place and that they are expected to attend. It is useful to give orienting information about the group: that the group's purpose is to help members adjust to hospital life or to help learn how to deal with mental illness and its consequences in family life and other relationships. Patients are usually told that the group sessions are a required aspect of the overall treatment program, but more vulnerable patients are told that they can leave group sessions any time they become too uncomfortable.

Because repressive groups that function in psychiatric hospitals focus on coping with events and feelings in the here and now, and because it is the duty of hospital staff members to keep each other informed of patients' thoughts, feelings, and behavior as they affect and are affected by treatment, confidentiality is not required of the patients or volunteered by the staff.

Members of repressive groups need not be asked to report outside contacts with group members if they are confined to the same area of the same institution. They certainly should be encouraged to report contact with each other outside the confines of the institution.

When repressive groups are conducted as classes of finite duration, potential members should be enlisted for the entire course and attendance at each session encouraged for the reason that going back and reteaching a missed lesson penalizes the group as a whole.

Ego-Supportive and Evocative Groups. Leaders of ego-supportive and evocative groups commonly build three provisions into their therapeutic contracts: (1) that outside contacts between group members be reported in the group, (2) that the material discussed in the group is confidential, and (3) that the individual group member stay with the group for a certain minimum time, or that he agree to give sufficient notice of intent to leave so that his decision can be dealt with by other members of the group. Those contracts are made during individual sessions before entering group therapy, and are reiterated in the group sessions. Outside contacts need to be reported to deal with subgrouping. Confidentiality is important for maintaining trust. Contracting for a minimum stay in the group is a means to prevent fleeing in reaction to the anxiety of entering a new group. A period of consideration before dropping out of a group is partly to help deal with acting out and partly to emphasize the responsibility of each group member toward the other group members.

Preparing Adolescents and Their Families. Confidentiality is a major issue for many adolescents. Adolescents should be asked their wishes about confidentiality, and they should be asked their feelings about the therapist contacting their parents. With some older adolescents, it is possible to avoid all contact with the parents by seeing the child first and agreeing that conversations with the parents are off limits, except for a telephone call by the therapist to introduce himself or herself to the parents, to explain the need for avoiding contact with them, and to ask if they feel there is some important information that the therapist ought to have. Adolescents who insist on an exclusive relationship with the therapist are often trying to conceal significant aspects of themselves and their relationship with their parents.

The therapist can ordinarily agree that the content of sessions will not be discussed with the parents. The exception is when the child is in danger. The teenager who is close to losing control of his aggressive or suicidal impulses needs to be told that the therapist reserves the right to breach the confidentiality specifically as it applies to that impending danger.

The contract with adolescents includes ascertaining who will be responsible for transportation and informing the child about fees for missed appointments. Older adolescents can be told the fee, and if they are seen without the therapist having been in touch with the parents, should be asked who will pay the bill. Again, it is unwise to accept an adolescent's word that the parents will pay. Therapists owe it to themselves, their patient, and the parents to obtain direct confirmation. Misunderstandings of this sort have arisen in the author's practice with dependent children as old as 27.

The therapeutic contracts of adolescents directly involve their parents. Parents usually make the initial contact and, excepting older adolescents, see the therapist first. Some therapists do not have direct contact with the parents of adolescents with whom they work unless the child is present. The rationale is to demonstrate an alliance with the child. By establishing such a contract, therapists may rob themselves of a useful alliance with the parents and of a source of information about the child. While therapists must accept the adolescent's point of view as legitimate, it is often useful to have another point of view or to have background material the child cannot provide.

Most parents understand the importance of a confidential therapist-patient relationship if it is adequately explained. Parents tend to object when they do not receive adequate explanation of the need for confidentiality or when the child's behavior is frightening. Occasionally, parents are so intrusive that they will not allow therapy unless given a direct pipeline into the therapy sessions. Unless the adolescent is institutionalized, the therapist had best refrain from contracting with parents who are that intrusive. If the parents cannot tolerate a minimal amount of individuation on the child's part, psychotherapy alone is not likely to be of great value. The therapist must firmly, but politely, hand the problem back to the family until they decide they can afford to let an outsider in, or one of the family out.

Therapists can, on the other hand, welcome input by the family, but can also indicate that they will pass along the information to the adolescent. This ensures that families will think twice before calling and that the information provided can be used by the patient for self-understanding or for understanding his impact on the family.

Periodic progress reports from family to therapist and therapist to family are very useful. Their frequency usually depends on the degree of tension generated by the identified patient. The reports need not always be direct, but may be funneled through a colleague to whom the family turns for periodic advice or ongoing therapy.

Renegotiation of Contract

Therapeutic contracts are periodically renegotiated as group members progress or fail to progress, or as their view of their problems changes. People whose initial goal was symptom relief often become intrigued with the possibility of understanding themselves. People whose initial goal was insight often find it unrewarding and opt for advice or behavioral measures.

Situations arise in which therapist and patient are unable to renegotiate a contract that is appropriate for the patient. Those cases usually involve a strong transference-countertransference bind in which the therapist, the patient, or both cannot shift. The best approach to such an impasse is to have a consultant help resolve it by working with the therapist, the patient, or both.

Dealing with Spouses or Other Concerned Relatives

Dealing with spouses and other concerned relatives of adult patients is particularly important when the identified patient's judgment is poor and there is substantial need for others to provide information and to be prepared to take action.

Brushing aside spouses or concerned relatives can complicate the treatment of any patient. It gives the spouse or relative a real reason to be angry, and that anger is likely to be acted out against the patient in the form of derisive remarks or overt efforts to disrupt the therapeutic relationship.

Family members can be told that direct contact with the therapist will not be frequent, that it is welcomed if there is considerable stress or distress in the family, and that it will be reported to the patient. The provision that contacts will be reported tends to minimize calls and keeps the therapist from having to referee family fights.

If therapists deem direct contact with the family to be inadvisable, they need to offer an explanation and someone to whom the family can turn to deal with their concerns about the patient.

Fees

Many group therapists attempt to minimize potential attendance problems by charging a flat rate for the entire duration of a short-term group or a monthly flat rate for a long-term group. Charging a flat rate or a monthly rate emphasizes the group members' responsibility for their own attendance and avoids debates over justifiable versus unjustifiable absences.

Furthermore, the flat or monthly rate eliminates an avenue for the patient to punish the therapist financially by cancelling visits.

Patients occasionally comment that charging for unperformed services is unprofessional and unfair. They use the analogy of charging for an unperformed operation. However, a fee for group therapy is more like the rent one pays for an office or apartment. It is available for one's personal use, and cannot be assigned by the lessor to another person. The lessee has the option of deciding whether or not to get his full value. Unlike individual therapists, group therapists cannot make up for the income lost if a group patient is absent; they cannot replace a person in a group for one session.

Institutionally based group therapists often pay inadequate attention to fees. Frequently, they are trainees who do not feel their services are of value. Often, they are acting out against the institution the anger that they feel about being students or about their relationship with a particular supervisor.

Patients often act out their wish to be taken care of or their anger through nonpayment of the bill. Failure to pay the bill is treated like any other resistance at a level appropriate for the group. In any type of group, failure to pay the bill has the real consequence of eventual termination from the group and, in some instances, is the only way the patient can say that he or she wants to quit.

Working Through

Prospective group members usually have reservations about entering a group. They fear disclosure of their weaknesses, expecting that other group members will be as unaccepting and judgmental as they are of themselves. They express doubts that others in the same emotional circumstances can help one another and they fear the stimulation of their own and others' repressed impulses.

The prospective group therapist, after introducing the possibility of group therapy, therefore needs to ask prospective group members their knowledge or concerns about group therapy, and to give prospective members a chance to communicate that knowledge and their special concerns.

Therapists can allay the concerns of prospective repressive and ego-supportive group members by emphasizing the positive aspects of a group experience, or can allow prospective evocative group members to develop fantasies about and associations to the idea of being in a group. After dealing with the resistances to entering a group, therapists set a starting date. They then may allow apprehension to build again while prospective patients await entry into the group, or may continue dispelling tension and creating an attitude of positive anticipation as time nears to enter the group. Should severe regression or significant acting out occur during the waiting period, therapists may postpone entry of prospective group members until their ego is more intact and impulses are under better control.

Frequently, prospective group members' concerns about the group are displaced onto issues such as smoking, confidentiality, and where people are seated in the group. It is important to recognize those issues as displacements, but it is also useful to give concrete answers in addition to dealing with the questions as expressions of concern about entering the group.

Observing prospective group members' means of defense and adaptation to the prospect of entering the group also gives therapists valuable insight into each person's overall coping and defense mechanisms, especially in relation to new life situations. It is important that therapists not become so caught up in alleviating prospective members' anxiety that they overlook this important opportunity.

When a group experience is added to individual therapy with the same therapist, themes of sibling rivalry and the need to compete for the therapist's attention are common. Referral of an individual therapy patient for conjoint therapy raises the issue of separation from and abandonment by the original therapist.

Summary

Making the arrangements for group psychotherapy is more complex and tedious than for individual psychotherapy, but careful attention to those aspects of the treatment enable group leaders and groups to function more effectively. Developing institutional cooperation, preparing themselves and the physical environment, and providing for recording all work together to ensure the best possible setting for therapy and help to keep the therapy on course.

Therapy is initiated during the patient's preparation for group sessions. The evaluation, offering of a contract, education about the group, and working through patients' resistances to group therapy prepare patients to be effective group members who can be readily assimilated into an ongoing group, or who are sufficiently guided and supported to be able to deal with the tensions of a beginning group.

8

Leadership and Coleadership

GROUPS DO NOT HEAL THEMSELVES. They require leadership to do their work. Although highly interactive and highly responsive to group members, leaders set themselves apart from their groups. They are less emotionally involved, have greater technical expertise, and are better able to focus on long-term goals. Leaders do not become fully a member of groups because they would thereby lose their therapeutic leverage. It is a lonely business for the therapist—perhaps more lonely than individual therapy because therapists witness the formation of emotional ties without being able to partake equally of them. In that sense, conducting group therapy may strain interpersonally deprived professionals more than individual therapy (Grotjahn 1975).

Therapists become exposed as people to their groups as a result of their interactions with individual patients, enabling group members to recognize their therapists' likes and dislikes and their reactions to certain personalities and types of behavior. Through consensual validation during and after meetings, group members come to know much about their therapists' assets, blind spots, needs, and prejudices, especially in unstructured groups and in marathon groups where leaders participate in an active, personal way.

Being a group leader stimulates therapists' exhibitionistic urges and their defenses against them, and may lead to inappropriate activity or passivity. The exposed position of group therapists makes them more personally vulnerable than individual therapists because patients' observations are more likely to be accurate. As a group member, the therapist responds to group pressures and is likely to tell himself or a group member, "What you say about me is true," instead of investigating the source of the group member's perception. In that way, therapists are vulnerable to psychological injury or manipulation by patients who are aware of their need for praise, acceptance, or other kinds of input.

Participation of the Leader as a Person

The personality of the therapist impinges strongly on the therapeutic process, regardless of his attempts to be a neutral therapeutic instrument. The therapist's reactions and interventions are colored by his values, his personality, and his personal needs.

Through experiences as a group and individual therapist and through life experiences, supervision, and personal therapy, group leaders become aware of their personalities and the impact of their personalities on others (Weiner 1983a). The best information about the impact of the leader's personality on groups and the impact of groups on the leader's personality comes from direct observation of his or her interaction in groups by a more senior coleader or by a supervisor reviewing videotapes of the leader conducting a group (Gladfelter 1970). All therapists evolve a style of interaction with certain kinds of patients and certain kinds of groups. A group leader's awareness of his or her style becomes a means to detect unusual types or amounts of emotional pressure in the therapeutic situation. Departure from one's usual style of dealing with certain types of people and situations indicates a need of the leader to detect the source of the emotional pressure (or lack of pressure) and to ascertain the impact of this change of style on the therapy (Weiner 1982a). In addition to changes in therapeutic style, there are other indications of unusual types or degrees of involvement by the therapist, such as preoccupation with or indifference to certain group members and recurrent dreams about them (Langs 1973). In those situations, the therapist's mental checklist includes:

1. How am I reacting?
2. Is my behavior congruent with my feelings? If so, why? If not, why?
3. What am I reacting to in this patient or group?
4. What in myself am I reacting to or acting on? Personal values? Personal needs? Countertransference?
5. Does my behavior need to be altered?
6. If it needs to be altered, in what way?

All therapists are vulnerable to certain attitudes or behaviors of patients or groups. As therapists grow professionally, they become aware of their vulnerabilities and attempt to deal with them or compensate for them.

Many sensitivities of therapists are related to their personal lives: marital conflict, conflict with parents or children, or losses through personal illness, divorce, or death.

Therapists must also be aware of the ways in which their group members conform or fail to conform to their cherished values, whether they be education, upward mobility, or interest in automobiles or athletics. It is difficult for many therapists to tolerate patients whose life values differ significantly from their own. For example, most therapists would have difficulty managing their feelings toward persons who regularly indulge in violent acts or criminal behavior that endangers the lives of others.

The nature of the leader's participation as a person relates to the type and goal of treatment, the real relationship between leader and group members, group members' feelings about the therapist, and the therapist's feelings toward the group and its members.

Type of Treatment

Leaders' participation as a person differs in different types of groups.

Repressive. In the lay-led Alcoholics Anonymous (Alcoholics Anonymous 1955) and Recovery, Inc. (Low 1952) groups, the therapeutic process begins with the leader's disclosure of the problems he shares in common with other group members and his or her triumph over them. Each person accepts the devalued aspect of himself or herself through identifying with the self-acceptance of other group members, including the leader. The subsequent enhancement of self-worth makes possible a limited abandonment of denial, a shift to more constructive value judgments, and the development of new, more realistic ideals and behavior.

In professionally led repressive groups, therapists instruct, advise, promote discussion of important topics, and actively question group members, but ordinarily refrain from injecting much of themselves as persons into the group interaction.

Ego-Supportive. Disclosing therapists' here-and-now feelings can be useful feedback in ego-supportive groups. By stating their feeling reactions to patients, therapists can enhance patients' awareness of their impact on others and can validate or correct patients' perception of others' reactions. The latter is shown in the following example.

> After several years in a therapy group, Mrs. A.D. came to perceive the other group members as disinterested in her, or hostile and rejecting. The group leader said he did not feel hostile but noted that she responded to nearly everyone's attempts to talk to her by feeling attacked and launching hostile counterattacks. The group members whom she had most vigorously attacked followed suit over the next few sessions, declaring that, although they felt positively toward her, they had been driven away by her hostility. She was unable to assimilate the transference interpretation that she was leaving herself out of the group as she had rejected her own mother, presuming in both cases that her dependence would not be tolerated. She was, however, able to hear the therapist's real neutrality and willingness to include her in the group.

Therapists can be models of self-acceptance. They accept the responsibility for their own feelings and behavior and examine aspects of their behavior that endanger or compromise their own welfare and the welfare of the group. Role playing by therapists is at times effective, but it must be identified as such. If therapists do not identify their deliberate role playing to their groups, they may come to be seen as manipulators who cannot be trusted. While manipulation is sometimes imperative in human relations, it defeats one of the prime requisites of the group: being and saying what one is.

Evocative. Aspects of the therapist as a person are seldom deliberately introduced in psychoanalytically oriented group psychotherapy. Gestalt therapists and psychodramatists touch and role-play but ordinarily disclose little about themselves in the process. Leaders of marathon groups use self-disclosure to elicit responses from patients (Rachman 1969; Kovan 1968; Gendzel 1970).

Mintz (1971), a marathon group therapist, reveals her feelings and shares her personal experiences only insofar as she judges they will be helpful in the therapeutic situation. She is often spontaneous, but if she is bored, antagonized, or irritated by a patient, she ascertains whether or not she is reflecting her own personal problems before expressing herself. She shares her own emotional problems only to maintain an intimate relationship with a patient or a marathon participant. She feels free to laugh and cry, but does not ask patients to weep over her personal griefs. Although she acknowledges that there are problems in her outside life and within herself, she does not use the therapeutic relationship to solve them.

The Real Relationship Between Leader and Group Members

There are very few communities in which therapists and group members can be totally unknown to each other. Therapists need not exclude all people whom they have ever met from their groups, but should not undertake the treatment of someone over whom they have real influence (aside from hospitalized patients), or someone who has real influence over them, such as the manager of their office building.

Real relationships also develop during the course of therapy. Leaders and group members come to appreciate each other as real people. They learn to enjoy each other's company and, to a certain extent, learn to tolerate each other's interpersonal liabilities as each becomes important in the other's support network. For that reason, long-standing groups may lose their ability to effect change. The leader and members become stable parts of each other's emotional economy. In that case, the therapist attempts to disrupt the links that maintain the status quo by challenging long-standing alliances, by introducing new members, by transferring members to individual therapy or other groups, and, at times, by dissolving the group.

Group Members' Feelings About the Therapist

Therapists can dispel unreasonable expectations by allowing patients to disillusion themselves in the process of therapy or by disclosing their personal limitations. Therapists need not actively disillusion patients who enter a well-functioning ongoing group. The older group members generally reduce unrealistic expectations of therapists without their active self-disclosure.

Groups usually tolerate therapists' human failings and react sympathetically to therapists' obvious mistakes. Sophisticated groups are also aware of therapists' attempts to avoid responsibility by pleading human error. For that reason, group members can protect themselves from incompetent therapists better than patients in individual therapy, who cannot validate their reactions to their therapists.

Feeling reactions based on distorted perceptions of therapists are readily spotted and interpreted by experienced group members. At times, all group members may seize upon some aspect of a therapist as a means to devalue him. That is especially true when members are involuntary participants and seek to discredit the therapist or the therapy instead of learning about themselves.

The Therapist's Feelings

Therapists' feelings during groups sessions can help them become aware of group and individual resistances. As therapists' boredom or irritation indicates avoidance of issues by group members, they can interrupt a silence by asking questions. Small talk can be steered to a more profitable topic. After group cohesion has been established, group leaders can use their own reactions to deal with group resistances. They can express boredom or restlessness in response to small talk, establishing a tie to the group members who are avoiding discussion of their anxieties.

Countertransference

Finally, therapists must develop tools for self-exploration to enable recognition of countertransference. The source of countertransference reactions can be sought in therapists' dreams, the quality of their behaviors and feelings toward the person(s) in question, therapists' associations, and the types of fantasy therapists can produce in relation to the troublesome group members.

If therapists' countertransference feelings do not alter their behavior with the patient(s) or group in question, nothing needs to be done for their sake. Therapists, on the other hand, may wish to satisfy their curiosity or alleviate their own discomfort, which they can do by introspection, by discussing their feelings with colleagues, or by seeking supervision or personal therapy.

When therapists behave in ways that they regard as nontherapeutic and cannot alter their behavior, they have many courses of action. They can call their behavior to the group members' attention and ask for their reaction as a means to help understand. They can videotape and review their sessions with the group, by themselves, with peers, or with a supervisor. They can acquire a coleader. They can seek supervision or personal therapy or, if all else fails, can transfer the patient or group to another therapist.

Coleadership

Coleadership is a unique aspect of group therapy that offers different advantages to group leaders at different points in their careers (Rosenbaum 1971). It is the best way to introduce group therapy to trainees (Anderson et al. 1972). The cotherapy role is better for trainees than the observer role. Although the latter is less threatening to the novice, a commitment to act as a therapist engages the trainees' attention and encourages the development of their resources.

Coleadership is also useful to more experienced group leaders. They can learn new therapeutic techniques by joining other therapists' groups to learn their style or technique, or can have a visiting therapist for a few sessions in their ongoing group or an especially designed marathon.

Long-term cotherapy relationships are part of many group leaders' practices. Having a coleader makes it easier to observe and react to events in the group, enables each leader to objectify his impressions, and helps reduce the professional loneliness of being a psychotherapist.

Coleadership is an intimate relationship. The two therapists come to know the other's personality and professional assets and liabilities. They confront and support each other and resolve differences between themselves when possible. Cotherapists can offer their relationships as a problem-solving model to the group, but their openness in discussing and dealing with problems between them must be carefully timed and dosed. Early in the life of a group, it is best that they work out disagreements in private lest the overt tension between them destroy the group. After the group has developed the ability to tolerate and deal with tension, coleadership problems can be occasionally introduced in the group by mutual agreement of the coleaders, when they feel that a specific purpose can be served.

Selection of a Coleader

Masters and Johnson (1970) suggest a male-female cotherapy team for the conjoint treatment of sexual disorders. Kaplan (1974) questions the need for male-female coleadership, and to date, there is no evidence that a mixed-sex cotherapy team has significant advantages over a like-sex pair. The most important qualities of potential coleaders are their ability to withstand the confrontations necessary for resolving conflicts between them (McGee and Schuman 1970), and their agreement in attitudes toward working with patients in groups. Personality differences between therapists can be useful if they result in the therapists working in a complementary fashion (Davis and Lohr 1971).

The professional qualifications of the coleaders are less important than their ability to work together. Many physicians in training who are insecure about their own professional identity resent coleadership with a more experienced nurse or social worker. That can often be worked out (Benjamin 1972), but at times pairing persons in the same profession is best.

Prospective coleaders need one or more preliminary conferences to discuss their theoretical orientations, their goals for the projected group, and their commitment to the project. They can also explore each other's areas of difficulty in dealing with patients, and the areas in which each considers himself or herself to be strong. What each knows of his or her own style can also be shared. The cotherapy team can agree to joint supervision or consultation as needed.

Advantages and Disadvantages to the Group

The advantages to the group are continuity of leadership, opportunity for multiple identification and multiple feedback, modeling of a cooperative relationship, working through of multiple transferences, splitting of transferences, and protection of group members from the negative aspects of each therapist's personality.

Through coleadership, a group that cannot tolerate alternate sessions or deal with loss can be assured of continuous leadership. That is especially important with inpatient groups who require a sense of stability and continuity, or groups whose members have little impulse control and are likely to act out in response to feeling deserted.

Every leader is limited by personality in what he or she can offer for identification, and at times certain aspects of a leader's personality block some group members' ability to identify with him or her. The more healthy identification models are, the greater likelihood of group members making a constructive identification with the therapist instead of a defensive identification.

Defensive identifications are often based on transference-distorted perceptions of therapists (Freud 1946). Other harmful identifications are the incorporations of therapists as a whole that occur in highly suggestible patients or persons with poor ego boundaries. Those incorporations can prevent patients from developing their own assets and coping mechanisms, relying instead on mechanisms that fit poorly with their own personalities. Therapists with whom patients identify defensively or whom patients inappropriately incorporate have difficulty seeing the nonuseful or defensive nature of these reactions because they mirror qualities they value in themselves. Coleaders are in an ideal position to detect the defensive or nonuseful quality of such identifications. They can help their colleague to become aware of their fostering antitherapeutic identifications and can also help point them out to the patients.

Because each coleader has a different point of view, there is opportunity for multiple feedback. One coleader may be more sensitive to problems of dependency. The other may be more alert to sexual issues. Their different reactions allow a multifaceted response to each group member.

Group members can identify not only with the personality attributes of the cotherapists but with aspects of their relationship to one another. The cotherapists' relationship can be a model for mature dependency, conflict resolution, and cooperation that can be applied by group members to their own interpersonal relations.

In addition to increasing opportunities for identification, a coleader makes it possible to work out more transferences than a single therapist can. Each therapist, because of the limitations of his personality, can arouse only a few of the possible transference reactions for any given patient. The differences in coleaders' personality and style are bound to evoke different transferences, allowing greater access to their group members' unconscious conflicts.

The presence of two leaders can also split the transference so that formerly unavailable or unexpressable thoughts can be dealt with openly. Group members are often unable to recognize or deal with their negative feelings toward a single therapist for fear of losing his support (Weiner 1974a). When there are two therapists, patients can maintain their positive ties with one while expressing negative feelings toward the other.

Cotherapists can also help protect group members from the inevitable lapses of any therapist, whether they be due to life crises, overwork, fatigue (as occurs in marathon sessions), or intrapsychic problems.

There are also disadvantages, including cultivation of excessive dependency, excessive or conflicting models for identification, intensification of transference resistances, excessive dilution of transference, and the impact of a poor cotherapy relationship.

A group that functions without a break may promote excessive dependence and may not allow enough separation to encourage the individuation of group members.

Group leaders whose personality attributes differ markedly may confuse group members. In an effort to establish a stable identification with one, group members may need to label one as good and the other as bad. Because of that splitting, the transference to either leader may become so strongly defended or defended against that it cannot be worked through. On the other hand, multiple leadership can dilute transferences to the point that they cannot be worked on at all.

Unresolved communication and cooperation problems between coleaders can undermine group members' hopes of resolving their own interpersonal tensions and can also recapitulate traumatic experiences. Coleadership can also encourage the leaders to act out. Coleaders may regress in the cotherapy relationship and act on their impulses, allowing the other coleader to function as their ego and conscience under the guise of allowing themselves to be spontaneous.

A final drawback of cotherapy is the negative impact of group members' awareness of the therapists having a special relationship from which they are excluded. That can restimulate strivings from all levels of psychosexual development, including clinging, attacking, and competition with one or both of the group leaders.

Advantages and Disadvantages to the Leaders

The advantages to the leaders include opportunities for new learning, for relief of alienation, and for ease of observation and dealing with groups. Having a cotherapist allows coleaders to work more intensively with certain group members without other group members feeling abandoned or rejected. It makes taking vacations easier because groups need not be disrupted if critical events occur when one leader is planning to be away. A cotherapy team can observe group interactions more effectively. One therapist can view the group in operation as the other interacts, and in that way obtain a broader perspective. Noting differences in group members' styles of relating to each cotherapist can point to important transference elements. Interventions can also be made by the therapist to whom a given group member is more receptive at that time.

The disadvantages to the leader are having another personality to cope with, spending the extra time necessary to operate as coleader, and the temptation to regress and act out.

The most effective format for coleadership is a brief premeeting to review the last session and discuss impending issues and their management, and a longer postmeeting to review the group session, including the leaders' interactions. Premeetings can be as short as five minutes and postmeetings as short as 10 minutes, but they are an extra time commitment.

The Coleaders' Relationship

In their pregroup and postgroup sessions, the cotherapists review their reactions to the group members and to each other. In that way, the irrational elements of the cotherapy relationship can be brought out and not acted upon in the group.

Coleadership calls for each to know enough about the other to facilitate trust and to maintain a positive, ongoing relationship. Coleaders need not know about each other's early life. They do need to know the current reality problems that impinge upon their working relationship, and to know something of each other's personality. They must be able to compliment and criticize each other. Neither can treat the other as a neutral therapeutic instrument. As in the therapeutic relationship, some gratification of ordinary object needs makes the relationship worth continuing. An absence of emotional reaction to one another suggests that important elements in the relationship are being glossed over and that crucial elements in the group itself are not being faced. On the other hand, the development of intense emotional reactions, whether loving or hostile, suggests the operation of factors outside the real cotherapy relationship and calls for appraising the unconscious forces at work. Transferences may be in operation, as well as displacements from each other's daily life. If unable to identify and work through the obvious areas of conflict in their relationship, they can clarify matters by asking group members to comment on their perception of the cotherapist relationship, by reviewing audio or video tapes, or by seeking outside consultation (Levine and Dang 1979).

To avoid overstimulating group members' feelings, it is reasonable that cotherapists avoid exhibiting extremes of feeling toward one another in the group session. Fond embraces and angry outbursts between group leaders have little place in the group; they stimulate jealousy, rivalry, and feelings of exclusion. There is certainly room for expressing and exchanging positive and negative feelings in words attuned to the level of feelings that the group can tolerate.

Use of Cotherapists in Training

The most common cotherapy team in training institutions is an experienced trainee paired with a trainee who has had no group experience, supervised jointly by a faculty person. If there is no trainee with group experience, the process can be initiated by pairing an inexperienced trainee with a faculty person. After six months of faculty-trainee coleadership, the faculty member can be replaced by a trainee and the faculty member can assume a supervisory role.

The joint supervision of coleaders is a better teaching-learning experience than the supervision of a single group therapist because the coleaders are forced by the supervisor to deal with their own relationship as it facilitates and obstructs the movement of the group. That creates an in vivo group experience for the coleaders instead of a reporting session.

Because they are pushed to deal with issues between them, one of the coleaders often resists the supervisory process by frequent absences. The supervisor can use that to advantage by asking the coleader who is present his or her impressions of the other coleader's activities in the group. Invariably, themes of envy and rivalry present and can be dealt with during meetings with both supervisees. Or, the supervisor can request an individual supervisory session with the frequently absent coleader to deal with the resistance that will almost always be blamed on the other trainee, who is described as inept or boring. As the supervisor prompts each member of the pair to deal with the other's perceived shortcomings and to support the other's strengths, the cotherapy pair usually develops a positive working relationship and mutual respect. For example:

> A self-doubting, self-effacing male trainee was paired with an independent, aggressive female trainee. During the process of supervision, it was possible to deal with his lack of assertiveness in relation to his coleader, whom he first described as a manipulative person to be feared, and later reacted to and dealt with as a competent coprofessional with whom he could actively disagree.

Burnout

Much attention has been given to the phenomenon described as professional burnout (Edelwich 1980). Burnout encompasses a number of dysphoric symptoms that were formerly attributed to intrapsychic conflict: restlessness, ennui, and feelings of inadequacy and little worth, among others. They are now attributed to job stress, and because of their change in name, it has become respectable to have symptoms and blame them on one's work. There are stresses in being a mental health professional (Groesbeck and Taylor 1977), but the issue is much broader. The average mental health professional prepares for his or her profession, but not for life. One's life is supposed to be an appendage of one's career. If the career goes well, supposedly so will life. But the professional needs more than a profession.

Psychotherapy is taxing and often tedious. Therapists need sufficient satisfaction in their personal lives to bring enthusiasm to the office, and they must be open enough to education to bring fresh perspectives to their professional practices.

New professionals should be thoroughly grounded in at least one theory of psychopathology and one theory of therapy. As they mature professionally, they can expose themselves to other theories and other forms of practice. In addition, therapists need secular education that prepares them for life by developing both sedentary and physically active interests that give a balance to life and are available under many different conditions. Therapists need an education that stimulates curiosity and a religious or philosophical grounding that gives a reason for being to sustain them through life's inevitable tragedies. They also need to acquire and maintain sustaining interpersonal relationships.

Peer support through professional organizations and informal professional socialization is valuable (Nobler 1980). It relieves professional loneliness and allows sharing of frustrating professional problems. As suggested earlier, support groups led by peers or outside professionals can be valuable as well (Weiner and Caldwell 1981).

The Ideal Therapist

Ideal therapists are self-aware, recognize that they cannot be all things to all people, and recognize personality types or types of psychopathology that they deal with poorly. They also have sufficient self-awareness to recognize situations that commonly lead them to be defensive or to overreact. While they are able on the one hand to control their impulses, they also have controlled spontaneity: the ability to make an association at the right time to catalyze an important intrapsychic or interpersonal process (Foulkes 1968). Controlled spontaneity involves therapists being in touch with their unconscious processes and being able to verbalize their empathic awareness.

Ideal therapists have sublimated their aggression well and can use it to comfort, to defend themselves, and also, through humor, to reframe group members' views of themselves in ways that enable them to see more clearly and cope more effectively (Schimel 1980).

Ideal therapists enjoy being potent as therapists, but also enjoy seeing group members deal effectively with themselves and with life for their own sake. They take responsibility for their own conduct and, instead of rationalizing or blaming others for their mistakes, use self-examination, supervision, or personal therapy to help change aspects of themselves that are counterproductive with patients.

Ideal therapists know their level of expertise, especially their ability to teach principles of psychologically healthy functioning, their sophistication about psychopathology, their mastery of psychological interventions, and their self-awareness. Good teachers with little sophistication about psychopathology and little formal awareness of group techniques can often conduct repressive groups well. Leaders who teach well, who are sophisticated about psychopathology, and who are technically well equipped can conduct ego-supportive groups well, even if they lack great awareness of their own unconscious processes. By contrast, leaders of evocative groups need not be talented teachers, because their therapeutic medium is confrontation and interpretation, not explanation or modeling. However, they must understand psychopathology well, must be able to employ group process to facilitate the emergence of material from the unconscious, and must be sufficiently self-aware to enable them to guide the group interactions without stimulating acting out (Weiner 1983c).

Summary

The group therapist has a more complicated process to deal with than the individual therapist, has less knowledge of it, and has less control of it. Consequently, therapists who need to be in control of the therapeutic relationship and to know with certainty where it stands at all times fare poorly as group leaders. Therapists who cannot lead or intervene actively in the group to move it in a direction they deem therapeutic are equally unsuitable group leaders. Group therapy appeals to many therapists because of its high level of interpersonal stimulation, but may also be a vehicle for them to act out.

Coleadership is an excellent means to train therapists. It provides the experienced therapist with peer supervision and the opportunity for further personal growth. Patients receive greater input and have greater opportunity for identification and for working through multiple transferences. On the negative side, coleaders introduce another variable into an already complex situation. An unhealthy relationship between coleaders can undermine the group and reinforce pathological identifications and patterns of interaction. To avoid such difficulties, the coleaders must communicate openly. Transferences and misunderstandings are bound to arise. Coleaders' personal integrity, mutual respect, and their professional relationship help them to resolve issues without distracting the group from its work.

Many psychotherapists become professionally disillusioned. The problem for most disillusioned or unhappy therapists is not their profession, but their inadequate preparation for life, their failure to develop a broad basis for living, and a lack of philosophical or religious values. Education is the best prophylaxis. Peer support groups, personal therapy, opening of one's self to education, and developing transcendent values are the best cure.

9

Starting a Group

BECAUSE THE FIRST SESSIONS of a new group are so anxiety-provoking for most new group therapists, they appreciate step-by-step directions to reduce their emotional tensions enough so that they can be effective leaders. This chapter, therefore, provides a detailed guide to initiating a group.

The therapist's tasks during the first few sessions of a group include, in addition to dealing with his own apprehension, a review of each member's therapeutic contract, reiteration of the group rules, setting limits, and establishing a positive interchange that will motivate the group members to return. The first session establishes the group norms and the level at which the group will function. It can also aid the psychodiagnostic process if the therapist is alert to the type of projections each patient initially makes on the group, the therapist, and other individual members. Those projections give clues about the structure of the patient's ego and superego, and the manner in which they deal with conflict and facilitate or inhibit the gratification of instinctual drives.

Group members who expect attack are often projecting their rage onto the group. Or, they may be projecting their own expectation of punishment for transgressions they have not yet revealed.

The First Two Group Meetings

The conduct of the first group meeting depends on the setting in which the group is held, the familiarity of group members with each other and with psychotherapy, and the type of group therapy employed.

As in any new group situation, group members recall similar events from their earlier experience and seek ties to others. The leader can facilitate the process by pointing out what group members have in common. In the first group sessions, some patients exaggerate their emotional distress to capture the therapist's attention, or call attention to themselves by silence. Themes of dependency, trust, and the wish for the ideal parent commonly arise during the first session (Bion 1959).

Most group members begin by presenting external difficulties such as problems at work, or with parents or children. The therapist ascertains how hard to push for deeper issues, and at what pace. During the first session, the therapist's attitude of optimism, confidence, and friendliness is important. Those attitudes enable the patients to feel at ease with each other.

In psychiatric hospitals, the mode of functioning of many groups is widely known, and the participants in the groups are known to each other. In outpatient settings, potential group members may have had little practice being patients and no previous acquaintance with one another.

Typical Problems of First Sessions

The therapist's main concern during the first session is to mold the members into a functioning group. Despite their widely varying personalities, problems, and interests, he or she establishes common bonds, such as their desire for treatment. The therapist may sympathetically comment on the difficulties of getting started and help bring the members' attitudes, thoughts, and feelings into the open by gentle questioning. Another method is encouraging members to react to each other, or to reinforce one's positive comment about another.

Conscious and unconscious resistances appear from the very

beginning of a group. Conscious resistances include refusal to discuss extramarital relationships, skipping school, or other matters that are likely to be disapproved of. Patients who consciously resist may need combined treatment until they feel more secure with other group members.

Protracted silences should not be allowed in the first session, whether repressive, ego-supportive, or evocative. The therapist can break the initial silence by asking people to introduce themselves and to say a few words about why they are in the group. Later in the session, there can be discussion about each member's fears concerning the group. Starting off with a discussion of fears about the group will generally paralyze any group interaction.

The first sessions of repressive, ego-supportive, and evocative groups are more highly structured than the following sessions, but repressive groups remain highly structured, while peer interaction is fostered in ego-supportive groups and evocative groups. At the beginning of the first session in all three types of groups, the participants are introduced. Later in the session, the contract and group rules are reiterated.

During the group, the leader parcels out the time so that those who are willing to talk are able to have roughly equal amounts of the group's attention. The leader also begins to exert gentle pressure on all to eventually participate at a level commensurate with their abilities.

Repressive Groups

In repressive groups, therapists often take the lead and introduce each group member to the others, or ask the participants to introduce themselves in turn. The leader may ask each member to make a brief statement about his or her reason for being in the group, or may first give a general description of the group members' problems and the means by which they will be dealt with. The leader may start by saying that the members have been selected for group therapy to help them adjust to living in a psychiatric hospital or residential treatment center, or that all the members are gathered to learn how to stand up for themselves in difficult personal relationships. He may then turn to each group member and ask for specific problems with

which they would like help from the group. Or, the therapist may describe problems that group members are likely to experience and ask if any group member has had such problems. When those problems are brought forward by one or more group members, the leader underscores their similarities as a means to develop universalization, group cohesion, and identification.

Depending on the experience of the members with groups, their experiences with discussing their problems, and the general level of group tension, the leader can encourage group interaction or respond directly with advice or suggestions to the material presented. Instructional tools, such as pamphlets or other assigned reading, a blackboard and chalk, or audiovisual aids such as slides, videotapes, or movies, can be useful means to transmit information, reduce the anxiety of group members, and provide commonly shared material for discussion.

The following first-session vignette from a time-limited group consultation illustrates the elements of starting a repressive group.

> A group therapist was asked to conduct a four-session group consultation for the 12-member social work staff of a pediatric hospital. He arrived five minutes early, armed with pen and note pad. The group therapist was introduced briefly by the chief social worker, who then turned the meeting over to him. The group therapist began by stating his impression of the group's purpose: to help the group identify and formulate means to deal with job-related stresses. He asked the group members for confirmation, and there was consensus on that point. He next stated his understanding that they would have four sessions together, with the option of increasing to six sessions. Again, there was general assent. Then, he asked the group members to introduce themselves and to state in what area of the hospital they worked. That stimulated discussion about recent changes in assignment, the stresses of working on certain units, and the hiring of new social work staff.
>
> The group therapist was uncertain of what area of work difficulty to enter. He therefore presented his perception of the stresses of working in a hospital, including the heavy work load, dealing with frightened and grieving families, facing severe illness and death, communicating with the medical staff, and mediating between families and medical

> staff. Finally, he mentioned the possibility of difficulties within the social work staff such as miscommunication or differing goals. Sensing that group morale was high, he asked the group members to comment on their relationship with the chief social worker. They enthusiastically endorsed her leadership, and that endorsement united the group in a positive camaraderie. Group members touched briefly on intragroup tensions, but settled into a discussion of the enormous work load and their sense of obligation to see as many of the patients' families as possible. As the group members raised those issues, the group therapist noted them and then asked members of the group who felt themselves to be coping successfully with those issues how they dealt with their work load and with their feelings about their inability to serve everyone equally. They gave useful suggestions to which the others responded well.
>
> Toward the end of the session, the group therapist commented that the group had high regard for its leader, had good morale and worked together well, and suggested, as their agenda for the second session, that they continue discussing the work stresses that had been brought up, and that the group therapist would himself discuss techniques that he found of value in dealing with physically or emotionally demanding work pressures. He terminated the group session by stating that he looked forward to their next session and then said, "It's time!"
>
> During the group session, the group therapist attempted to draw out each member of the group (only one remained silent), established eye contact with each person, and when possible, addressed each member by name as a means to develop personal ties that would be supportive should conflict arise in the group.

In terminating the first session of repressive groups, the therapist gives encouragement, restates the group contract, and selects issues to be discussed in the next session. Homework can be assigned. That may involve reading a pamphlet, practicing skills developed during the session, or applying what has been taught during the session to real-life situations. Group members can be asked to report on their homework at the next session.

Having given the group leader information about themselves during the first meeting, group members may lapse into a state of complete leader dependence in the second. That serves the leader of a repressive group well. The repressive group leader begins the second session by recapitulating what was learned in the first session, by asking if there are questions about that, and by requesting reports on homework. If there was no homework, the leader takes up the agenda for the day, after asking group members if there are topics they would like to add to the day's agenda or substitute for the planned agenda. The therapist tries to establish enough contact with each group member to ascertain and reinforce the positive aspects of the first session. He also seeks areas of sensitivity that may have been bruised and then devises ways to avoid further traumatizing group members.

Ego-Supportive Groups

After the initial introduction, leaders often begin the first session by stating that the group offers members an opportunity to talk about their feelings and to understand their own patterns of behavior, and that members will not be compelled to expose themselves. However, leaders will also state that communicating freely will help members gain an understanding of their problems.

The leader of an ego-supportive group may encourage the group members to introduce themselves and briefly describe the problem or problems for which they are seeking help in the group. An alternative ice-breaker is asking members of the group in turn to tell something they like about themselves, and then asking the members in turn to tell something they dislike about themselves. While telling about themselves, interaction between group members is stimulated by asking their reactions to one another's statements.

Although leaders of ego-supportive groups usually assert less control over the group interaction than leaders of repressive groups, they try to ensure that no group member is embarrassed or humiliated and interrupt extensive revelations by individual group members by asking others if they experience similar thoughts or feelings. While opening the way for discussing problems, the positive attributes of the group members are also underscored during the first group session, so that the therapist will not be seen as an extension of group members' own self-criticisms. The following vignette illustrates the basic principles of starting an ego-supportive group.

> In beginning a demonstration ego-supportive group, the therapist asked the group members what issues they were dealing with in their daily lives. Two of the women indicated that they were dealing with their children leaving home. A man said that he was dealing with being a new stepparent. Another man talked about difficulty with intimate relationships with women. The leader acknowledged that all of those were difficult issues, but encouraged the person who showed the most emotion to continue talking about her situation. As she did, she cried, and the other group members responded with empathic tears. Instead of giving advice on managing her separation from her child, the group leader focused on the special role her child played in her life and encouraged her to experience and express her feelings of loss. After a period of time, the therapist asked other group members how they had responded to the woman's show of emotion, by which she herself was embarrassed. They responded with warmth and admiration of her openness and her ability to face her emotions. Several members indicated a feeling of emotional closeness to her.
>
> The therapist did not attempt to resolve this woman's grief during the session, nor did he attempt to turn the group to a less emotional topic. Instead, he used her expression of emotion to set a group norm of expressing inner feelings concerning interpersonal issues. Toward the end of the session, he thanked the group members for their openness and expressed the hope that they would continue to feel free to discuss their feelings.

In terminating the first session, the ego-supportive group leader summarizes the content of the session, noting the fear group members had of dropping social facades and the courage they displayed in doing so. He asks for the members' reactions to the first session and to each other as people, keeping the interaction as positive as possible. He attempts to reduce tension by explaining that all beginnings are difficult, but cites the openness that group members were able to achieve during the session, and lets the group members know that some will have misgivings about having been so open, and that those misgivings are important to explore in the group.

In the second session, the group leader focuses first on the reactions of group members to the initial meeting and to each other as people. If the group members seem excessively tense or anxious, he can start by asking them what they liked or responded to positively about each other. Here again, the going-around technique is a useful means to overcome resistance to talking. If there is less resistance, the leader can ask for responses to each group member's reactions and observations. Much as in repressive groups, the leader can emphasize the positive attributes group members have in common. As group members settle in, the therapist focuses on feelings and attitudes that are potentially divisive.

Evocative Groups

The leader of an evocative group may begin by asking members to introduce themselves and tell a bit of their main problem. After minimal introduction of those problems, the leader may ask if anyone dreamed the night before or experienced a daydream or fantasy earlier in the day. After a member's dream, daydream, or fantasy has been introduced, the leader indicates that the purpose of the group is to stimulate each member in such a way that the workings of his or her unconscious mind can be understood and dealt with in the group.

The leader regulates gently the flow of advice-giving and mutually supportive statements, allowing enough so that cohesion develops, and noting when various group members feel impelled to give advice or to interrupt the flow of another's comments or disclosures. As the group becomes less anxious, the leader introduces the idea of their giving associations to each other's thoughts, feelings, and behavior. The purpose of group interaction is therefore to stimulate reflection; the group leader pursues the meaning of events in the group for individual members and does not attempt to stimulate strong bonding between group members. Strong positive or negative bonding would distract from intrapsychic events and draw group members into the interpersonal sphere. The group leader must, on the other hand, point out when the process of exploring associations leads to unprofitable intellectualization about what the group members' dreams or actions *really* mean.

The evocative group leader uses Wolf's (1949) technique of "going around" to terminate the session, ascertaining each member's feelings and associations in reaction to the group meeting and to one another. He attempts some closure at the end of the session with a general statement to the effect that the group is already doing its work of stimulating the feelings, thoughts, and fantasies that will be the subject of the group's work in the sessions to follow.

The second session can be initiated by asking about dreams or fantasies that followed the first session or preceded the second. If the leader senses overwhelming anxiety, he can use repressive or ego-supportive techniques until the level of group tension is reduced. Although tension and anxiety are an important driving force in evocative groups, it is better at first to underestimate the group's ability to tolerate tension than to overestimate their anxiety tolerance and disrupt or paralyze the group.

Summary

The first group sessions are the most threatening for therapists and prospective group members. Their success depends on the therapist's own preparation and that of the group members, and the therapist's ability to maintain his or her anxiety and theirs within tolerable limits: not great enough to increase members' defensiveness so much that they flee, and not so little as to establish a group climate of avoiding important issues. Although the first session sets the tone of the group, the emotional intensity of the first session needs to be controlled and the interaction structured in general conformity to the level at which the therapist intends to work. Cohesion is developed, but not at the expense of the group task.

10

Dreams and Imagery

WE HAVE DEALT WITH GROUP PSYCHOTHERAPY thus far as an interchange of verbal symbols. In this chapter, we will consider the role of other symbols in group psychotherapy: the visual and kinesthetic symbols of dreams and of fantasies, and imagery. The fundamental difference between dreams, fantasies, and imagery is that dreams take place when conscious thought and will are partially suspended by the biological process of sleep, while fantasies and imagery are active products of conscious thought and will. We do not know the exact meaning of dreams, and we do not know how the human imagination works. We do know that since ancient times, the direction of many lives has been strongly influenced by the interpretation placed on dreams and fantasies (Dodds 1971). One can reasonably state that the accuracy of a dream's interpretation is less important than its aptness. Finding the "true" meaning of a dream is less important than ascribing a meaning that contributes to the dreamer's progress in therapy. In a different way, the same is true of fantasy and imagery. Because they can be consciously controlled, they impart a sense of potency and control over one's own destiny. The fantasies or images conjured up by group members are probably less important than their sense of being in charge of themselves and not helpless victims of fate.

Dreams

Physiologically, dreaming results from the spontaneous activation of nuclei in the phylogenetically older portions of the brain that trigger activity in specific neural circuits (Hartmann 1980). Biological investigators of dreaming conclude that dreaming has a role in the human body's protective, defensive, and regulatory apparatus. Dreaming is associated with rapid eye movement (REM) sleep, which occupies approximately 20 percent of adult sleeping time. Experiments in dream deprivation indicate that a certain amount of REM sleep is necessary to preserve psychological integrity, and that deprivation of REM sleep leads to an increased biological pressure for REM sleep and dreaming.

Sigmund Freud viewed dreaming as the ego's means to preserve sleep (Freud 1900). According to Freud, dreaming incorporates residues of the present day's concerns and activities, experiences that occur during sleep (such as hunger or the need to urinate), and material from childhood that has been repressed into the unconscious. The dream results from the sleep-weakened ego's attempts to blend day residue, nocturnal sensations, and material repressed during childhood. The dream thus gratifies symbolically the infantile wishes striving for expression and thereby avoids threatening the ego enough to cause awakening. At times, the ego's dream work fails, and the sleeping person awakens in a state of fright or tension.

The part of a dream that is remembered is its manifest content; the disguised underlying motives and conflicts of which the dreamer is unaware are the latent content. The structure of a dream is identical to the structure of a neurotic symptom. Its symbolic expression of forbidden id drives allows their partial gratification and partial symbolic expression (Brenner 1973). The dream work of the ego involves displacement, symbolization, and condensation, as we can see in the following example.

> Mr. W. had an irrational fear that he might have cancer. His fear was unrelieved by numerous medical checkups. Mr. W. reported a dream that his Aunt Millie had her left arm under her coat. In the dream, he accidentally brushed against her and noticed that her forearm was soft, almost absent, but her hand and elbow felt intact. She told him in the dream that she had been operated on for cancer, and that the cancer had been removed.
>
> Mr. W. was asked to tell his associations to each part of his dream. His associations to Aunt Millie were that she was athletic, the mother of four, and that she might have been recently hospitalized. His next association was his mother-in-law's treatment for a uterine cancer. He related Aunt Millie's absent forearm to concern about his sexual potency. He then expressed concern that if he developed a cancer, the treatment might cause impotence or disfigure him so that he would be sexually unattractive.

In the above dream, Mr. W.'s concerns about himself were *displaced* onto Aunt Millie, whose soft, almost absent forearm *symbolized* his concern about his sexual abilities and, by *condensation,* his fears about his physical appearance and his life as well.

There are other psychological theories of dreaming. Alfred Adler (Ansbacher and Ansbacher 1956) suggested that dreams express the dreamer's total life-style and personality and are attempts, during sleep, to resolve problems of living. Adler's view is similar to that of Carl Jung (1964), who theorized that the manifest dream *is* the dream and that there is no latent content. Jung viewed the dream as a creative symbolic expression of images that reflect the dreamer's mental life or some aspect of his or her life to which insufficient attention is being paid. For example, a psychotherapy patient dreamed she was becoming blind. Referral to an ophthalmologist confirmed the dream. She had been aware of her failing eyesight, there were serious psychological problems she literally did not wish to see, and she was also having psychological problems as the result of her dimming vision (Wilmer 1982).

Perls (1969), the founder of Gestalt Therapy, treated dreams as projections, and suggested that each part of a dream represents a projected, disowned aspect of the dreamer. He emphasized a here-and-now orientation to dreams, tying their content to the dreamer's relationships in and out of the group. The Adlerian, Jungian, and Gestalt approaches are applicable to repressive and ego-supportive groups.

Repeated redreaming of a traumatic event is the hallmark of the post-traumatic stress disorder (American Psychiatric Association 1980). Observations of post-traumatic stress disorders suggest that dreams lessen the impact of experiences that have traumatized the ego by exceeding its capacity for absorbing affect-arousing stimuli (Krystal 1978). Repeated dreaming of traumatic events such as the horror of combat gradually reduce their impact (Freud 1920), perhaps through a process similar to desensitization.

Group Members' Dreams

Group members produce dreams and discuss them to the extent that group leaders invite their introduction and discussion. Reports of dreams can be stimulated by the leader, who can ask if anyone has repetitive dreams or recalls a specific dream since the last group session. He can also ask about daydreams or fantasies about the group. Like any other sort of activity, telling and discussing dreams can become a resistance, and the group leader needs to actively direct the discussion toward implementing the overall therapeutic goals for the group.

The quality and nature of dreams brought to the group by its members often gives clues to the dreamer's perception of the group as receptive or rejecting, friendly or hostile, and also gives important clues about the nature of the group interaction (Locke 1957). For example, when one group member reported a dream of driving his car into a lake, it was evident to the therapist that the patient was aware of the hostile response he was getting from the group (equivalent to "go jump in a lake") and his own role in stimulating the group's hostility.

From dreams, therapists can obtain valuable information concerning psychodynamics, defenses, ego strength, self-concept, and transferences. What a therapist does with the dream depends on his impression of the information it contains and the stage of treatment of the individual and the group when the dream is reported. He must decide how deeply the group members are ready to explore the unconscious content of a dream. The involvement of group members with the symbolic language of dreams or their attempts to disregard them may provide important information on their involvement in the group (Kaplan 1973).

The appearance of other group members in a dream can have many kinds of significance. It may indicate acceptance of others in the group as real people and the development of meaningful relationships with them. It can also mark their beginning role as transference objects and as dream symbols (Whitman 1973).

Many dream symbols are quickly grasped by the group, as shown by this comment from one member to another: "In your dreams you never walk straight. You're always zigzagging and never find what you're after. If you try to walk a straight road for once, instead of being devious, you may get what you're looking for, and it won't take as much time as this useless backing and filling." That response related to the dreamer's manifest present difficulty and to his total life-style (Kadis et al. 1974).

Dreams in Repressive Groups. The therapist who is presented a dream in a repressive group uses it to teach a practical lesson in living. The leader usually assumes sole responsibility for dealing with members' dreams. He focuses on the aspects of the dream that reflect everyday concerns, conscious feelings and attitudes, and the dreamer's characteristic patterns of behavior. The leader ordinarily suppresses elements in the dream that stimulate emergence of further material from the unconscious. The dream is used to aid the problem-solving tasks of the group, as seen in the following example.

> A woman diagnosed as having borderline personality disorder told her group of a dream in which she turned her car over and went to a hospital, covered with blood. She found herself going to work from the hospital. The therapist dealt with her dream as her wish for and fear of psychiatric hospitalization instead of suggesting her probable unconscious wish for fusion with the therapist and her fear of being torn apart by him.

In a repressive group, the therapist uses the dream material to tie the dreamer to his or her present life situation. Unconscious elements are noted by the therapist, but not explored with the patient.

The therapist usually does not ask for dream material in repressive groups, but it may be offered spontaneously. The manifest dream content is linked with the patient's real world and its latent content used for the therapist's guidance of the therapy. The manifest content is used to reduce anxiety while strengthening the ego through better coping with reality and life's demands.

Dreams in Ego-Supportive Groups. In an ego-supportive group, the therapist employs dreams to explore the unconscious defenses and conflicts of the dreamer and the other group members. The therapist shares the responsibility for dealing with dreams with the group as a whole. Dreams are tied to the dreamer's interpersonal relationships in the group and his life outside the group. The therapist avoids intrapsychic issues and uses the dreams to break through group members' denial and rationalization of their self-defeating interpersonal behavior. Group members are asked if the dream indicates some aspect of the dreamer that was hitherto disowned. The group members are encouraged to use their experience with the dreamer to back up their observations, in the hope that the dreamer will begin to acknowledge and assume the responsibility for behavior he fails to see or rationalizes as a reaction to others' behavior.

In the following example, an intrapsychic issue was avoided and the therapist dealt with an interpersonal issue.

> A man with claustrophobic symptoms reported a dream in which he was unable to board an airplane—a crippling symptom that had interfered greatly with his work for many years. Instead of dealing with the castration anxiety that was suggested by his history, the therapist tied the dream to the man's guilt over aspects of his relationship with his wife. The therapist selected that topic because the patient had in many ways accepted a castrated status in his work, and the area in which he seemed to have the greatest opportunity for change was in his marital relationship. It also allowed discussion of

> his behavior toward the women in the group, whose attention he actively sought.

Dreams in Evocative Groups. In an evocative group, the therapist employs dreams to explore the unconscious defenses and conflicts of the dreamer and the other group members. Investigating dreams for latent content is reserved for evocative groups. The leader does not supply interpretations of group members' dreams. Dreams are used to approach group members' unconscious conflicts and wishes. In that regard, it is important to ascertain the context in which the dream occurred, including the events of the day and the significant tensions the dreamer was undergoing at the time. Then, the dreamer is asked to associate to the elements of the dream, whether they be names, places, or objects. Other group members are also asked to associate to the dream as though it were their own. On occasion, the therapist can reveal his or her own associations (Weiner 1983a). Those associations frequently spark the dreamer's making new associations to his or her own dream material.

At first, the leader takes the initiative in dealing with dreams. As the group becomes more sophisticated, the leader becomes less active in dealing with dreams and allows the group members to deal with each other's dreams and their resistances to dealing with their own dreams.

The therapist need not explore all of the dreams that are reported and only spends as much time on each as seems in the best interest of the group as a whole. Relating a dream produces anxieties, mobilizes resistances, and reinforces defenses in the dreamer and other group members for whom it carries a special meaning. The therapist deals with those anxieties, resistances, and defenses in all members of the group (Kadis et al. 1974). In the following instance, the group leader's associations helped dispel the resistances of the dreamer and the other group members.

> Mr. A.K. dreamed that he and his wife were naked at a movie. In the dream, they felt that everyone else should have been naked, too, that it was somehow the natural thing to do. In a second dream reported at the same time, the therapist had a huge penis and was raping a prepubertal girl.

> The patient's association to being undressed was a dream he had in grammar school of being at the water fountain with his pants off. Other group members were too uncomfortable to respond to the dream. The therapist revealed his association of boys comparing penis size. The therapist asked Mr. K. if that had ever been a concern. He replied negatively, but then went on to describe cosmetic surgery he had undergone at age 19 to increase the size of his chin. An injury at age 12 had arrested the growth of his lower jaw. It was later corrected by bone grafting, but that had left him with a conspicuously small chin. The other group members relaxed at this logical explanation of the dreams.

The therapist deferred dealing with the rape aspect of the second dream until a later time. At the time the above two dreams were reported, the patient's two conscious concerns were that the therapist was trying to control or sexually assault him. Later, the patient was better able to deal with his wish to be penetrated by the therapist and his concomitant fear of being torn apart by anal sexual assault (Weiner 1983b).

Group therapists have reported that patients who had special difficulties with dreams in psychoanalysis begin to experience meaningful dreams in group therapy (Kadis et al. 1974). At times, group members do not respond to others' dreams. They fend off discussion by relating their own dreams or by changing the subject. The therapist must recognize that as a resistance that can stem from feelings about the therapist or the dreamer.

The way in which a dream is presented, or the dream itself, may be a resistance. Many patients do not recall dreams. Some relate only dream fragments, while others minimize the importance of dreams. Kadis et al. (1974) suggest dealing with this resistance by indicating the usefulness of dreams in the therapeutic process. They suggest to group members that dreams are a way to express emotions a person cannot ordinarily express while awake; that when we sleep, the mind's censoring mechanisms relax and allow those emotions to be expressed in a disguised way so that sleep is undisturbed. By examining dreams, they suggest, we are better able to understand the unconscious conflicts and feelings that create psychological problems.

The way and the time at which a patient introduces and

relates a dream are important. A group member may tell his dream to only one person—the therapist or another group member. Or, he may tell the dream to the entire group without looking at any one person. He may relate his dream only during a private session with the therapist, only in an alternate meeting, or in a regular meeting only after having told it to the therapist individually. At times it is appropriate for the therapist to point out the circumstances under which a group member brings up dreams.

Dreams can elicit associations by the dreamer and other members that help to overcome the dreamer's initial reluctance to "own" his dream and help work with it on many levels. A dreamer's resistances may be loosened if the other members' associations are given first (Klein-Lipshutz 1953), but the dreamer's associations may be colored by what he has heard, or sidetracked altogether.

Dreams can be related in group sessions to universal problems and conflicts, such as birth, death, aggression, and sexuality. The multiplicity of associations to a single dream helps to reveal many aspects of the dreamer's problems and the therapeutic situation with its multiple transference manifestations.

Certain group members may avoid discussing a dream presented to the group. They try to change the subject by bringing up personal crises, asking questions, or offering dreams of their own for attention. The therapist must decide whether or not to continue focusing on the dream or to allow temporary sidetracking to diminish group members' anxiety. Later, the therapist can call the group's attention to their overlooking the dream.

Interruption of discussions is inherent in the group situation, but it does not hinder the associative process, and helps the therapist and group members understand the dream. In addition, postural or behavioral changes from the moment the patient enters the room or starts to tell a dream can be noticed and brought up in relation to the dream (Berger 1958).

The Gestalt Approach

Gestalt Therapy has made a significant contribution to the use of dreams in group psychotherapy, using technical innovations reminiscent of Psychodrama. The essence of the Gestalt approach is treating the elements of the dream as disowned parts of the dreamer.

Polster and Polster (1973) find that patients who experience frightening dreams are relieved when they identify themselves as the terrifying forces as well as the victims in their dreams. In a dream of a thunderstorm or a flood, the dreamer can be encouraged to see himself as both the victim of forces in and around himself and the source of power. That reinforces a sense of potency. To make dreams into a vivid here-and-now experience, the therapist may ask the patient to speak for a person or object in one of his dreams. He may be asked to talk to the object or person as if it were really present, by imagining it to be in an empty chair and addressing himself to the imaginary object or person. He can then be asked to switch chairs, take the role of the imaginary object, and talk back to himself. That can result in an animated, emotional dialogue. As the dreamer begins to experience the elements of his dream with immediacy and emotional intensity, his physical behavior may change. He may clench his teeth, stiffen, or relax. The therapist or other group members can point out this behavior and ask what he wishes to say, from whom he is withdrawing or with whom he would like to relax. If he replies, for example, that he wishes to express angry feelings toward his mother, he is encouraged to experience the feeling as deeply as he can. He is encouraged to say over and over again, "I am angry with you, mother!" until he experiences the feeling fully and becomes able to penetrate to the next emotional level, which may be a wish for closeness.

To help make the dream more real, the therapist or group members may role-play parts of the dream, again giving the dreamer a chance to work through his feelings in a here-and-now situation. The emphasis in Gestalt dream work is on bringing patients into better contact with the group, the therapist, and themselves, and on staying out of the patients' private, idiosyncratic world. That goal is no different from those of other ego-supportive modalities, but the action techniques of Gestalt Therapy that actively assert the dreamer's ownership and ability to control the elements of his dream are a useful technical innovation.

Therapeutic Imagery and Guided Fantasy

Fantasies and visual images or kinesthetic sensations suggested by the therapist can be used therapeutically (Korn and Johnson 1983). Imagery has been used in desensitization and implosive techniques that reduce the power of feared objects or situations by introducing them in fantasy in graduated intensity (Stampfl and Leavis 1967). It is used in Psychodrama to initiate the interaction between protagonists and in Gestalt Therapy to unite preconscious and conscious feelings, attitudes, and desires. Singer and Pope (1978) have reported the use of positive imagery and a variety of fantasies in direct interventions with neurotic patients. Singer (1974) has suggested that imagery may be a more effective means for uncovering intrapsychic material than free association.

Visual imagery and guided fantasy can be used in groups in many ways. They can serve as a rehearsal for anticipated life situations or can help shed light on intrapsychic conflicts. A fantasy can be constructed by a single group member or with the aid of other group members who role-play significant persons in the member's life; alternatively, as in Psychodrama or Gestalt Therapy, the group member can enact significant aspects of himself or herself. A person seeking a job can be asked to role-play an interview in the group to help discover self-defeating behaviors and attitudes, and to reinforce useful attitudes and behaviors. A person who has difficulty becoming aware of his self-critical aspect can have another group member role-play his conscience, and then reverse roles and play the other person's conscience.

Schorr (1974) suggests a number of imagery techniques in groups. The leader can assign an imagery task to a single member, such as the fantasy of being held by each member of the group, and imagining their responses. Other group members can be asked to create a fantasy about a particular group member, or to respond to that group member's fantasy with a fantasy of their own. Fantasies can concern the past, present, or future of the group members. For example, each group member can be asked to imagine himself or other group members as they were as children, as they are in relation to their spouses, or as they will be in five years.

The group leader assigns a fantasy or visual image according to individual members' needs or the needs of the group at the moment. Sensing that one group member is being actively excluded by other members of the group, the leader may ask that the group construct an imaginary wall around the excluded member and then help him break out. Or, when the group as a whole appears resistant or stalemated, they may be asked to imagine themselves in a prison and to seek a way out. If caught up in intellectualizations about behavior, the group members may be asked to fantasy about their bodies, or about their bodies coming into contact with or being seen by other members of the group.

By suggesting specific types of imagery or selecting specific persons, the leader helps to overcome resistances that are part of supposedly free or spontaneous communication, which is always inhibited by unconscious defense mechanisms. The leader's use of a nonthreatening imagery assignment may allow members individually or as a group to approach a previously avoided topic.

Finally, it must be said that imagery, too, can be used as a defense against dealing with feelings or events that arise in the group, and the use of imagery must be carefully balanced with direct questioning and confrontation.

Dreams Versus Guided Fantasies

Certain negative aspects of using dreams are circumvented by guided fantasy. Interpretation of dreams by the leader is often experienced by patients as the therapist's special power to read minds. That can create a troublesome situation for patients who strongly wish and fear fusion with other persons, or who have difficulty establishing firm ego boundaries. The leader supplying a "correct" interpretation also helps create or foster a dependence on outside authority. "Having" a dream also suggests that the dreamer is the victim of forces in his unconscious mind that are beyond his control, thus reinforcing a sense of helplessness.

The use of fantasy, on the other hand, places patients in an active role in which they control their own minds, following the suggestions of the group leader. Patients are free to discontinue or change the fantasy at any time and can clearly see that the therapist or the group does not control their minds. The use of dreams or guided fantasy can stimulate either regression or a sense of greater self-control. The therapist then guides the use of the dream or fantasy in the most helpful direction for the patient and the group.

Summary

Dreams and imagery enable group therapists and group members to express and deal with highly complex, emotionally charged issues that are sometimes inaccessible through ordinary verbal interchanges. Therapists' use of dreams and guided fantasy depends on their goals for individual patients and their groups.

In repressive groups, the leader can use dreams and imagery to assert his or her authority and to facilitate dealing constructively with day-to-day reality. Interpersonal interaction in the group and in daily living can be highlighted in ego-supportive groups, and evocative groups can be helped to uncover unconscious material. Guided imagery and fantasy allow group members to confront aspects of themselves that may be unconscious or merely avoided.

The strong emotions attached to dream symbols and the amount of emotion that can be provoked through guided imagery enable catharsis, but also pose the danger of overwhelming an inadequately defended ego. Therefore, the ego strength of the individual group member and the ability of the group as a whole to lend support are important considerations when considering delving into dreams or promoting guided imagery as a means of intrapsychic exploration. On the other hand, dreams and guided imagery can be used as repressive or ego-supportive techniques when modified appropriately.

The most important function of dreams and imagery is introducing symbolic thinking into the group discussion, stimulating the interest of group members in each other's psychological and interpersonal lives, helping group members feel that they can be understood, and helping them feel and become more potent or more accepting of guidance when needed.

11

Special Patients and Situations

CERTAIN PATIENTS AND CIRCUMSTANCES require unique modifications of the leader's role and the structure and composition of the group. Until this point, we have viewed the differences between group therapy patients in terms of ego strength. We will now deal again with the issue of ego strength, with certain constellations of ego defenses and coping mechanisms, and certain life tasks.

Ego strength is a primary consideration in determining the type of group therapy employed with different patient populations. Ego strength includes the ability to tolerate anxiety, the ability to make and carry out rational plans based on an accurate appraisal of internal and external reality, and the ability to delay action. Substance abusers, including alcoholics, and many persons with personality disorders may have little anxiety tolerance or may be reluctant to give up the intense libidinal gratification associated with their activities. Other considerations are patients' psychological mindedness, the reactions patients stimulate in therapists, and the nature of patients' real-life problems. Physical disorders, for example, are often triggered or aggravated by emotional influences, but many of the people with those disorders are not psychologically minded and respond best to groups in which concrete suggestions are made for managing their illnesses. Borderline and other acting out personalities strongly tax the emotions of the therapist, who must deal with their acting out as their fundamental problem. Finally, the elderly must cope with increasing disability and dependence. All of these populations require differing therapeutic attitudes and techniques.

Group Therapy with Psychiatric Inpatients

Patients are generally hospitalized because their ego strength is temporarily inadequate to cope simultaneously with their emotional difficulties and the difficulties of daily living. Early group therapists working with psychiatric inpatients used a repressive approach (Lazell 1921; Marsh 1931). Later therapists, attempting to deal with seriously ill persons through stimulating feelings and dealing with intrapsychic conflict, found it damaging to their patients (Frank 1963). Kibel (1981) finds that exploring intrapsychic conflict is unhelpful for inpatient groups because most hospitalized patients have little conflict-free ego available for self-reflection or interpersonal self-observation. In that circumstance, attacking a psychological symptom or a symptomatic behavior is equivalent to attacking the person as a whole and causes further ego disintegration.

In recent years, inpatient groups have focused on overcoming social isolation, developing social skills, improving contact with reality, and developing positive coping behavior (Horowitz and Weisberg 1966; Edelstein and Noy 1972). The following sections delineate the general principles of treating hospitalized persons.

Psychotic Patients

Working with a group of psychotic patients is taxing. It requires much activity by the group leaders in structuring the group and guiding the conversation (Leopold 1976; Betcher et al. 1982). Because the attention span of the group members is short, group sessions are best limited to one hour and should be held more than twice a week to maintain continuity. It is useful to have an agenda for these groups and to tell patients that, during group sessions, problems common to all group members are discussed. Typical agenda items include the following: how to stay out of the hospital, how to look for a job, what to tell others about one's illness, where and how to seek help should one's mental difficulties recur, reactions to the hospital and its staff, and plans for returning to home and family.

Two coleaders can usually manage a group of six to 10 patients. Patients should not be admitted to the group until they have had a few days to settle down and adjust to the hospital routine, and until they evidence significant contact with reality and some ability to tolerate social interchanges. They should be actively encouraged by the staff to attend the group after they are designated appropriate candidates, and may even be escorted to the group by staff members. If they cannot tolerate the group, they can be allowed to drop out and can be encouraged to reenter at a later date if they wish. Patients should also be free to leave during the course of a group meeting.

A routine coffee break can be a valuable tension-reliever in these groups and is also a reality-based task which the group can address. For example, a different member of the group can be elected to make coffee for each meeting or can be responsible for getting coffee for the group. In that way, cooperation with and recognition of other persons is stimulated.

The group leaders begin sessions by asking new members to introduce themselves and by having each member of the group identify himself to the new members. New members can be added as often as there are openings in the group, except for crises such as the elopement or suicide of a group member that call for a period of working through. It is also useful to ask new members how long they have been in the hospital and why they are in the hospital. That frequently leads to a comparison of diagnoses and a lessened sense of being uniquely afflicted. Patients are also encouraged to talk about their medication, its dosage, its positive effects, and its unpleasant side effects. Patients often fail to recognize dizziness related to postural hypotension, constipation, and dry mouth as side effects of their medications. Information about side effects is useful in maintaining patient morale, encouraging cooperation with the prescribed treatment, and increasing patients' physical comfort.

Going around is a helpful technique in this type of group—asking each member to react in turn to a particular subject or asking each member to react to a statement made by one of the group. Advice-giving is encouraged. Patients who give constructive advice are praised by the leaders and the other group members. Patients who give unhelpful advice are not criticized by the group leaders. Instead, their suggestions are turned over to the group for its reaction, which is usually a sensible revision of the original suggestion.

The group leaders need to convene briefly before and after the group. Beforehand, they agree on the day's agenda, which usually includes topics left over from the last session or designated for the current session. After group, they assess the progress of the group members and communicate patients' progress and concerns to other members of the staff. Group leaders should be rotated frequently, perhaps every six months, because the extreme repetitiveness of this type of group rapidly drains the leader's enthusiasm. This type of group can be led by an inexperienced staff member paired with a more experienced staff member, such as a senior staff nurse.

The group frequently becomes a vehicle for expressing legitimate complaints and constructive suggestions by group members who do not raise those issues in the regular ward meetings, or who do not raise them with their primary therapists. Patients' complaints that their doctors do not spend enough time with them are taken seriously, as are suggestions that the ward staff be identified by name tags, that the name of the head nurse on each shift be posted, and so forth.

Nonpsychotic Inpatients

The structure and content of the therapeutic group for neurotic and personality-disordered hospitalized patients differs from that of the group for psychotic patients. The group sessions can be longer, up to 90 minutes. They require a different structure and a different type of activity by the leaders. The focus of this type of group is on recognizing symptoms and behavior as products of one's feelings and reactions to his interpersonal world. In addition, the group discusses the impact of each member's behavior on the other group members and supplies interpersonal feedback to help make ego-alien the behavior of the personality-disordered patient and the secondary gain of neurotic symptoms. Group members are encouraged to take more responsibility for their own lives and to stop blaming their parents, spouses, and jobs for their unpleasant feelings (Stein et al. 1955).

Accomplishing those goals calls for the group leaders to be confronting, and requires that they be comfortable with their own aggression. It is also important that the leaders know enough about the overall progress of their patients that they do not press too hard when group members are highly taxed or frustrated. In that way, they can avoid triggering violence, suicide attempts, or elopements.

The leader's knowledge of psychodynamics is more important in this group than in the group for psychotics, which has the unidimensional focus of living in the real world. Dealing with affects and interpersonal confrontations requires a background in psychodynamics, psychopathology, and individual psychotherapy. Because these patients' thinking is more like the therapist's than that of the psychotic patients, leaders of this type of group are more subject to manipulation and involvement in conflicts between patients and unit staff.

Although leading this type of group is more complicated than leading a group of psychotics, its complexity makes it more interesting. In this type of group, the therapists approach the patients at multiple levels and deal with multiple levels of response, including feelings and behavior.

Coleadership is important in groups of psychotics because it provides relief for each leader during the session, provides a model of healthy relatedness, and provides continuity of leadership should one of the leaders be absent. Those aspects of coleadership are less important with neurotic and personality-disordered patients. The function of a coleader in this type of group is to help deal with manipulation and to provide multiple figures for identification.

Short-Term Inpatient Units

A repressive approach that helps build coping mechanisms and does not attack defenses is the best group therapy technique for the psychiatric patient whom one is trying to return rapidly to the community (Erickson 1984).

In a short-term inpatient unit, with patient stays of one to three weeks, patients recovering from psychosis are better dealt with in groups separate from patients with neurotic or characterologic problems. The focus with psychotic patients is on improving reality testing. With neurotic and personality disordered inpatients, emphasis is placed on their dealing with feelings through verbal expression instead of symptoms or action. In an acute care unit, it is best to exclude the persistently mute, physically violent, incoherent, or severely regressed patient (Maxmen 1978).

Yalom (1983) suggests that the primary functions of groups on an acute inpatient unit are to introduce patients to talking therapy and to provide an experience so relevant, comfortable, and effective that patients elect to continue in therapy after hospital discharge.

As a result of his own experiences and his study of 25 short-term inpatient units, Yalom suggests that psychiatric inpatients on acute units be treated in two different types of groups: team groups and level groups. The team group includes all of the patients assigned to one treatment team who are able to attend a group discussion; it is used to assess patients' progress and to foster positive patient interaction. The level groups operate at two levels: that of the nonpsychotic patient who is able to identify and discuss interpersonal issues, and that of the psychotic patient who is having difficulty focusing attention, listening to others, and communicating clearly. Yalom recommends that team groups and level groups each meet five times a week. He also recommends that group therapists curtail their therapeutic ambition and be content with demonstrating that talking helps, identifying problems to be worked on in future therapy, developing social skills, and dealing with problems caused by hospitalization.

Yalom notes that many inpatient groups deal with issues outside the group or with administrative issues and that therapists try to work from common themes that they identify in group members' verbalizations, including the verbalization of hostile feelings toward other group members. He finds all of these unhelpful in short-term units and suggests instead that therapists regard the life of each group as one session and attempt to teach or tell each member something positive about himself at each session. To that end, he recommends highly structuring the groups, dealing only with here-and-now issues in the group, and rapidly reducing intrapsychic and interpersonal tension. He agrees with Richmond and Slagle (1971) that expression of hostility between patients threatens their sense of safety. Yalom does not provoke anger, aims for rapid conflict resolution, and encourages angry patients to get out their anger before it becomes intense and while it is directed toward issues and procedures instead of others in the group. He detoxifies anger in the group by distancing it, as in, "Mary, what would you say *if* you were going to express your anger to John?" Or, "John, would you be willing to role-play what you think Mary is feeling?" Anger can also be circumscribed by allowing a patient one minute to express it. Conflict between patients can be dealt with by asking them to objectify it. "What can we learn from the conflict between John and Mary?" Role reversal can help, as well as suggesting that members avoid making global statements such as, "You *never*. . . . " or "You always. . . . "

Yalom also recommends another departure from the traditional therapeutic stance. He finds personal openness about the therapist's here-and-now feelings to be useful, especially in the lower-functioning group, in which he suggests that the therapist participate as fully as the patients. Yalom's finding is in agreement with the author's view (Weiner 1983a) that poorly integrated patients need the sense of another person's presence instead of a blank screen, and that prudent disclosure of here-and-now feelings limits the development of transference and fantasy and helps patients stay in reality.

Yalom (1983) suggests that the group for psychotic patients have no more than seven members and meet for 45 minutes. He suggests a specific structure, including a two- to five-minute orientation and preparation period, a five- to 10-minute warmup, 20 to 30 minutes of interpersonal exercises to foster concentration, listening, and communicating to others in the group, and a five- to 10-minute review period at the end of the session.

The leader meets and prepares the patients in each group session by stating that the group is to help members learn how to talk to others, to concentrate, to listen to others in the group, and to share information with other group members. The warmup can include physical activities, such as tossing a ball from person to person. In doing so, the ball-tosser names the person to whom he tosses the ball and makes an observation or a positive statement about him or her. A similar exercise can be done without tossing a ball, by asking group members in turn to make observations about each other's dress or feeling state, or to state a good or bad thing that happened that day. During the interpersonal exercise period, self-disclosure can be facilitated by asking patients to complete statements such as, "I really enjoy . . . " or "I'd like people to know that I. . . . " Empathy can be facilitated by each patient naming a strength that he or she feels another patient possesses. Interaction can be promoted by asking patients whom they know best in the room, or whom they most resemble. At the end, the leader can review the group interaction with the help of a blackboard, helping members remember what happened, helping them to point out positive aspects of the meeting, and encouraging them to make positive comments about each other's performance.

During the course of the meeting, the leader interrupts the formal agenda to deal with events in the group, explaining their dynamics and then teaching useful concepts. For example, in response to a patient's outburst that other people in the group hate him, the leader can say that the hate he feels is not coming from others in the room. It is his disappointment and anger with himself for not living up to unreasonably high standards. The leader asks other group members how they actually respond to the member who feels hated, and points out that people don't always feel toward a person the way he feels about himself.

Yalom proposes that the group for higher functioning nonpsychotic patient have three to 12 members and meet for 75 minutes. The group's focus is working on relationships between people in the group, using their here-and-now reactions to each other as the substance of the session. Yalom finds that a good structure for the group is three to five minutes of orientation and preparation, 20 to 30 minutes of agenda-making, 20 to 35 minutes of work on agenda items, and 20 minutes of wrap-up. The wrap-up period includes 10 minutes of discussion by the therapist with observers (who may be trainees, supervisors, or both) and 10 minutes of discussion by the patients of their reactions to the therapist-observer interactions.

Agenda-making is the most crucial element of Yalom's therapeutic scheme. It is a type of contract-making in which each patient ascertains and selects an attitude or behavior that manifests in the group to examine and alter. Arriving at an agenda item with the help of the therapist and the group involves patients actively in their treatment, trains them to state their needs explicitly, helps them think about themselves systematically, and involves them in performing and completing a task.

Examples of agenda-making are helping a patient refine a statement such as, "I want to get over feeling helpless," to "I want to tell you how I feel about you, John," or refining "I'm tired of being depressed," to "I'm going to stop withdrawing from you, Mary, when there's something I really want from you."

The agenda-filling stage involves the therapist stimulating hope, building cohesion, encouraging patients to help each other, helping patients to universalize, and cultivating socializing techniques. The therapist facilitates interpersonal interchanges by enabling members to request, receive, and provide interpersonal feedback by disclosing themselves in a trusting way that leads to mutual support.

The wrap-up period of 20 minutes is divided equally between the therapist-observer interaction and the patients' discussion of that interaction. Yalom finds that patients are strongly attentive to discussions of themselves by others, and that the therapist, in discussing the group with observers, models constructive interaction, especially in seeking and taking advice and suggestions.

Groups in Long-Term Facilities

Long-term hospitalization may be required for persons with severe personality disintegration, great dependency needs, chronic inability to control aggressive or suicidal behavior, and few environmental supports. On the other hand, long-term hospitalization is not a constructive means for personality reconstruction. Many patients require psychiatric hospitalization because of their therapists' overly vigorous attempts to uncover unconscious conflict (Kernberg et al. 1972) and remain in hospitals overly long because of the staff's desire to resolve those intrapsychic conflicts instead of reestablishing coping mechanisms. Personality reconstruction can come about only when a person has sufficient ego strength to cope with living in the real world. Therefore, the aim of groups for persons who are hospitalized long-term is to acquire sufficient coping skills to live and function better in the hospital and eventually in the outside world.

Groups in long-term facilities can accommodate a variety of patients, including the chronically regressed and chronically psychotic. Being accepted by others as part of the group stimulates the hope of reentering meaningful human relationships. Groups can organize games, parties, and trips to encourage members' involvement with one another and to help them redevelop the ability to plan, organize, and carry out activities with others. Groups also allow patients to deal with the staff about problems in the hospital system itself, and can facilitate the hospital's goal of meeting the patients' needs (Klapman 1956).

Patient government is a useful type of group activity for chronically hospitalized persons. It helps develop leadership skills, encourages the flexibility of roles among hospital patients, and helps patients assume responsibility for themselves.

Outpatient Groups for Chronic Mentally Ill Persons

Some studies indicate that the chronic mentally ill are less frequently hospitalized and continue longer in aftercare if they are seen in groups than if they are seen individually (Levene et al. 1970; Shatton et al. 1966).

Groups for the chronic mentally ill emphasize learning how to interact with others, self-care, and adapting to ego impairment—accepting limitations and meeting one's needs as is. For many, returning to work or to high levels of function are not possible, and those persons are helped to find self-esteem, enhancing activities such as sheltered workshops or group activities in day care centers.

Attempts at promoting self-reflection have proved ineffective. Outpatient groups with the chronic mentally ill are often found to be tedious, emotionally barren, and lacking interaction, but many of the difficulties with these groups are generated by the therapist. Therapists have tended to value fostering intrapsychic insight and self-reflection over developing ways of helping patients to cope from day to day and to develop simple social skills. Thus, they have missed creative opportunities for themselves and their patients.

Substance Abusers

Substance abusers are best treated in homogeneous groups (Lowenson and Zwerling 1971). Substance abuse is the repeated voluntary taking into the body of substances that affect the central nervous system and lead to behavior changes that are regarded as extremely undesirable in almost all cultures. DSM-III (American Psychiatric Association 1980) defines substance abuse as having a minimum duration of one month, social complications such as impaired social and occupational functioning, and a pathological pattern of use, such as the inability to reduce the use of the substance or remaining intoxicated through the day. Substance abuse includes substance dependence, which is defined as the development of tolerance or avoidance of withdrawal.

The substances of abuse and dependence are alcohol, barbiturates and the similarly acting sedatives or drugs prescribed for sleep, opiates (including heroin and synthetic narcotics), amphetamines and similar stimulants, and marijuana. Substances that are abused but widely believed not to cause physical dependence are cocaine, phencyclidine (PCP) and similar substances, and hallucinogens.

The user of hallucinogens, singly or combined with substances such as marijuana and amphetamines, presents a difficult problem, but one that is less common now than in the 1970s. Although a variety of people experiment with drugs, the typical chronic marijuana or psychedelic user is a psychologically or socially impaired adolescent or young adult (Blocker et al. 1966; Hochman and Brill 1973).

There is no common psychodynamic factor in substance abusers. Substance abuse can occur in any type of personality and can accompany many types of psychiatric disorder. Substance abuse is often associated with personality disorder, but there are many substance abusers for whom drug use was first a socially acceptable form of recreation.

The most important principle in dealing with the person who abuses one or many substances, serially or simultaneously, is that substance abuse is the central problem (Heilman 1982). Once habituated to intoxication by a substance or to the use of substances to relieve emotional tensions, the habituation must be dealt with before dealing with other issues.

Successfully addressing drug abuse may involve removing the abuser from his usual environment, in which substance abuse may be the norm and abstinence deviant. It may involve the temporary use of external institutional controls. It certainly involves developing a support network in which abstinence is rewarded and nondrug tension-relieving mechanisms are readily available (Zarcone 1981).

Dealing with a substance abuser's emotional problems must wait until the abuser can deal with his or her reality without resorting to drugs as a means to cope or escape. The substance abuser's anxiety tolerance is low (Kaufman 1983), in large measure because one or more drugs have become that person's principal defense against unpleasant feelings. The best treatment is therefore a repressive treatment.

Experience has taught that identification is the primary therapeutic vehicle for substance abusers. They work best in groups of people struggling with the same problem. Positive identification with nonabusers is difficult until there has been a period of abstinence. Mental health professionals tend to be over-idealized or devalued and seen as objects for manipulation by the substance abuser, and are therefore not adequate models for identification. Furthermore, they cannot personally provide the immediate round-the-clock support that is necessary.

Contemporary substance abuse involves multiple substances. It frequently begins with alcohol abuse and often ends with alcoholism. There is growing evidence that alcohol abuse can be treated as part of a total drug abuse program (Heilman 1982), but until further evidence of the efficacy of combined programs, we will deal with alcohol abuse separately.

Group therapists who wish to work with abusers need to be familiar with relevant state laws and must be willing to deal periodically with law officials. If abusers are to be seen in a clinic or agency, the policies of the institution must be carefully considered, including the question of reporting to a law enforcement agency. Withdrawal must be accomplished before group therapy is undertaken, and facilities for withdrawal and detoxification must be available for referral in the event of renewed abuse.

It is important to maintain liaison with medical help. Group therapists should be aware of the dangers of the substances abused by their patients: life-endangering withdrawal syndromes from barbiturates and other sedatives; suspicion, aggressive behavior, and transient psychosis with continued use of stimulants and cocaine; and unpredictable violence with PCP (Grinspoon and Bakalar 1980). They should also understand the psychological aspect of their patients' substance abuse, whether it is escape from the oppressiveness of reality, excitement, a reaction to peer rejection, or an attempt to fit in to a particular subculture.

The most frequent difficulty with abusers is the disruptions resulting from absences and/or the inaccessibility of persons who come to group sessions when "high." Generally, a member who is intoxicated should be excluded from the group (whether heterogeneous or homogeneous) for that session (Ben Yehudah 1980).

Attendance is an important issue, and part of the responsibility of the group as a whole is to stimulate and maintain the attendance of individual members (Khantzian and Kates

1978). The departure of a group member may provoke guilt in the others because they feel they have let him down or have been unable to help him. They may also feel, through their identification with him, that their problems are insoluble and that they, too, will be dropped or forced to leave (Kadis et al. 1974). The group therapist can explore the identification of the members with each other, as well as the feelings toward the person who has left. The tensions stimulated by the departure may also be reduced by the therapist clarifying the realistic factors involved in the member's need to leave.

At times, treatment may be possible only in a controlled environment, such as a drug-free sheltered community (Densen-Gerber 1973). Unfortunately, many relapse on return to the street (Freedman 1980). When patients' personality structure or physical condition will not tolerate abstinence, substituting a less disabling substance may be indicated: methadone for the heroin abuser (Lahmeyer 1982) or regular doses of codeine for the chronic pain patient who has become an opiate abuser.

Alcohol Dependence (Alcoholism)

The basic treatment of alcohol abuse is achieving abstinence (Vaillant 1981). Attempting to reduce the need for alcohol through resolving conflicts is ineffective unless the person has been self-treating with alcohol a psychiatric disorder such as depression (Vaillant 1981). Formal group psychotherapy is often employed in the treatment of alcoholism (Mullan and Sanguiliano 1966; Doroff 1977). The most successful formal treatment for alcoholism has been active membership in Alcoholics Anonymous, which is often incorporated into the overall treatment program of alcoholics whose alcohol dependence requires a controlled environment as a means to begin abstinence (Alcoholics Anonymous 1955).

Alcoholics Anonymous promotes a feeling of belonging and offers controls and support that cannot be obtained outside of a hospital. Such controls and support include taking care of alcoholics when inebriated and staying with them and preventing them from drinking when they experience intense cravings. The aid available through other members diminishes alcoholic patients' tendency to act out and to make unacceptable demands on others.

Alcoholics do poorly in heterogeneous groups, as do other substance abusers. The other members may accept the fact of their alcoholism, but may not be able to tolerate drunkenness in group sessions. While drunk, alcoholics may also express hostility toward other group members and stimulate intense counterhostility. That may be used by other members to reinforce their own resistance to therapy or to stimulate their own acting out (Kadis et al. 1974).

Alcoholics' families are a very important factor in their recovery, and family members are encouraged to join Alanon, the organization for family members of alcoholics, and Alateen, the organization for their teenage children. It is also important that therapists maintain contact with their patients' support networks.

Psychosexual Disorders

From a psychodynamic standpoint, the psychosexual disorders result from diverting the *aim* of the sexual drive away from genital union, or changing the *object* of the sexual drive from the genitals of another person to another object. From that standpoint, voyeurism is a change in the aim of the sexual drive from appropriate sexual contact to peeping; pedophilia is a change of the object of the sexual drive from the genitals of an adult to the genitals of a prepubertal child.

Ego-Dystonic Homosexuality

Ego-syntonic homosexuality is not classified as a mental disorder in DSM-III (American Psychiatric Association 1980), because many homosexuals are satisfied with their sexual orientation, show no significant signs of psychopathology other than the sex of their love object, and function socially and occupationally with no impairment (Bell and Weinberg 1978). The term ego-dystonic homosexuality refers to homosexuals who are disturbed by, in conflict with, or who wish to change their sexual orientation.

Ego-dystonic homosexuality can be treated in heterogeneous groups, but is best treated in homogeneous groups in which confrontation by other group members with the same problems cannot be regarded as rejection based on their different sexual preference (Hadden 1966). In addition, members of homogeneous groups are better able to spot and confront rationalizations and to encourage more adaptive behavior through modeling and identification (Bieber 1971). Persons with ego-syntonic homosexuality who have other emotional problems can readily be treated in groups with mixed sexual orientations.

Emotionally Influenced Physical Disorders

Emotional states can trigger and exacerbate many physical disorders (Reiser 1975). Emotions often trigger asthma attacks, migraine headaches, and some forms of dermatitis. They aggravate the course of peptic ulcer disease (Cobb and Rose 1973), and the type A personality has been implicated as a significant risk factor for developing coronary artery disease (Jenkins 1976).

In all chronic diseases, psychological factors influence patients' willingness to acknowledge the presence of physical dysfunction, to cooperate with the prescribed treatment, and to alter unhealthy habits (such as smoking in emphysema and coronary artery disease) to reduce environmental risk factors. Emotions may also influence the body directly through the overflow of neural impulses into the autonomic system or hypothalamic stimulation of the neuroendocrine system (Knapp 1980).

Physical disorders such as peptic ulcer disease and coronary artery disease can be understood and treated as concomitants of certain acute and chronic emotional tensions that act in conjunction with genetically determined and environmental predisposing factors. There is no evidence that those physical disorders have a primary function of defending against anxiety, but they are often used to avoid unpleasant or threatening situations. For example, many people whose exercise tolerance has returned to normal after heart attacks do not return to work (Gulledge 1975), usually for situational or emotional reasons.

Many people who suffer from physical disorders that are directly aggravated or precipitated by emotional factors are not psychologically minded and do not see significant connections between their patterns of behavior, their emotions, and their disease. A subgroup of these people has been described as alexithymic (Lesser 1981): unable to put feelings into words and therefore largely unsuitable for a psychological treatment that connects symptoms with thoughts and emotions (Sifneos 1975).

Optimal therapy for many of these people, such as the postcoronary patient and the diabetic patient who is recurrently hospitalized because of mismanagment of his or her diabetes, is convalescent groups during and after hospitalization that use repressive techniques. The groups can include patients and their families. Patients and families are taught about the disease through discussing the physiology of the disease, diet, exercise, etc. Patients and families are asked to voice and to share common problems and to give each other advice and support. The group leader helps prepare patients and families for postdischarge anxiety and tries to reduce invalidism by helping families to understand when it is appropriate to have the patient continue in a dependent role and when, both physically and psychologically, it is important that he or she be pushed toward self-care.

When a person with a disorder such as migraine or tension headaches, mucous colitis (spastic colon), asthma, or neurodermatitis feels that there is a significant emotional component to the physical disorder, the therapist must consider the advantages and disadvantages of individual, group, and combined treatment. Since the person's emotional tensions may exacerbate the organic malady, the group psychotherapist must evaluate the potential effect of the group on the individual patient. The therapist must also determine whether the goal should be direct relief of emotional tension or an attempt to change personality factors that produce emotional tension. The therapist must consider the anxiety tolerance of the patient and whether he will be merely upset by the group or will gain insight into his psychological problems and cope more effectively with them. The therapist should be careful not to create unrealistic expectations. It is helpful to inform patients that psychotherapy will not cure their physical disorder, but may diminish its severity as anxiety or maladaptive patterns of behavior are reduced (Karasu 1979).

It is usually best to place patients who complain only of physical symptoms in a homogeneous group, in which all members speak "organ" language.

There is little evidence that physical disorders serve as defenses against anxiety in the same way as repression, denial, displacement, and the other psychological mechanisms of defense. It is more likely that vulnerable organ systems react as a result of nonspecific emotional stresses or the sheer amount of psychosocial stresses that occur in a given period of time (Rahe et al. 1970). The eating disorders, however, are the exception. We will consider the group treatment of obesity. At present, there is insufficient data on the group treatment of anorexia nervosa or bulimia to draw generalized conclusions.

Obesity

Obesity may be operationally defined as a body weight that is in excess of standard life insurance norms by 20 percent. Severe obesity is the product of long-standing eating habits, environmental factors, psychological factors, and in many cases, a significant genetic factor (Stunkard 1980). The treatment of severe, prolonged obesity is often most unsatisfactory. The overeating that leads to severe obesity is best conceptualized as an impulse disorder. Severely obese persons have learned to reduce emotional tensions by snacking or by filling their stomachs. They experience secondarily lowered self-esteem and social inhibitions that further stimulate their eating.

To date, the best treatment for chronic over-eaters is lay-led groups, such as Weight Watchers, which operate at a repressive level and give practical advice and 24-hour-a-day support to overeaters. Positive feedback from the group for weight loss and negative feedback for weight gain, identification with members who have lost weight, and meeting people with similar problems seem to be the significant advantages of this type of group.

Attempting to foster insight into the unconscious conflicts of people whose primary complaint is overweight stimulates further overeating. It is possible, however, that once an overweight person has developed some self-control (as with the alcoholic) he or she may be able to profit from introspection.

Borderline Personality Disorder and Acting Out

Borderline personality disorder is a new diagnostic entity that describes people with minimal ego strength who are impulsive and have unstable personal relationships, poor emotional control, identity disturbances, and rapid mood swings (American Psychiatric Association 1980). Their impulsiveness, lack of anxiety tolerance, and lack of impulse control result from using primitive ego defense mechanisms: splitting, primitive idealization, projection (including projective identification), denial, omnipotence, and devaluation (Kernberg 1975).

Because persons with borderline personality disorder may present with neurotic complaints such as free-floating anxiety, they may not be detected until they have entered the group. After entering the group, they are readily detected because of the turmoil created in the therapist and other group members. They viciously attack the leader and the other members and then expect their support. They manipulate and extract without regard for the needs of others, project their hostile feelings onto others, and then react as though they were being attacked.

Group therapy has been recommended as an adjunctive treatment for borderline patients to help them develop more awareness of their interpersonal behavior and its impact on others (Wong 1980), but including borderline patients in groups may overtax the resources of the group and the therapist, and the therapist should not hesitate to remove a highly disruptive borderline patient from a group before everyone becomes thoroughly demoralized.

Borriello (1979) suggests that the first task for acting-out group members is to become reflective, to become curious about their behavior, and to inventory their life crises and notice how many times similar crises have occurred, in the hope that they will realize that similar crises are bound to recur if they do not change.

To accomplish that task, Borriello proposes norms that must be established in groups for the members who act out: continuous attendance, adherence to confidentiality, being honest in the group, self-exploration, assuming responsibility for their behavior, tolerating emotional discomfort, expressing feelings through words instead of action, acknowledging the self-destructiveness of acting out, realizing the adverse effect of manipulation, and actively attempting to control impulses. He also suggests that the acting-out group members be made aware that their behavior has roots in the past and consequences in the present and future.

Acting out must be regarded as the central problem of the acting-out patient, and the behavior must be dealt with before attempting to deal with underlying psychodynamic issues. Thus, continued attendance and promptness at group sessions is praised. Slips in attendance or repeated tardiness may be regarded as possible reasons for expulsion from the group, and violation of group members' confidence may actually necessitate expulsion from the group to allow an atmosphere of sufficient trust to foster open interchange. Persons who act out with extreme violence are generally not helped by outpatient group therapy (Lion et al. 1977).

Narcissistic Personality

Narcissistic personality is also a new diagnostic entity. It is characterized descriptively by an over-inflated sense of importance or uniqueness and preoccupation with achieving unlimited wealth, power, beauty, or intellectual feats. There is a need for constant attention and admiration, and minor failures produce intense emotional reactions. At an interpersonal level, there is a lack of empathy, a sense of entitlement, and a tendency to exploit others (American Psychiatric Association 1980). In the treatment situation, the therapist becomes aware that the patient regards him only as a tool and not as another sentient, equally entitled human being (Kernberg 1975). Kohut (1971) has noted the tendency of the narcissistic person to develop idealizing and mirror transferences; the therapist is overvalued and the patient expects the therapist to be a source of admiration and approval.

Wong (1980) recommends combined individual and group therapy for narcissistic patients. In the group, the idealizing transference can be modified through the observations and comments of peers. The raw aggression of disappointed narcissistic patients is also tempered by the group, and patients are taught that their needs will be better met by people if they are treated kindly than if they are abused. The patient is allowed to idealize the therapist and experience the therapist's positive regard in the group and individual sessions as a means of maintaining the patient's ego integrity, while he or she is concomitantly frustrated by the group's refusal to allow its members to be exploited (Stone and Whitman 1977).

The Elderly

Persons over age 65 are the least homogeneous of any age group (Butler 1975). They vary greatly in their physical and cognitive abilities, but are commonly seen by others as uniform in their problems and behavior, a stereotype referred to by Butler (1969) as age-ism. Much as the physical complaints of the elderly are no longer regarded as inevitable consequences of advanced age (Busse and Blazer 1980), emotionally disturbed elders are no longer seen as merely senile.

The emotional problems of elder persons are sometimes exacerbations of earlier, repressed conflicts, but are more commonly reactions to multiple losses, disability, illness, loneliness, and lack of satisfying employment or recreational pursuits. The reactivation of conflicts in elder persons results from the weakening of intrapsychic defense mechanisms such as reaction formation and rationalization. During late life, the increased dependency due to limited financial resources and physical infirmity often reactivates early feelings of inadequacy (Burnside 1970). When unable to find emotional support, elderly persons may become isolated or use physical complaints as a means of contact with others. Withdrawn isolates frequently become lethargic, unkempt, and forgetful. Because of the person's age, those symptoms are often misinterpreted as organic deterioration (Wells 1977).

Group work with the emotional problems of the elderly may be limited to helping older persons accept restricted activity and guiding them in limited activities (Berger and Berger 1973; Saul and Saul 1974). Ego-supportive (Berland and Poggi 1979) and evocative techniques (Krasner 1974) have been employed successfully. After working intensively with elderly people for two decades, Krasner (Kadis et al. 1974) concluded that the psychotherapy of choice for elderly patients is combined individual and group psychotherapy, with the group homogeneous for age.

When elderly persons are seen individually, they experience the intimacy and support of a one-to-one relationship. Age-homogeneous groups enable older persons to depend on peers instead of young therapists, whom patients often experience as a child on whom they are forced to depend. In psychotherapy groups with younger adults, most older patients try to be good parents to the younger members. The transference-based acting out of the younger members toward the elderly is experienced as rejection and often results in hostility or withdrawal. The issues of dependence, trying to be a good parent, and the intense, related negative affects are more readily worked through in a homogeneous group. Levine and Poston (1980) modified a "coffee lounge" group by having an initial period for refreshments and socialization and then getting down to the work of the group—listening to and empathizing with each other.

Perhaps the most important difficulty in dealing with the elderly is the stereotyped attitude of younger therapists toward the elderly. Younger therapists easily project onto the elderly their attitudes toward their own parents and grandparents, including their wish to be nurtured by parental figures who now turn to them for nurturance. Recognizing the sexual needs of the elderly is difficult for younger therapists who wish to deny their parents' own sexuality, and the sexual attraction of elderly men or women toward younger therapists is often met with much defensiveness by their therapists, who see it as a breakdown of ego defenses instead of a reawakening of adult interests.

Other Populations

Group techniques are now widely used to deal with the emotional consequences of medical illnesses (Lonergan 1982). Modified group therapy has been employed to help the newly blind adapt to their changed and changing world (Kübler-Ross and Anderson 1968; Oehler-Giarratana and Fitzgerald 1980). Groups are used to help persons recovering from myocardial infarction (Bilodeau and Hackett 1971) and to help the terminally ill (Yalom and Greaves 1977).

Other groups help persons in life crises such as rape (V. A. Sadock 1980, 1983), divorce, bereavement (McCourt et al. 1976; Granvold and Welch 1979), or working in high-stress environments (Mohl 1980).

There is an increasing tendency to develop groups that focus on a common problem dealt with by all group members. Women's groups have been established for persons with problems they experience as related to being female (Daley and Koppenaal 1981). Sharing reactions to an illness or common life problems creates a supportive bond that cannot be provided by relationships with health care professionals, and enables people in various types of life crisis to depend on each other instead of the health care system.

Summary

This chapter indicates the special modifications required to meet the treatment needs of certain special populations. There are many therapeutic techniques available. They can be creatively applied to different situations, and can be used as adjuncts to other types of treatment for emotional and physical disorders.

Group therapy has its limitations. Inpatient group therapy is largely confined to developing communication and coping skills. The treatment of substance abuse disorders must begin by facilitating or enforcing abstinence. The emphasis in dealing with persons who act out is on observing, taking responsibility for, and controlling their behavior. Through painful failures, we have learned that group and other psychotherapies are primarily useful as adjunctive treatments in the so-called psychosomatic disorders and that there is no simple one-to-one connection between emotions and physical disorders. In group treatment of the elderly, the attitude of the therapist is the primary obstacle. Other specialized groups are still in the process of development.

12

Resolving Impasses

GROUP THERAPISTS SOMETIMES FAIL to help people change. Many failures manifest abruptly when a group member suddenly and prematurely terminates therapy. Other potential failures present as prolonged stalemates or impasses in which there is still a possibility for a positive action if the impasse is recognized and dealt with.

Dynamically, impasses result from investing more energy in sustaining resistance and from valuing opposition more highly than its resolution (Liff 1970). Because impasses are the product of an interaction, alternating one or more elements of the interaction can relieve the impasse. Therefore, we can look for the antitherapeutic aspects of the therapist–group–group member interaction instead of branding certain patients as intractable or their therapists as incompetent.

Impasses stem from therapists' inability to receive and understand necessary information from the patient, therapists' inability to respond appropriately to patients on the basis of information received, patients' inability to receive and integrate information from the therapist and other group members, and patients' inability to respond appropriately to the therapist or the group based on that information. The same problems also occur between group members (Weiner 1983b).

Impasses may arise from any or all of the above factors during the contract-making phase of group therapy.

Contractual Impasses

Contract-related impasses are generally due to interfering reality factors, an unclear therapeutic contract, inappropriate enforcement of group rules, an invalid therapeutic contract, a poor fit between member and group, or a poor therapist-patient fit.

Reality Factors

Therapists must consider realistic aspects of their patients' lives, such as their inability to obtain regular transportation, to be regularly absent from the job, or to pay the bill for treatment. Inability to attend the group regularly for any reason has the potential for stalemating treatment. Another type of stalemate occurs with patients who cannot afford individual therapy and are placed in a group as a less expensive alternative. Group therapists must be aware that individual sessions may be required to deal with issues that cannot be dealt with in the group. That in turn raises the question of foregoing needed individual sessions, thus risking inadequate treatment, or raises the problem of altering the fee for the individual session. Doing so may establish the transference expectation of the therapist as an all-giving parent and may place the patient in the position of the exceptional child, which may stimulate his narcissism or enhance his guilt and block therapeutic progress.

Unclear Therapeutic Contract

The therapeutic contract includes the goals for therapy and the rules of the therapeutic situation. Ideally, each group member and the therapist agree on long-term and short-term goals. If no progress is made toward the short-term goals, the therapist and the individual group member examine those goals in the group. An impasse may occur because therapist and patient have different conscious goals for treatment. For example, the therapist's goals may be to help his patient understand his relationship with his peers. The patient's goal may be solely to make his relationships more comfortable and may therefore stalemate the group as a whole by interrupting the flow of intense feelings when they arise and focusing on mutual advice-giving.

Patients' unconscious goal for treatment often differs from the therapist's. For example, the wish for an omniscient parent frequently underlies patients' expressed desire to understand themselves. It can undermine a contract to work toward self-understanding by causing uncritical acceptance of the therapist's formulations instead of thoughtful consideration and integration of them.

Therapists attempt to determine their patients' unconscious wishes, and then decide to gratify them, sidestep them, or bring them to consciousness and partial or full resolution. The differences between patients' unconscious wishes and therapists' treatment goals are always dealt with at some level, and their resolution is frequently the heart of the therapeutic process.

Failure to establish explicit goals for therapy often stems from therapists' unwillingness to tell their patients that they cannot get what they want from therapy and patients' wanting to avoid knowing the limitations of therapy. When therapists place the burden of explaining the nature of the group process on the group members, they often become the target of anger displaced away from the therapist and then respond with impasse-producing counteraggression.

If a group leader fails to obtain an agreement to abide by the group's rules, that seeming oversight may point to significant characterologic or countertransference problems in the therapist that will significantly affect the course of a group member's therapy.

Enforcement of Group Rules

The enforcement of group rules or the failure of group leaders to enforce rules or to deal with infringements of the rules can be an important source of impasse.

Rules facilitate the function of groups and serve as norms. When they are eventually violated by one or more of the members, they become important subjects for discussion—for example, an agreement made between two group members to avoid sharing certain information with the others. Group members who secretly become sexually involved with one another frequently do so to avoid issues with the therapist. The sexual involvement can symbolize oedipal rivalry or the gratification of an incestuous wish, to name only two of the possibilities. Without disclosure to the group, investigation and interpretation are impossible.

Therapists who deal legalistically with violations of group rules often produce impasses. A threat of termination is needed, however, if a group member's behavior literally endangers others in the group (Weiner 1970). Ordinarily, the best approach to violations of the group contract is dispassionate exploration of the circumstances surrounding the violation, of the possible reasons for the violators, and of the reactions of the group members. The therapist and the whole group can then determine if the violation demands action or if group discussion alone is sufficient. In the rare instance of repeated absences, prolonged disruptive behavior in the group, or recurrent betrayal of group confidences, a group member may be asked to leave.

Invalid Therapeutic Contract

Group psychotherapy calls for a willingness to share information about one's self and actively implement what one learns as a consequence of sharing. Unmotivated patients frequently do not hear that they share the responsibility for the work of therapy.

Patients may be taken into groups because they will not accept more appropriate therapy. Therapists make such compromises because their patients will not accept hospitalization or medication, and they wish to offer some treatment, instead of no treatment. In those situations, the therapist's collusion with the patient's wish to remain in control of his treatment may result from his countertransference or his narcissism. The therapist fails to let the patient suffer the consequences of his decision to avoid or postpone appropriate treatment because of his unconscious reactions to the patient or the patient's appeal to his omnipotent fantasies.

An invalid therapeutic contract also results from misdiagnosis—usually an overestimation of coping ability or impulse control. A misdiagnosis is less likely to occur if the therapist evaluates the patient in more than one interview and over a period of time, carefully noting the quality of the interaction while taking a detailed history with emphasis on coping ability and impulse control, as reflected in the patient's ability to complete schooling, hold jobs, and maintain stable, positive relationships. If the group therapist is in a hurry to fill his group or performs a hurried evaluation for a reduced fee, he may miss his prospective patient's concrete thinking and his primary concern with direct alleviation of symptoms.

A negative placement frequently invalidates the therapeutic contract. Negative placement is avoiding the recognition of negative feelings toward a patient by referring him to a group (Kadis et al. 1974). It not only avoids awareness of uncharitable feelings toward the patient, but also avoids the negative feelings of the patient toward the therapist. Therefore, patients who antagonize or frustrate their therapists are frequently told that they need a group experience. If carried out, the group experience may devastate the patient and the group alike. The patient's anger at his former therapist, whether transference-based or a reaction to his real behavior, is acted out in the new group, and, if caught at a vulnerable moment, the group and the therapist may react with destructive counterhostility.

Therapists can avoid making negative placements by asking themselves, when contemplating referral of a patient to a group, "What am I avoiding by making this referral?" Group therapists can avoid experiencing a negative placement by adequately evaluating patients referred for group therapy, regardless of the referral source.

Inappropriate Group

Group therapy may be the treatment of choice for a particular person, but he or she may be referred to an inappropriate group. Sometimes inappropriate placement occurs because a therapist has an opening in only one group or an institution is in need of a new member for a certain group.

Group placement may be inappropriate not only for the kind of group (repressive, ego-supportive, evocative) but for the life of the group. Patients who are introduced into a group during a crisis in its life are likely to be traumatized or stalemated for long periods of time.

The composition of an otherwise appropriate group may make certain goals temporarily inappropriate. One can, of course, flow with the direction taken by the group, instead of insisting that the group conform to the therapist's original intended level of function. Thus, a group in which the majority of members have marital difficulties can shift from its original goal to examining marital interactions. If the therapist sees a focus on marital difficulties as an important resistance by the group, he can deal with it by interpretation as part of the avoidance of an important transference issue.

Inappropriate Therapist

The therapist should be a person with whom the patient can establish a positive partial identification. The therapist must be prepared to deal with the patient's reaction to those aspects of his dress and mannerisms that he knows to be highly idiosyncratic in a neutral, nondefensive manner, just as he may need to deal with any other potential obstruction to therapy.

The most subtle and most potentially destructive factor is the therapist's narcissistic vulnerability (Saretsky 1980), his need to be treated in certain ways by patients in order to treat them. Certain patients deny therapists the gratification that they need to do effective psychotherapy. It is up to the therapist to ascertain quickly that his personal limitations make it impossible to work with a particular patient and to arrange for transfer to someone with whom the patient can work. On occasion, a therapist-patient encounter at the outset of therapy in which each agrees to modify a significant aspect of himself in order to establish a therapeutic relationship can herald a significant positive change for both (Kohut 1977), but we must also heed Kernberg's (1975) warning to avoid feeding our own narcissism and the messianic hopes of our patients.

Process Impasses

Process-related impasses are stalemates that result from errors in the conduct of therapy in which the initial contractual agreement was sound.

The principal process-related impasses are due to ordinary human error, an inadequate therapeutic alliance, an antitherapeutic alliance, adverse transference reactions, countertransference, and inappropriate transference gratification.

Human Error

Human error is readily corrected once the therapist becomes aware that he or she failed to understand, failed to act appropriately, or acted destructively. It is best dealt with by the therapist's admission of his or her error. Profuse apologies or protracted explanations are not called for (Weiner 1983a). Rather, the therapist and the patient attempt to reach agreement on the facts, with the therapist encouraging the expression of the patient's feelings and thoughts in response to the error. Then, therapy continues, with the therapist alert to changes in the patient that may result from the error. If errors occur repeatedly with one patient or a particular group of patients, the therapist needs to determine if one or more of the factors discussed below is operative.

Inadequate Therapeutic Alliance

The positive working relationship between the patient's rational, mature, health-seeking aspect and the therapist's rational, mature, professional aspect does not develop instantaneously. It requires a period of interaction, during which the relationship is held together by the patient's positive expectations. Those expectations are partly based on the therapist's expertise and partly on the hope of finding an accepting, powerful parent or the unconscious longing to return to a satisfying parent-child relationship.

At times, it is not possible to establish rapport. Failure to develop rapport may be due to the patient's psychological makeup, transference factors, the therapist's feelings or attitude toward the patient, or a poor match of personalities. If a positive relationship cannot be developed in the assessment and orientation sessions with the group therapist, group treatment must be postponed until a positive relationship can be established. Otherwise, the patient's negative feelings will be acted on in the group but will be uninterpretable because interpretation depends on the therapeutic alliance for its effectiveness. Without the therapeutic alliance, the therapist's comments are seen as hostile, critical, and demeaning. They reinforce the patient's negative feelings and make change impossible. The group also reacts to the negative relationship between the therapist and the patient by directing anger felt toward the therapist onto that patient, a scapegoating that can be unconsciously fostered by the therapist who is frustrated by his or her inability to reach the patient in a positive way.

Antitherapeutic Alliance

The following antitherapeutic alliance was based on an error in the assessment of the patient's ego strength and led to a prolonged impasse.

> Mr. S., a 30-year-old group therapy patient, was referred for evaluation because his chronic depression was worsening. He was described by his therapist as a bright, capable man with much potential who could achieve a doctorate in a technical field if he could mobilize himself.
>
> Mr. S. was a tall, physically unattractive man with a passive, shrinking demeanor who reported episodes of severe depression over the previous five years. He said that his depressed states were changing from a longing for companionship to bleak, anxious, hopeless spells in which he thought of suicide. He had worked with his present therapist intermittently over his five-year period of difficulty and had also tried other therapists without significant success. He had obtained some relief while hospitalized for a period of four months, but soon after hospital discharge four months prior to the consultation, he again felt depressed in spite of various antidepressant and tranquilizing medications.
>
> This man had few social contacts and no sexual experience. He worked part-time in his father's business and was working part-time on a master's degree in the hope of leaving his father's business and securing a high-paying technical job.

> He stated that he was getting little from his group experience, that nothing new ever happened, and that he'd learned every catch word in psychotherapy. He said that he had learned a lot about how his personality had been formed, but that this information was not particularly useful to him.
>
> In this case, it seemed that the therapist had overidentified with the patient and greatly exaggerated his ability to change. The consultant suggested a different type of antidepressant medication and less encouragement of the patient to strive for a higher level of adaptation. Because he got along well with his father and liked the business, he was encouraged to enter his father's business full-time and to stop dividing his energy between school and work.
>
> When seen by the consultant a month later, the patient reported his depression considerably improved.

Because of the group therapist's overidentification with this man, he was being pushed to operate at a level beyond his capacity at that time. As a result of the consultation, the therapist reduced his expectations of the patient. When the patient was encouraged to invest more energy in work and less in change and was given a more effective medication, his mental state improved.

An antitherapeutic alliance develops readily with adolescents. It is tempting to allow adolescent groups to be chatty and to digress into social conversation when tension builds. In allowing digressions, the therapist perpetuates disruptiveness, negativism, and avoidance of age-appropriate responsibility. Conversely, the therapist must take care not to reinforce overly punitive superego precepts and become a moralizing parent-surrogate.

Adverse Transference Reactions

Many adverse transference reactions stem from inadequate appraisal of the patient's ego strength or a failure to appreciate his or her dynamics, coping mechanisms, and defense mechanisms. It is important to be aware that an individual psychotherapy patient who requests group therapy may be acting on transference wishes or fears and that placement in one's own group is not useful in dealing with an overwhelming transference gratification to the therapist.

> Mrs. A.B., an individual therapy patient with borderline personality disorder, requested group therapy as a means of dealing with her growing dependent and romantic attachment to her therapist. She reasoned that, in the therapist's group, their relationship would be diluted, her feelings would diminish, and she would be better able to verbalize because she would have less concern about pleasing him and winning his favor.
>
> Mrs. A.B. was the youngest child of a large family. Entering the group recapitulated her position in her family. In the group, she at times withdrew, trying to be a good girl, and at other times occupied the center of the group by staging tantrums, thus becoming the bad child that she had been in her own family. She was unable to tolerate the warm feelings between the therapist and an older woman in the group and eventually withdrew from group treatment.

Mrs. A.B.'s group treatment failed, but there was little alternative. She had not been able to bear the anger she had projected onto a previous therapist, and with the group therapist she was unable to bear the intensity of her own positive feelings.

As the case material presented above suggests, severe transference regressions occur in the borderline patient. For many unfortunate patients, the diagnosis is made only after a severe decompensation has occurred.

Countertransference

Many of the therapist's emotional reactions to his patient are reasonable responses that are not based on unconscious processes.

> Mrs. Z., an intensely narcissistic divorced woman, spent several years in group therapy attempting to discover the best way to find a new husband. To her way of thinking, marriage was the ultimate solution to her problems. She was totally unable to see men as individuals. Each was only a prospective spouse. All other qualities were ignored or were wished away. Over the years, the group and the therapist became angry over their inability to communicate that message to her and her inability to see them as more than a source of advice on husband hunting or as people with whom to lament the loss of her most recent prospect. Eventually, all

> acknowledged that she was getting nowhere in group therapy, which she terminated in favor of individual treatment, in which she fared no better. (Weiner 1982b)

In the case above, the anger of the therapist and the group was based largely on real frustration. The countertransference aspects were reactions to frustration of the therapist's and the group members' omnipotent strivings. Countertransference factors were much more important in the following case.

> Mr. A. reentered group therapy after an absence of two years because of recurrent depression and loss of interest in his work and his family. When he reentered the group, his attitude toward the group and the therapist was strongly positive. Shortly afterward, he had a heart attack and dropped out of the group for three months. On his return, his attitude toward the group and the leader changed radically. He was very critical of the group members and of the group leader. He complained that the group sessions were boring and requested individual sessions. When the therapist pushed for dealing with his feelings in the group, he began to express doubts about the leader's competence.
>
> Out of concern that an impasse was developing, the therapist referred him to a colleague for consultation. The consultant felt that Mr. A.'s recent heart attack had considerably increased his oral needs and that a significant source of his anger was the therapist's refusal to see him individually. (Weiner 1974b)

Mr. A. was a large man and had been a street fighter as a youngster. The therapist was afraid of him. On understanding that Mr. A. was angry because he wished an individual relationship with the therapist and not because he wanted to hurt him, the therapist agreed on weekly individual sessions in addition to group therapy. Soon afterward, Mr. A. discontinued group therapy. They successfully concluded his individual therapy a number of months later.

Transference Gratification

Transference gratification, the therapist's attempt to directly fulfill the infantile wishes or to assuage the infantile fears expressed in therapy, is an important source of impasse. One cannot make up for or undo traumas suffered by the patient in the past, whether they occurred in reality or resulted from the patient's reactions to fantasies. The therapist can deal only with the altered attitudes and perceptions generated by the original real or imaginary experiences (Goulding and Goulding 1978).

Partial transference gratification is necessary in all therapeutic relationships. The therapist's genuine interest, acceptance, and willingness to set limits within the therapeutic relationships are all minor transference gratifications.

Major transference gratifications are sometimes indicated, generally in the treatment of severely ego-impaired persons unable to deal with the demands of reality or their own superegos. Those patients frequently require that the therapist literally behave as a good parent, giving reasonable permissions and setting limits on behavior outside the therapy hour.

Some requests for advice and guidance are demands for transference gratifications, but many are legitimate requests for professional expertise. The therapist differentiates on the basis of his awareness of the realities of the patient's life, his dynamic formulation, and his clinical judgment (Weiner 1980).

A demand for physical contact, whether overtly sexual or not, is usually a demand for transference gratification. It is sometimes the direct outgrowth of a transference wish, at other times a defense against transference, and sometimes an appropriate response to the therapist's behavior. A push for sexual intimacy by a patient is frequently a reaction formation against sexual fears. It may be a way to avoid expressing hostile feelings or to defend against highly regressed clinging to the therapist.

Physical contact with borderline patients is to be avoided. They react to physical contact as an entrée for making further regressive demands, and it stimulates their wish for and fear of engulfment.

Working Through Impasses

Having established that an impasse exists by noting an absence of change or an actual worsening over time, the therapist faces the issue of resolving the impasse.

Some impasses are extremely difficult to resolve because they result from an entanglement of the needs and defenses of therapist and group member, and may actually be supported by the group. The first step is the therapist arriving at an assessment of the impasse as contractual or process, or based on transference or countertransference. While aiming his intervention at correcting the problem, it is often useful for the therapist to call the attention of the group member and the group as a whole to the therapist's observation that nothing positive (or something negative) is happening. Doing so unites the therapist with the individual group member or the group in jointly addressing the problem, and so mobilizes the resources of all.

After recognizing an impasse, but being uncertain as to its cause, the therapist may need considerable support to reverse the situation and extricate himself and his patient. At times, that requires peer consultation or following the recommendations of a paid consultant. Often, it is useful for the stalemated patient to work with a consultant or for therapist and patient to work together with a consultant. Ongoing supervision or therapy for the therapist may also be necessary. In the event that all of the above measures fail, the patient may require transfer to another type of therapy or another therapist. At times, a vacation from treatment will break the deadlock. When an entire group is stalled, a consultant can view videotapes or join the stalemated group to help break the deadlock.

Untangling a process impasse can involve years of struggle by the therapist and the patient, as the following example illustrates.

> Mr. A.K., a 29-year-old married man, was referred for group treatment by his individual therapist. He had entered individual therapy because of chronically low self-esteem, difficulty in initiating and maintaining social relationships, and more recent feelings of depression and feelings that people were laughing at him.
>
> Mr. K. had injured his lower jaw at age 12. The injury gave him a severe overbite until it was surgically corrected when he was 19. His deformity had been a significant source of embarrassment when trying to eat in public because food often dropped out of his mouth.
>
> In the group, he monopolized much of the group's time in a stereotyped replay of his internalized relationship with his

parents, in which he felt he had to pay the price of subjugation for the love and acceptance that he wanted. Positive responses by group members were brushed aside or provoked intense anger, which he recognized as irrational. Confrontation, clarification, and interpretation of his behavior did not help, nor did interpretation of the group's behavior toward him. He was too caught up in the transference.

After more than three years, the other group members unanimously demanded that he leave the group. The issue was discussed at length with him in the group, and it was decided that it was in the group's and his best interest for him to continue in individual psychotherapy, where he could be given the therapist's individual attention.

He and the group therapist continued individual psychotherapy, at first sporadically and later regularly, over the next four years. During that period of time, he came to recognize that, whether demanded actively or passively by him, he saw any intervention as an anal sexual assault. Even that recognition was not sufficient to diminish his defensiveness until the therapist recognized that his empathic smile and his unsolicited attempts to summarize and clarify were acting out the sadistic aspects of his own countertransference feelings. Then, with the patient's agreement, the therapist adopted a neutral, passive role toward him until Mr. K. demanded feedback directly by him.

As they dealt with the transference-countertransference aspects of their relationship, Mr. K. became less socially handicapped; however, because of continued social disability and a wish for a protected interpersonal arena for developing his social skills, he reentered a therapeutic group.

In the new group, he soon began his old behavior of soliciting advice and becoming angry when it was given. Because the therapist had a better idea of Mr. K.'s dynamics, he asked members of the group to refrain from giving him advice and asked them to signal to him when they felt he was running on or interpreting their remarks as attempts to control him.

At that point in his psychological development, he was able to tolerate frustration by the group and was aware that his demands to be nurtured by the group made him feel the need to submit to them and please them—it was not their demand. Because of Mr. K.'s increased understanding and better control of his behavior, the group's anger toward him was less intense than the anger of the previous group, and the new group was able to support him. Mr. K.'s impasse in group four years earlier was gradually turned into a positive group experience that enhanced his ability to establish and maintain social relationships. (Weiner 1983b, pp. 332–334)

At the beginning of Mr. A.K.'s group therapy, he was blocked from receiving input from others. That blockage eventuated in the group members' decreasing ability to respond to him in a useful manner. In later individual therapy, the therapist was able to correctly receive information from the patient, but acted inappropriately. When the therapist's inappropriate activity was resolved and the patient became less provocative, it was possible to place him in a group in which he did not overtax the group's ability to listen and to respond appropriately.

Summary

The resolution of impasses is facilitated by dealing with them as interactional processes instead of fixed aspects of the therapist, the individual group member, or the group as a whole.

Both contractual and process impasses result from the interaction of factors that alter the therapists' understanding of and reactions to patients and factors that affect the patients' understanding and reactions to their therapist. The same factors operate in patient-group interactions.

If group therapists examine impasse situations from a dynamic standpoint, instead of labeling patients as uncooperative or untreatable, and can then shift their therapeutic approaches within a coherent frame of reference, many treatment stalemates can be resolved successfully.

13

Termination

TERMINATION IS ORDINARILY REGARDED as the last stage in the life cycle of a group (Powers et al. 1974), but most terminations from group therapy occur early and are unplanned by the therapist. Yalom (1966) reported a dropout rate of 10 to 35 percent in the first 12 to 20 meetings of trainee-led groups at Stanford. Lothstein (1978) reported a 29 percent dropout rate in the first 12 sessions of groups conducted by professionals of several different disciplines at different levels of training. Those dropout rates are not higher than the dropout rates reported from individual psychotherapy in clinic settings (Weiner 1982a). In a study of analytically oriented group therapy, Stone and Rutan (1984) reported a 37 percent dropout rate by the end of the first year and 64 percent by the end of the second year, and 90 percent of group members had terminated at four years.

It is safe to assume that many persons terminate their treatment because it does not offer what they hoped for, or it makes demands they do not choose to meet. In this chapter, I will discuss termination as part of the overall therapeutic experience—the aspect of therapy that is the most significant for persons who need to learn how to deal with leave-taking and with loss, and for those who were unable to adequately assimilate positive introjects in their earlier lives. In closed groups, termination is an event shared by all at the same time and can be dealt with only in fantasy before the group's actual termination. Open-ended groups give each member a chance to experience termination vicariously before his or her own turn to leave.

Types of Termination

The types of termination are proposed termination, enforced termination, circumstantial termination, and inappropriate or premature termination.

Proposed

A proposal of termination by the therapist can indicate to a group member that he or she has accomplished the tasks set forth in their contract. It gives the group and the group member a chance to evaluate his or her progress and compare it with the therapist's view. It may also raise other issues that the individual group member has postponed dealing with. A proposal of termination can be initiated by the therapist stating that the group member has accomplished what he or she set out to do and by raising the issue of whether the member in question has thought about possible termination. If further issues do not arise over a period of time, the therapist initiates the leave-taking process.

Enforced

An enforced termination is a unilateral decision by the therapist that continuing in group is against the individual member or the group's best interest, and is employed with the group member who is worsening in therapy or too deviant to be tolerated by the group.

It is also fitting for persons who substitute the group for social lives of their own; they may be referred to social clubs or other organizations whose chief purposes are socialization and recreation.

Circumstantial

Circumstantial terminations from group therapy are quite common. Group members become physically ill, transfer in the course of their employment, or return home from college at the end of a semester. In clinics and training institutions, the turnover or graduation of personnel may necessitate termination of a group.

Groups on college campuses can be geared to circumstantial terminations and be scheduled to meet only during the school year. In training situations, groups may also be time-limited if transfer to another group leader will not be possible at the end of the therapist's period of service or at his or her graduation.

Groups need not be discontinued because of a prolonged absence of the leader. In my own experience with a prolonged illness and with the illness of colleagues, one therapist can readily stand in for another for months at a time, helping group members deal with their leader's illness and temporary loss, and furthering their treatment. There is insufficient information about the death of the group leader to know whether those groups are better terminated or carried on by another therapist (Rosenthal 1947; Aronson et al. 1962).

Premature

As noted earlier, many group terminations are premature in the sense that patients have not attained the benefits from therapy that one would expect if the group member had stayed.

Lothstein (1978) suggests that the dropout phenomenon is part of the normal selection process, and that persons who drop out prematurely do not fit well with the other group members' goals. However, the reported studies of group therapy dropouts come from settings in which new group members seldom had an ongoing relationship with the leader before entering the group, and had little or no opportunity for a one-to-one relationship with the leader or another therapist during the course of the group experience. The author's experience with a variety of patients in private practice is that patients with little ego strength and impulse control tend to drop out early. Even with continued individual support available, approximately 25 percent of persons referred for group therapy had dropped by the 10th session, and 40 percent had dropped by the 20th session, the majority of those early terminators being unimproved (Weiner 1984). It is possible that a highly screened and highly selected group of patients with strong ties to the therapist and much support from therapist and group might have fewer dropouts, but because of the complexity of human interactions, it will never be possible to retain all of the patients who are selected for any group.

Occasionally, group members will discontinue group sessions without giving notice. More commonly, there are warnings of an impending premature termination. Increasing dread of group sessions is a frequent sign, as is unwillingness to disclose in the group. Overdisclosure is also an indicator of a potential premature termination. The group member who reveals his or her sex life or moral misconduct in great detail during a first group session is likely to drop out because of the angry or rejecting response he or she anticipates from the group or from actually stimulating the group's anger.

When a group member unaccountably fails to appear for one or more sessions, it is the group leader's responsibility to establish contact and determine what is going on. Undisclosing group members' reluctance to be open can be gently dealt with, and overexposing group members may need to be questioned about their tendency to disclose prematurely and the effect those disclosures have had on relationships.

Premature terminations in early group sessions are probably due to a poor fit between a member and the group (Yalom 1966). Premature terminations at later points may have many precipitating factors.

Seasonal premature terminations are common. They occur shortly before, during, or after the therapist's vacation. They are partly related to feelings of being deserted by a parent and left with nonsupportive siblings and partly an identification with the aggressor—becoming one who leaves instead of one who is left. Seasonal terminations may also be influenced by the time of year. Therapists usually vacation during the summer, the time at which work and school pressures often diminish.

Intrapsychic factors play an important role in premature termination. Group members often fear that they or other group members will lose control of their sexual or aggressive impulses. Patients may also fear their own self-punishing tendencies in interpersonal relationships, or project the disapproving aspects of their superegos onto the group. Or, the group may recreate a painful family situation.

Therapists can forestall many terminations by carefully selecting group members and by building a pretermination delay of one to four weeks into the therapeutic contract. They can also be alert to hints suggesting potential flight from treatment, including missed appointments, tardiness for group sessions, and failure to pay the bill. Patients may in those ways stimulate group leaders' anger and then rationalize their leaving the group as a reaction to the therapist's anger or disapproval.

In repressive groups, the leader may insist that it is best for a group member to remain for the period of his therapeutic contract and encourage the fleeing member to stay. The leader can also turn to the group to support his position.

The leader of an ego-supportive or evocative group encourages the expression of feelings about the proposed termination. He begins by asking the group's reaction to the member's suggestion of termination. Members are encouraged to discuss the impact of that group member's leaving on themselves, and the significance of his or her leaving on the group. In evocative groups, the emphasis is on feelings and associations of other group members to the prospect of being left by one of their peers. In both ego-supportive and evocative groups, the member who is considering leaving is asked to respond to the other group members' reactions, thus underscoring the fact that his or her contemplated act has interpersonal and intrapsychic consequences.

Proposing a cooling-off period can give time for the therapist, group member, and group to deal fully with the reasons for, and consequences of, an early termination.

At times, a premature termination can be averted by examining the group member's reality situation, as shown in the following vignette.

> Mrs. J., who had a strong commitment to her group treatment, announced that she would need to terminate soon. Her husband had been out of a job for several months, and they were in dire financial straits. The therapist asked if she would consider using her group insurance at her place of employ-

> ment. She was startled and pleased to learn of this previous unexplored possibility. She used her insurance and was able to continue. (Weiner 1973)

Many patients are unwilling to discuss financial difficulties in the group, thus preventing consideration of alternative action or even a temporary adjustment in fee until the time of crisis has passed. Thus, individual sessions with a group member planning to terminate prematurely may be used to explore difficulties not mentioned in the group because of embarrassment or reluctance to ask for special consideration.

Methods of Termination

It may be possible to wean a group from therapy by decreasing the length and frequency of sessions. Weaning of individual group members from a group is not ordinarily feasible because absences of a member disrupt the flow of the group. The exception is large repressive groups, in which the addition or subtraction of a group member has little impact on the group as a whole.

The two principal methods of termination are vacation from therapy and outright termination. Vacation from therapy is useful under several circumstances. At times, a group member's job or finances will not allow continuation in therapy. For example, when Mr. A.K.'s job required that he be out of the country for several months, the therapist and group members agreed to hold his place open for him. Patients in financial straits for whom the therapist feels it unwise to reduce or forgive the fee may also be placed on vacation status with the stipulation that they may reenter the group as soon after they reapply as the group can accept them.

Vacation from therapy is also a useful means to terminate persons who do not tolerate well the idea of permanently losing the therapist or the group. For those persons, leaving the group is made equivalent to taking a job away from home, but being able to return if it does not work out well. There is no single diagnostic category of persons who cannot accept outright termination. The common denominator may be inadequate ability to introject or identify, or the inability to face symbolic death or permanent separation. Patients who require termination by vacation from therapy usually indicate their need for that type of termination by expressed fear of permanent separation or severe regression when faced with the prospect of permanent separation from the group.

Termination of Individuals: Indications and Process

There is no single criterion for terminating group treatment. Group treatment may be terminated because it has been partly or fully successful, because the termination process is the crux of therapy, or because patients are becoming worse. Termination may also be indicated when the therapist or his group is unable to tolerate a member, when an unresolvable impasse has developed, or when a member's diminished motivation makes further therapy unproductive.

Success

Success can be gauged by the goals established at the outset or during the process of therapy. It can be evaluated only in relation to patients' former level of maladjustment or discomfort and their life situation. Some treatments aim only to prevent decompensations; others work toward changing a limited segment of a patient's psychological and interpersonal life, while still others attempt more global change. Defenses are reinforced in some patients, while others are encouraged to relax their defenses and explore themselves.

Most group therapists use their observations and patients' subjective reports as indicators of progress. Recently, tests such as the Beck Depression Inventory (Beck et al. 1979) have been used to follow the course of depression, but few group therapists use objective measures of their patients' progress.

Repressive Groups. From the therapist's point of view, termination should occur when the patient has accomplished the educational task prescribed, such as a former psychotic patient recognizing that he or she has an emotional illness, or an abusing parent adopting healthier means for controlling children and managing his or her own aggression. When adequate repression or suppression has been stimulated and sufficient defenses have been mobilized against the eruption of primary process or raw, unsublimated impulses, patients are usually better able to deal with certain concrete tasks. Former psychotic patients may return to their jobs and abusers may establish reasonable limits for their children, and both types of patients thereby experience greater self-esteem. Termination from a repressive group may consist of a transition from formal therapy to a mutually supportive semisocial relationship with others facing the same problems.

In a repressive group, individual or group leave-taking may be highly ritualized and culminate with a graduation party in the group. On the other hand, leave-taking may be treated as a matter of course. Grief is sidestepped. Because intense feelings have been minimized, they require no working through. The final meeting is used to reiterate what the group members have learned and to reinforce the positive feelings between them.

Ego-Supportive Groups. The therapist looks for evidence of more effective interpersonal coping in the group, with the substitution of appropriate dependency and autonomy for overly dependent clinging or pseudo-independence. Ego defenses are modified and superego demands are eased. There is greater cooperation and mutuality in the group, and that is reflected in group members' day-to-day relationships. Patients' self-esteem is enhanced as a result of their improved interpersonal relationships and their taking responsibility for themselves instead of blaming others or being unable to turn to others for help at times of need.

Evocative Groups. Evaluation of a patient for termination from an evocative group is more complicated because there is less disturbed behavior and disturbed relationships to serve as markers, and the patient's complaints may have been largely subjective. Usually, however, there is sufficient disturbance of interpersonal relationships manifesting in the group to allow some objectification of the patient's progress.

Psychodynamically, patients use fewer neurotic and immature defense mechanisms (Vaillant 1977) and become more willing and able to face and assume responsibility for parts of themselves that were previously disowned and to take action in ways that were formerly blocked.

The formation of friendships attenuates the impact of termination in all three types of groups. That is frequently desirable in repressive groups in which one wants to avoid burdening group members with the difficulties of separation. It is also desirable in ego-supportive groups because of the real supportive value of friendships. The formation of friendships in evocative groups, while again desirable, helps avoid facing separation from the group and dealing with the process of leave-taking. However, the value of friendship probably outweighs the value of dealing with separation from the group. After all, living is in great measure a denial of loss and death (Yalom 1980).

When a member of an ego-supportive or evocative group decides to terminate, the therapist searches for evidence of resistance, especially a transference resistance. For example, the patient may be attempting to determine his value to the therapist. If the patient's proposal of termination does not involve resistance, the therapist can then deal with his own resistance, if any, to separating from the patient. If the therapist proposes termination, he first explores his own motivation for wanting to terminate that patient's treatment and later helps the patient work through concerns about separation.

Even when the decision to terminate therapy is mutual, understanding why is still useful. The therapist may be angry with the patient. The patient, sensing the therapist's anger, may be trying to avoid it.

In ego-supportive and evocative groups, the first step after agreeing to terminate is to allow the entire group to express their feelings. The next step is to set a date. Leave-taking from an ego-supportive group may require a few weeks to a few months. Leaving the group is treated as a positive step forward, and the ambivalence of patient and group is minimized.

There are additional steps in leaving an evocative group that may take a year or longer (Spotnitz 1961). Group members are encouraged to feel and express their reactions to the anticipated loss, to express feelings that develop during the separation process, and to deal with reactivated feelings from other losses. Ambivalence on the part of the group and the departing member usually runs high, and mild regressions often occur. A process of mutual decathexis begins, and new relationships outside the group develop as further evidence of readiness to depart.

After graduation of a group member, the therapist and group deal with the loss and then look forward to adding other new members.

Termination as the Crux of Therapy

In a sense, object relations exist only because we cannot remain physically attached to our mothers. We need to replace our umbilical circulation as the source of our nourishment. Many persons have not faced the task of psychological separation from the significant persons in their lives, and therefore have not been able to introject and identify adequately with them and have not developed the skills to establish new relationships.

Many group members whose overall levels of function and self-awareness have improved do not wish to take the next step of taking in what has been learned and leaving the people from whom they have learned. Based on Freud's (1923) observation that relinquishment fosters identification, one means to encourage the process of introjection and identification with the positive aspects of the group is through termination.

The process is introduced to the group members as part of growing up. It becomes necessary at some point to give up those we love and value and those on whom we depended earlier in life, to make new attachments, and to make what we have learned part of ourselves.

Deterioration or Regression

Some group members are harmed by their psychotherapy (Lambert et al. 1977). When a person's psychological condition is worsening, active consideration must be given to terminating the group treatment and ascertaining what type of treatment, if any, is more appropriate. Worsening does not refer to the occasional acting out that occurs in response to an overly vigorous intervention or a failure of the therapist to intervene. It is a steady deterioration of job performance, interpersonal relationships in and out of the group, and the appearance of more primitive psychological defenses and coping mechanisms.

The regressing group member can be removed from a repressive group without dealing with the issue in the group and with a comment to the effect that another form of treatment seems better. In ego-supportive and evocative groups, members who are worsening need to be discussed in the group and, in some instances, the group as a whole can be included in deciding if the worsening members should stay or leave. Groups often feel such loyalty to each member and so guilty when they are unable to help that they cannot relinquish group members who are beyond their ability to help. It is then the responsibility of the group leader to remove a regressed member over the other members' objections. Afterward, there is usually a sigh of relief as the other members acknowledge that they were holding on because of their guilt and their fear that they might be abandoned by the group if they became equally distressed. The therapist emphasizes that the group member was not abandoned, but transferred to a more effective therapeutic medium.

The Deviant

Occasional group members are so deviant from the others in the group that they significantly hinder the group's progress. At times, they are persons with borderline psychosis or persons whose thinking is more concrete or symptom-oriented than the group leader was aware. Such persons usually drop out of the group after a few sessions, but at times the group leader will need to acknowledge an unsuitable placement and suggest that group treatment be discontinued.

Terminations of a Group: Indications and Process

Groups are terminated as a whole when the therapeutic contract for the group as a whole has been fulfilled. Repressive groups are often terminated as a whole because they are frequently time-limited. Ego-supportive and evocative groups are usually open-ended and are terminated when they can no longer effectively function as a group or when a leader cannot be replaced for administrative or other reasons.

A group may need to be discontinued when there are too few members. There are times when so many members drop out or graduate that the remaining members, including the leader, become demoralized and can no longer function together effectively. It is possible to carry temporarily a group of two members provided they can be encouraged to work together and the leader can maintain his self-esteem—a factor that is often tied to the number of group members. In most cases, it is best to dissolve a group whose membership is reduced to two and place those persons in other groups or individual therapy.

The loss of a leader through graduation, transfer, or suicide may so impair the functioning of a group that it must be terminated. However, Dumont (1966) reported a group of hospitalized schizophrenic patients whose group interaction survived the suicide of their therapist after an initial period of disorganization.

Departure of the leader of better-functioning people and groups can be a positive or negative experience for the group, depending on the leader's management of his departure (McGee 1974). A departing leader can undermine the group's ability to function with another leader through excessive transference gratification or failure to deal with the group's anger or sense of desertion. In the case of excessive gratification, the group regresses and demands to be fed by the new leader. When the group's anger over its loss is not dealt with, that is often acted out against the new leader, who is literally driven out of the group. Group members may also flee rather than face desertion again.

When a group's regression cannot be reversed, when its acting out cannot be dealt with, and when its fear of desertion precludes its acceptance of a new therapist, it may be best to dissolve the group and place its members in other groups or individual therapy to deal with the intensified resistance.

Terminating the Group as a Whole

Terminating a group as a whole is much like terminating individual group members. Termination of entire groups is common where periodic turnover of professional personnel makes it impossible for some groups to continue, or when only short-term groups can be offered (Budman et al. 1981). Group terminations are also important as part of therapists' training experience. They help therapists deal with the mechanics and emotional impact of leave-taking. Terminating a group as a whole has the advantage of leaving no one behind, but has the disadvantage that not all members are equally ready to terminate.

Because most terminations of entire groups are based on external circumstances rather than the needs of group members, much anger may be aroused in group members who feel they have been short-changed. The therapist, identified with the group members' plight, may feel much guilt. However, the most reasonable and useful attitude for the therapist is that he or she has given what has been possible under the circumstances, and that everyone and everything has its limits. The group members are then encouraged to use the process of leave-taking to strengthen themselves by learning to face that aspect of reality.

Arrangements need to be made for continuing the therapy of group members who require it, but many group members will elect a period of no treatment, knowing that they can obtain further treatment if they feel the need.

There are no specific stages of terminating a group as a whole. Kadis et al. (1974) found in terminating one open-ended group that the group members' reactions included surprise and happiness that they were considered well enough to terminate, doubts and ambivalence, anxiety, hostility and grief, reestablishment of earlier defenses against anxiety, resolution of transference and dependence on the group, and acceptance of termination and the real adjustment involved.

Hindrances to Termination

From the patient's point of view, termination may symbolize abandonment or loss of hope by the therapist that he or she can progress further. It may also imply loss of symbolic parental nurturance or a life style of authority-dependence. Resistance to termination can be a form of hostile clinging. Important unresolved transferences can often be brought into the open by the therapist's proposal of termination. When one therapist terminated a group, a member said that she had expected him to always remain as a surrogate parent and that she now had to deal with the therapist having needs and priorities of his own that he placed above the needs of the group members.

Hindrances to termination from the therapist's point of view include the convenience of continuing to work with the same group members, avoiding the issue of loss, the difficulty of finding and integrating new group members, countertransference, and the value of the group member to him as a person.

Effects of Termination on Therapist and Group

After the graduation of a group member, other group members feel left behind and somewhat envious of the departed person's positive accomplishments, including his or her ability to say goodbye to the group and operate without them. Often, termination by one group member triggers a wave of terminations by people who do not want to be left behind or to deal with their own problems. The therapist can help avert a transference-based stampede by stating that many people react to leave-taking by also wishing to leave, and encouraging group members to express those feelings instead of acting on them.

While a patient's graduation can be a source of pride for the therapist, he or she also loses an important person and suffers the narcissistic injury of realizing that the graduating member can do without the therapist's help. There is the further injury that the member may have graduated without fulfilling all of the therapist's wishes for that patient.

Viewed from a positive standpoint, losing group members encourages accepting the cycle of birth and death and prepares all for the numerous separations they will endure in the course of their lives.

Interminable Versus Brief Groups

A case can be made for lifelong membership in a therapeutic group as a necessary augmentation of impaired ego functioning when there are inadequate environmental supports. It can also be argued that lending permanent support discourages seeking support in ordinary social relationships. If permanent support is necessary, it probably requires only brief, infrequent visits and not weekly sessions (Weiner 1982b).

Recognizing that therapy often lasts as long as it is allowed to last (Stieper and Wiener 1959), there has been a recent emphasis on short-term groups (Budman et al. 1980). Short-term groups with discrete goals may be one means to avoid growth-thwarting dependency on therapy, and may be useful as a specific means to deal with various types of loss.

What Does Termination Really Mean?

Termination means that at a certain point in time, the therapist, group, or individual group member determines that the benefits of continuing in a group are minimal or outweighed by the time, expense, or other negative aspects of attending the group. It does not mean that a person is permanently cured of life's problems or that he or she will be able to handle all future problems with equanimity. It usually means that psychotherapy is no longer indicated or necessary for that person as a means to deal with life's problems, and that he or she can now make good use of inner resources, friends, or other support systems such as religion as forms of sustenance.

In the process of termination, the leader makes it clear that departing members are only human, that life is complex, and that turning to others for help in solving life's problems can indicate strength as well as weakness.

Summary

Termination is a complex process. It is the crux of therapy for many group members because it forces them to deal with issues of separation and autonomy and provides an opportunity to deal with separation-individuation issues (Mahler 1979).

Termination involves the active participation of the leader, the group, and the terminating member or members in dealing with the issues that have led to the decision to terminate, the process of termination, and the aftermath of termination.

Finally, termination from group psychotherapy is termination of only one step or one means of dealing with life's problems. It should leave the door open for further therapy should the need arise and should foster acceptance of a universal need for periodic support, nurturance, and guidance. Formal therapy is but one means, and its aim is to open people to the other means available in themselves and their families and communities.

14

Ethical and Legal Issues

GROUP THERAPISTS HAVE CERTAIN ethical obligations to the people whom they strive to help. The American Psychiatric Association's code of ethics (1973) applies to all mental health professionals. Mental health professionals have the ethical obligation to make a prompt and adequate diagnosis, to establish treatment based on that diagnosis, to obtain appropriate consultation, to avoid doing harm, and to maintain the privacy of communications made in confidence during the course of professional activities.

Group therapists who are licensed mental health professionals have certain legal duties in addition to their ethical obligations. They must provide the same standard of care that other adequately trained professionals of the same discipline would provide. They must make a prompt and adequate diagnosis. Informed consent for treatment must be obtained. That is, patients need to be informed, when possible, of the nature of the treatment, its possible benefits and possible harmful effects, and what is expected of patients in the treatment process. If appropriate treatment based on an adequate diagnostic evaluation is instituted, but is ineffective, there is an obligation to seek consultation in a reasonable length of time or to refer the patient to another therapist or treatment facility.

Malpractice

Regardless of the therapist's competence, there are times when therapy does not go well and harm is done (Bergin 1971). When harmed, the patient has a legal right to seek redress. The type of redress depends on whether or not the mental health professional belongs to a licensed profession. Failure to meet the standard of care of a licensed profession is grounds for a malpractice action. A group therapist who does not belong to a licensed profession such as medicine, clinical psychology, or nursing has no professional standard of practice and therefore cannot commit malpractice. An unlicensed mental health professional can, however, be sued for misrepresenting himself as a licensed professional, for assault and battery, or for practicing a healing art without a license.

Malpractice occurs when a patient is injured by a breach of the professional duties of skill or care or by a breach of their proper performance (Vaccarino 1977). The health care professional fails to perform his or her professional duty adequately or at all, or does not possess and exercise such reasonable skill as is ordinarily possessed by others in the same type of practice.

The legal criteria for determining adequate care are that the practitioner must possess the knowledge, skill, and abilities that others in similar practice in the United States usually possess, must exercise the same kind of care and diligence in applying that knowledge, and must use reasonably good professional judgment in carrying out his or her professional duty (Feld 1971). Adhering to local or regional standards of care is no longer adequate for medical specialists (*Naccarato v. Grob* 1970).

The legal criteria for malpractice are (1) that the health care professional owed a duty to conform to a particular standard of conduct, (2) that he or she failed in that duty by act or omission, (3) that because of the professional's failure the patient or a third party suffered actual damage, and (4) that the professional's conduct was the direct or proximate cause of the mental or physical injury (Rothblatt 1973). Establishing malpractice usually requires expert testimony. Occasionally, the court will rule that the health care professional's behavior was so deviant that it speaks for itself (*res ipsa loquitur*). In one case, for example, the therapist repeatedly struck his patient (*Hammer v. Rosen* 1960). If a patient does not profit from an appropriate, adequately conducted therapy to which he or she gave informed consent, there is no cause for malpractice action. There must be evidence of damage that directly results from the therapist's action or failure to act. Failure to cure is not grounds for malpractice (Fink 1972). If, on the other hand, the therapist has guaranteed a cure, he or she may be liable for breach of contract.

Legal actions against psychotherapists are uncommon; actions arising from group therapy are rare (Cohen 1979). The greatest cause of malpractice suits is not a bad outcome of treatment, but a failure to obtain or a disruption of a positive, cooperative therapist-patient relationship (Vaccarino 1977).

Proper Procedures

Much of a group therapist's professional routine has legal implications. That includes diagnosis, informed consent, group composition, confidentiality, the written record, reevaluation, the conduct of therapy, duty to warn or restrain, and abandonment.

Diagnosis

If a therapist has made an adequate evaluation and has recorded the evaluation and its findings, he or she generally will not be held liable for negligence or malpractice if the diagnosis is wrong. If, for example, an adequately examined patient who was found not suicidal should take his own life, the therapist is not guilty of negligence (*Baker v. United States* 1964) *if* the therapist was professionally qualified to evaluate a suicidal patient. If therapists such as social workers or psychiatric nurses who suspect mental illness or the possibility of suicidal behavior fail to obtain consultation by a professional more qualified to make that diagnosis, they may be liable.

Failure to diagnose is grounds for malpractice if there is no evidence (usually in the form of a written record) that an adequate evaluation was done.

Informed Consent

Therapists need to tell their patients enough about their condition and the proposed treatment so that they can decide whether or not to accept the treatment offered. Informed consent to group therapy might reasonably involve the number of members in the proposed group, typical activities of the group such as alternate sessions, and the contract for the group, including the therapist's charge for missed sessions, rules about socializing among group members outside the regular session, etc. Potential group members also need to be told if extensive physical contact is likely, and if so, the nature of that contact.

Informed consent is especially important for marathon sessions in which there is likely to be great stirring of feelings and physical interaction, both of which may severely upset people with marginal coping ability.

Failure to warn of the danger of treatment is acceptable in an emergency, especially when the patient is unable to judge risk for himself or if explaining the risk might result in failure to accept needed treatment (*Lester v. Aetna* 1957), but that is rarely the case with group psychotherapy.

Group Composition

Therapists are obliged to compose their groups to maximize potential therapeutic gain and minimize physical or emotional danger to group members. The gain for the patient when adding an acting out member must be balanced against the physical danger to the other group members. Therapists must also consider the emotional hazard to the group in adding a suicidal person in the event that person attempts or succeeds at suicide.

Confidentiality and Privilege

It is important that therapists discuss the issue of confidentiality with patients. Confidentiality is the professional or ethical obligation of mental health professionals to not disclose confidences revealed to them. Privilege is the patient's right to maintain the professional's silence. Because it is their right, patients may choose to waive their privilege under certain circumstances, and under those circumstances therapists may be obliged to disclose information that was originally disclosed in confidence. There is now privileged communication for psychologists and/or psychiatrists in 48 states (the exceptions are West Virginia and South Carolina), but the privilege statutes in many states have so many exceptions that they convey little protection (Shuman and Weiner 1982). In most cases, the privilege does not extend to other patients participating in groups, but to date there has been no case testing the liability of the group leader for a breach of confidence by a group member, and group members have not been called into court to testify about one another (Cohen 1979).

Generally speaking, therapists must keep confidences unless the patient presents an immediate physical danger to himself or others. Therapists are obliged to disclose if ordered to do so by a court, if the patient is making a legal claim in which his or her mental state is an issue, or when suing a mental health professional for malpractice. Therapists have a right to consult with other mental health professionals about their patients, but in doing so must take care not to reveal the identity of the patient, unless there is need for the consultant to know the patient's identity. In training situations, disclosing the patient's identity is often unavoidable and its concealment would unnecessarily complicate the supervisory process.

Therapists must be careful to avoid exposing their patients' identities when writing case reports. When extensive descriptions are given, the patient's permission to publish should be obtained. In one case, distribution of a published book was stopped by court order because the patient about whom the book was written claimed that her identity was insufficiently disguised and that her permission had not been asked (*Doe v. Roe* 1973).

The Written Record

The therapist's written record is the best means to follow the course of a patient's treatment. Failure to keep a written record that documents the diagnosis, treatment, and response to treatment endangers the patient and the therapist. It endangers the patient because, without a written record, the therapist has only his unreliable memory to record the initial diagnostic evaluation, the treatment plan, what has transpired during treatment, and what worked and what didn't. It endangers the therapist because lack of an adequate record can be equated by the courts with inadequate treatment (*Whitree v. State* 1968). It can be objected that keeping a written record potentially endangers confidences through the possibility of people gaining access to files illegally or through subpoena. However, the only data the therapist needs to record are the basic nature of the presenting problem, the treatment prescribed, and the progress of treatment. Highly sensitive information about the patient's business enterprises or sex life need not be included in the record unless they are the symptoms that led to treatment.

Reevaluation

A patient in ongoing treatment should be reevaluated periodically in terms of the presenting complaints and initial diagnosis. All therapists face the problem that the better they know their patients, the more difficult it is to make a single diagnosis. Almost every patient has symptoms of more than one diagnosable disorder. Histrionic people have obsessional thought patterns; obsessional people frequently use a great deal of projection, and neurotic people often have significant character pathology. Patients therefore need to be periodically reevaluated and rediagnosed according to the main presenting problem at that time. Reevaluation keeps the therapy on track and also shows that an adequate evaluation of the patient was done. Reevaluation should also include statements about the patient's present potential for suicide or homicide, especially if such thinking or behavior were part of the presenting problem.

Conduct of Therapy

In Trent and Muhl's (1975) report of 28 closed malpractice claims against psychiatrists between 1972 and 1975, none was attributable to the conduct of psychotherapy. The predominant source of malpractice actions against psychiatrists was improper commitment; pressing for fee collection was second. There was a single case of sexual impropriety.

In 52 complaints alleged against psychologists in 38 claims, the largest cause of malpractice complaint was fee disputes (11 complaints) and the next most common was sexual improprieties (Cohen 1979).

Group therapists have been highly innovative in their treatment approaches. While innovation is permissible, therapists' duty to their patients is to adopt or devise treatment that is well suited to their needs and that can be defended in court if necessary (Rothblatt and Leroy 1973). Departures from accepted professional norms need to be justified in the therapist's written record. If the procedure is experimental, the therapist needs to indicate its experimental nature and obtain the patient's consent for an experimental procedure.

Interestingly, sex between therapist and patient, although unethical according to the American Psychiatric Association (1973) and the American Psychological Association (1975), is not *prima facie* evidence of malpractice. It is poor judgment at best and exploitation of the therapist-patient relationship at its worst. In one case of therapist-patient sex, the court's finding of the therapist's liability for malpractice was based not on their sexual involvement, but on his mismanagement of the transference that made the patient vulnerable to the therapist's suggestions (*Zipkin v. Freeman* 1968).

Therapists must be careful whom they incite to what action in the group. They know the potential of people in groups for violence if incited, and their acts or failure to act can be the proximate cause of damage that may occur (*Woods v. Brumlop* 1962).

Duty to Warn

Mental health professionals have the option to warn others who are endangered if they perceive a patient to be dangerous to others (*Sealy v. Finkelstein* 1960). In some jurisdictions, they have an actual duty to warn (*Tarasoff v. Regents* 1976). Each therapist must determine his or her own state's position on protecting endangered third parties. Certainly, a group therapist needs to warn a group member if the therapist feels that another group member might do physical harm to him or her.

Duty to Commit, Restrain, or Supervise

If a group member's emotional condition makes him a danger to himself or others, the mental health professional has a duty to help that person or concerned friends or relatives seek a safe treatment environment for him or her. For psychiatrists, that may mean seeking commitment. For other mental health professionals, it means referral to a person who can evaluate the patient for possible involuntary hospitalization.

On the other hand, it is reasonable for group therapists to accept potentially dangerous persons for treatment as long as the potential benefits outweigh the risks, as in the case of persons formerly diagnosed as dangerous who are being reintegrated into the community from hospital care (*Eaves v. United States* 1969).

Abandonment

The American Psychiatric Association's ethical code (1973) states that therapists may discontinue their services only after giving adequate notice. Pope et al. (1978) suggest that adequate notice includes stating the reason for termination, a recommendation for further treatment if indicated, and help in securing that treatment.

Malpractice Insurance

Because mental health professionals are ordinary people, they make mistakes. Patients' entitlement to recompense for those mistakes is the basis for malpractice insurance. As a professional, the group therapist must be prepared to pay for his or her mistakes. Failure to secure adequate malpractice insurance is a disservice to the patient as much as to the therapist.

Malpractice insurance protects group therapists in other ways. Insurance carriers provide legal advice when malpractice threatens and pay the cost for legal defense of their clients.

The cost of a successful defense can be just as ruinous as a settlement paid to a patient.

The best nonfiduciary malpractice insurance is contained in the following suggestions.

How to Avoid Malpractice

Secure adequate training and operate only within your realm of competence. Keep up with developments in diagnosis and treatment. Do an adequate evaluation, and periodically reevaluate patients to evaluate their progress. Warn of possible consequences of suggested diagnostic and treatment procedures. Have a sound rationale for proposed treatments. Use consultants, peer supervision, and case conferences, especially when in doubt as to the treatment indicated, when treatment is stalled, or when patients are worsening. In all instances, protect patients' privacy.

Obtain informed written consent for recording, release of information, publishing case reports, and experimental techniques. Take direct, appropriate action with the patient who endangers himself or others. In some instances, warning an endangered third party is necessary. Select group members who will not violate the confidence of, or do physical harm to, their fellow group members. Confine relationships with patients to the office, except for certain specific treatment indications. Except for necessary examinations, handshakes, and other ordinary greetings, keep hands off patients except in the presence of witnesses and in the service of an acceptable therapeutic rationale. Do not abandon patients whom you have not been able to help, cannot help further, or do not wish to treat. Help them or a concerned relative or guardian find an adequate facility in a length of time consistent with his treatment needs. And, do not treat unmarried minors without parental consent. (Married minors can consent to treatment in many jurisdictions.)

15

Research

MUCH OF GROUP THERAPY PRACTICE has been based on the clinical lore of charismatic clinicians. As the field has matured, formal research has increased rapidly. The first book devoted exclusively to surveying group therapy research was published by Roback et al. in 1979. Unfortunately, there has been greater emphasis on process studies than outcome studies, so we know more about what is done in groups than we know about its effectiveness. Most of what we know about effectiveness is anecdotal, and very little has been objectified because of the difficulties in evaluating improvement. Few outcome studies have adequate controls. They often employ inexperienced therapists who treat chronically mentally ill persons for short periods of time (Bergin 1971).

Nevertheless, group therapies as a whole are shown to produce more change than no treatment, even when group casualties are taken into consideration (Lambert et al. 1977; Meltzoff and Kornreich 1970; Bednar and Lawlis 1971).

Therapist-Offered Conditions

There is much information on therapist-offered conditions that mitigate for and against successful psychotherapy. The therapist-offered conditions of genuineness, accurate empathy, and nonpossessive warmth, once held to be the sine qua non of successful psychotherapy, now appear to be only a part of the complex variables that influence outcome (Mitchell et al. 1977), including the therapist offering a cognitive frame of reference that the patient can accept and use (Strupp 1980).

Whitehorn and Betz's (1954) finding that people-oriented therapists (As) had better outcomes in working with schizophrenic patients than therapists who were more comfortable dealing with abstract ideas and concepts (Bs) has been investigated extensively, but has not been adequately reconfirmed (Razin 1977).

By contrast, Lieberman et al. (1973) found that the most damaging type of group leader has great charisma; is intrusive, aggressively stimulating, and highly challenging and confronting; and exercises strong control over the group. In other words, the leaders with the most casualties were the least sensitive to the needs of their group members and were intent on forcing their own frame of reference on group members. The victims predictably had high expectations and lacked the coping skills and self-esteem necessary to weather such an assault.

Patient Populations

Until the development of the cognitive and behavioral therapies, the problem of outcome research was compounded by the unstandardized way in which therapy was done. In most reported studies, it is difficult to determine exactly how the therapists applied their therapeutic frame of reference in the conduct of their groups. Nevertheless, the data are beginning to suggest differences in the effectiveness of group methods with different categories of patients.

Schizophrenia

The schizophrenias show strong biological-genetic factors (Kety 1978) and are comparable in that respect to diabetes, asthma, and hypertension. All are disorders with genetic predispositions influenced by emotional factors that often require chemical treatment of altered physiologic processes.

Cowden et al. (1956) showed that an antipsychotic drug plus group therapy was more effective in reducing disruptive ward behavior than group therapy or an antipsychotic drug alone, suggesting that groups may be a useful adjunctive to the treatment of the acutely and severely mentally ill. Their findings are supported by studies indicating that group therapy facilitates other forms of inpatient therapy (Parloff and Dies 1977). Pattison et al. (1967) find it unhelpful to use an evocative therapy with short-term hospital patients for whom the goal is immediate reconstitution, and Truax et al. (1966) find alternate sessions detrimental to psychiatric inpatients.

Claghorn et al. (1974) suggest that group therapy contributes little to preventing the rehospitalization, aiding the vocational adjustment, or increasing the social effectiveness of schizophrenic patients after they leave the hospital.

Authors who have surveyed the literature uniformly agree that group therapy, especially when insight-oriented, is a weak treatment technique for schizophrenia (Meltzoff and Kornreich 1970; Bednar and Lawlis 1971; Parloff and Dies 1977).

A few studies indicate the groups may be a better means to follow formerly hospitalized schizophrenic patients (Shatton et al. 1966; Levene et al. 1970). O'Brien et al. (1972) studied 100 schizophrenic patients who were randomly assigned to group or individual follow-up after hospital discharge. After a year, 76 percent of the group-treated patients remained in therapy in contrast to 46 percent of the individually followed persons; only 12 percent of the group-treated patients required rehospitalization in contrast to 24 percent of the individually followed patients.

Affective Disorders

Manic-depressive illness and severe recurrent unipolar depressions also show a strong biological-genetic component (Klerman 1978). There are no studies of group therapy in manic-depressive illness or severe unipolar depression, but the refractoriness of those disorders to a psychological treatment is well known to clinicians. Unfortunately, there are no objective data to confirm that clinical impression, and no data on group therapy as an adjunct to lithium or other forms of treatment. Preliminary studies suggest that group cognitive therapy may be effective for mild to moderate depression in outpatients (Hollon and Shaw 1979).

Delinquency and Criminal Behavior

Group therapy for severe delinquents and adult offenders adds little to overall institutionalization; recidivism remains about the same in most studies. One exception is a group of sex offenders on probation, reported by Peters et al. (1968), whose recidivism rate was one percent as compared to eight percent for the control group.

It could be argued that most forms of criminal behavior and delinquency are not psychological problems but social problems, and that social remedies might be more appropriate than psychological measures. Those who work with institutionalized populations of delinquents and criminal offenders find that they are outsiders dealing with subcultures in which the behaviors that led to incarceration are acceptable norms and members of those subcultures actively punish persons who attempt to deviate by conforming to the norms of society at large.

Substance Abuse

Parloff and Dies (1977) were unable to find convincing evidence that formal group therapy conducted by professionals has significant impact on alcohol or other substance abuse.

Vaillant (1981) has argued that the central problem for most alcoholics is alcohol abuse per se and that measures to increase self-understanding contribute nothing to dealing with the central treatment issue of becoming abstinent. He studied 268 men, prospectively followed from their sophomore year in college until age 50. Twenty-six of those men lost control over their alcohol use at some point. Half sought psychotherapy and received an average of 200 hours of treatment. Over time, half of the men achieved stable remission from their alcoholism, usually through abstinence. Psychotherapy seemed related to remission in only one case. In many other cases it seemed to divert attention from the primary problem.

Neuroses and Personality Disorders

According to the research literature, group therapy offers most to the neurotic or character-disordered outpatient who is managing his own life and has good ego strength (in contrast to the poor ego strength of the hospitalized person, regardless of diagnosis), values that conform with society in general (as opposed to the delinquent or criminal), and a measure of social competence. In fact, group therapies may be as effective as individual therapies for this group of patients. It is only in dealing with mid-range psychopathology that we find information about the specific types of group approach employed.

Barron and Leary's (1955) study of 35 group therapy patients and 42 individual therapy patients drawn from a population of psychoneurotics showed more similarities than differences in outcome. Frank et al. (1959) studied 54 neurotic and personality-disordered patients randomly assigned to treatment by second-year psychiatric residents and found no difference in outcome after at least six months of treatment.

Repressive group therapy and nonanalytic individual therapy were contrasted in a group of 67 patients largely diagnosed as having depression or anxiety states (Thorley and Craske 1950). Group therapy (57 percent improved) was as effective as individual therapy (62 percent improved).

Meltzoff and Kornreich (1970) reexamined Peck's study contrasting individual therapy with combined individual and group therapy for neurotics (1949) and found no significant augmenting effect.

Specific Types of Groups

It is doubtful that any group technique has the specificity of minor tranquilizers for reducing anxiety, or antipsychotic drugs for calming acutely psychotic or delirious persons. It is more likely that the success of any group therapy has much to do with the interaction of the therapist's personality and therapeutic style with the individuals in the group, their interaction with each other, and the overall configuration of the group—factors that are essentially unpredictable and not reproducible. We may therefore have to rely on anecdotal reports instead of analyzing data from the treatment of large numbers of group patients until group therapists can specify exactly what they do with specific patient populations.

While short-term groups are now receiving attention, the scientific basis for asserting their efficacy is slim. Melson et al. (1982) have reported positive results from an intensive group experience for two to five weeks as part of a day treatment program. They treated a variety of nonpsychotic disorders that presented primarily as physical complaints. There was significant improvement on several measures at termination of treatment and at six-month follow-up.

Donovan et al. (1981) reported on short-term groups whose members were largely between 18 and 35 years old, white, middle class, and highly educated (89 percent high school graduates and 53 percent college graduates), with a predominance of women. Most entered the group because of a marital problem or a broken romance. At termination, 91 percent of the group members rated the experience as helpful, and 95 percent liked the group. The therapists rated 75 percent of the members as improved. Improvement was said to have been sustained at one year follow-up, but the follow-up data are quite incomplete. Of 141 persons attending such groups over two years, 40 were not studied because they attended fewer than four sessions. Another 15 were excluded because they did not adequately fill out the initial evaluation form. Only 43 of 80 one-year follow-up forms were returned; therefore, only 30 percent of the treated population actually had a one-year follow-up.

In the first study contrasting the efficacy of one group technique with another, Lazarus (1961) showed a striking difference between group desensitization and insight-oriented interpretive group therapy in treating severe phobias. Group desensitization produced a 54 percent improvement rate in people with severe, chronic phobias, while none improved in the interpretive group.

Cognitive therapy was superior in one study (Rush et al.

1977) to antidepressant medication for depressed outpatients. Preliminary studies indicate that group cognitive therapy for depressed outpatients may be somewhat less effective and have a higher dropout rate than individual cognitive therapy, but still exceed the effect of the antidepressant imipramine (Hollon and Shaw 1979).

Thus, work of the behaviorists and the cognitive therapists brings us closer to developing specific group techniques with measurable outcomes applicable to specific types of psychological problems. Lazarus tested the effects of his desensitization work by challenging his phobic patients to perform tasks they formerly feared. The cognitive therapists have devised symptom rating check tests to objectify their patients' progress.

In a private practice setting, I evaluated the first 100 people whom I treated in groups for at least one session, using combined ego-supportive and evocative techniques (Weiner 1984). Patients were evaluated retrospectively at termination using the Menninger Health-Sickness Rating Scale (Luborsky 1962). The group was composed of 44 persons with mild to severe personality disorders (including six with borderline personality disorder), 34 with neurotic disorders, seven substance abusers, 12 with psychotic disorders, and three persons who presented with physical symptoms as a chief complaint. There was a 45 percent improvement rate for the group as a whole, but only nine of the 100 graduated from the group. One was a patient with borderline personality disorder who made only a small gain after 211 sessions. The others had mild to moderate neurotic or characterologic problems. A full 30 percent of the group members entered other forms of treatment, although half of that group (15 percent of the entire group) had improved at the time of transfer.

All members who stayed with the group for 60 sessions or longer showed some improvement, although improvement was minimal in several cases. Dropouts between sessions 30 and 60 correlated with low ego strength. Earlier dropouts seemed more related to individual motivation and fit with the group than ego strength. At least 11 of the 100 became worse during their group treatment. Seven required hospitalization, three became psychotic but were not hospitalized, and one committed suicide.

Of the 10 substance abusers, the only ones who improved

were alcoholics who were abstinent at the time they entered the group. Only two (17 percent) of the 12 persons with psychotic disorders improved, but 23 (68 percent) of the 34 neurotic patients and 18 (41 percent) of the 44 patients with personality disorders improved.

This study confirms the observation that persons with little ego strength do poorly in evocative and ego-supportive therapies, and that mildly to moderately neurotic persons are the patients for whom they are the most applicable. The exceptions in the neurotic group may be uncomplicated phobias or other monosymptomatic disorders for which behavior therapy may have the most to offer.

Hopefully, this uncontrolled study by a single rater retrospectively evaluating his own patients will be replaced by controlled prospective studies with independent evaluators. Research in group psychotherapy outcome can be done, and must be done if group psychotherapy is to become a body of rational treatment techniques.

Summary

As group therapists examine their work objectively, they find that as primary therapies, groups offer most to the persons who are also the best candidates for individual psychotherapy: persons with ego-alien symptoms who are coping adequately on a day-to-day basis.

Repressive group therapy may be useful in the psychoses as an auxiliary therapy to help cope with the effects of illness. Formal group therapy presently seems to have little to offer substance abusers, delinquents, or criminal offenders.

As group therapists have applied more specific, replicable techniques such as behavior therapy and cognitive therapy, there is evidence that those techniques may be of value for phobias and mild to moderate depression.

With the greater precision in diagnosis offered by DSM-III (American Psychiatric Association 1980) and with more precisely defined treatment techniques such as the cognitive-behavioral therapies, we will be able to elucidate more of the specific indications and contraindications for the types of group therapy.

Finally, group therapists should be aware that their groups are their laboratories and that every group and every therapeutic intervention in group is an experiment (Dies 1983). By keeping records of those experiments, quantifying them with instruments, such as the CORE Battery (MacKenzie and Dies 1982), and reporting them to colleagues, we can broaden the rational base from which we operate.

Appendix:
Teaching and Training Aids

Many films and videotapes of group treatment are available for purchase or rental. The following films and videotapes are only a few of the many teaching and training aids now available.

Films

All of the films listed are 16 mm and are shipped by mail. Many are in color. The running time of the film is indicated after the title.

Group Therapy: The Dynamics of Change: 31 minutes.

This is the best available enactment of psychoanalytically oriented group psychotherapy. It is a condensation of two and a half hours of an adult treatment group in private practice, with patients portrayed by professional actors. It was produced by Richard Abell, M.D., in 1971. The American Medical Association Film Library at 535 N. Dearborn Street, Chicago, Illinois 60610, rents the film for $15.00. It is restricted to professional audiences. The sound and photography are excellent, but the film is wearing out.

The Scream Inside . . . Emergence Through Group Therapy: 47 minutes.

Taken from videotapes of actual group sessions, the film demonstrates group process and the emergence of conflicts in a psychoanalytically oriented adult group in private practice. Sound and photography vary from good to poor. Made in 1969, it was produced by Milton Berger, M.D. The Film Department of Sandoz Pharmaceuticals, East Hanover, New Jersey 07936, will provide this film without charge. It is restricted to professional audiences.

Broad Spectrum Behavior Therapy in a Group: 29 minutes.

This film of psychology graduate students in behavior therapy is an excellent demonstration of behavior rehearsal, modeling techniques, group desensitization, and assertiveness training. It was produced by Arnold Lazarus, Ph.D. Audio-Visual Services, Pennsylvania State University, 17 Willard Building, University Park, Pennsylvania 16802, rents this film for $12.00 to professional audiences. Photography and sound are adequate.

Group Therapy: 60 minutes.

This film presents one session of an ego-supportive staff group that had met regularly for more than a year. Group members are caseworkers at a residential treatment center for children. It was produced by Allan King Associates. It rents for $40.00 to professional audiences only and is available from the Film Division, Grove Press, 53 E. 11th Street, New York, New York 10003. Sound and photography are good.

Turning Point: An Introduction to Group Psychotherapy: 32 minutes.

Turning Point is a good orientation to ego-supportive group therapy for lower middle class prospective group members. It gives a case history and simulated course of treatment. Group members are portrayed by actors. It is set in a psychiatric clinic and was produced by Hans Strupp, Ph.D. It is available from Hans Strupp, Ph.D., Department of Psychology, 134 Wesley Hall, Vanderbilt University, Nashville, Tennessee 37240. It rents for $30.00 and is for unrestricted audiences. Sound and photography are excellent.

Psychodrama of a Marriage: 100 minutes (2 reels).

The problems of a young couple are portrayed in this demonstration of psychodrama. It was made in 1964, produced by J. L. Moreno, M.D., and rents for $30.00 to unrestricted audiences. Contact Beacon House Publishers, P. 0. Box 311, Beacon, New York 12508. Sound and photography are fair.

A Problem of Acceptance (Part of Psychodrama in Process Series): 47 minutes.

A 17-year-old girl's homosexual problem is explored in this condensation of a two-hour session on an adult inpatient unit in a psychiatric hospital. The film illustrates the technique of psychodrama very well. It was made in 1969 and produced by Ira Pauly, M.D. New York University Film Library, 26 Washington Place, New York, New York 10003, rents this film to professional audiences for $30.00. The sound and photography are good.

Gestalt Prayer: 24 minutes.

In this Gestalt demonstration group, married couples develop a basic statement on responsibility of people toward each other. It was produced by Frederick Perls, M.D. Rental is $26.00. Contact University of California Extension Media Center, 2223 Fulton Street, Berkeley, California 94720. Audience is unrestricted. Sound and photography are fair.

Awareness: 27 minutes.

Four volunteers are used by Frederick Perls, M.D., to demonstrate Gestalt method. The film rents for $27.00. Audience is unrestricted. Contact University of California Extension Media Center. Sound and photography are fair.

Freeing Yourself From Fears: 23 minutes.

A student workshop for problems in coping demonstrates the use of a repressive technique with late adolescents by a talented teacher-therapist. It was produced by Milton R. Cudney, Ph.D. The film rents for $25.00 and is available without restriction. Contact Educational Media Corporation, P. 0. Box 21311, Minneapolis, Minnesota 55421. The sound and photography are excellent.

Self Control: Learning to C.A.R.E. for Yourself: 29 minutes.

A group of college-age students are taught to apply four basic self-control strategies in this demonstration repressive group conducted by Carl Thoreson, Ph.D. It may be rented for $30.00 from Educational Media Corporation, and may be shown to unrestricted audiences. Excellent sound and photography.

Behavioral Group Counseling: 28 minutes.

Following a pre-group interview, Dr. Carl Thoreson demonstrates behavior techniques with a group of high school students. Educational Media Corporation rents this film for $30.00. It may be shown to general audiences. It has excellent sound and photography.

Adlerian Family Counseling: 35 minutes.

In this repressive group conducted in the Adlerian style by Oscar C. Christensen, Ed.D., a biracial family deals with its problems before a live audience and becomes aware of the interactions between family members. The film can be rented from Educational Media Corporation for $40.00, and may be shown to general audiences. Excellent sound and photography.

The Use of Video Replay in Group Psychotherapy: 31 minutes.

In this psychoanalytically oriented adult outpatient group, immediate video replay is used to stimulate insight. It was produced by Milton M. Berger, M.D. Rental is $95.00. It is restricted to professional audiences. Contact Health and Education Multimedia, Inc., Suite 4B, 50 East 172nd Street, New York, New York 10021. Sound and photography are fair to poor.

Videotape in Couple Group Therapy: 35 minutes.

An insight-oriented couples group in a private practice in which therapist Ian Alger, M.D., demonstrates alter ego role-playing. It rents for $50.00, and is for professional audiences. Contact IEA Productions, Inc., 520 E. 77th Street, New York, New York 10021.

Journey Into Self: 47 minutes.

While not a therapy group, this superbly edited condensation of a 16-hour adult marathon group shows many aspects of ego-supportive therapy. It was made by Carl Rogers, Ph.D., in 1968, and is available for $45.00 rental from Psychological Films, Inc., 110 N. Wheeler Street, Orange, California 92669. Audience is unrestricted. Photography and sound are excellent, but the film is wearing out.

Three Approaches to Group Therapy (A series)

In this series of three films, a different therapist works with a newly formed group of novice and experienced members for an hour and a half on three successive days. Approximately half of each session is shown.

Part 1: 30 minutes. Everett Shostrom, Ph.D., demonstrates his technique of Actualizing Therapy.

Part 2: 40 minutes. Albert Ellis, Ph.D., demonstrates the Rational-Emotive approach.

Part 3: 38 minutes. Harold Greenwald, Ph.D., uses Decision Therapy in dealing with the group.

Each film rents for $40.00 and is also available in videocassette. Audience is unrestricted. Contact Psychological Films, Inc.

Videotapes

Videotapes in Couples Group Therapy: 35 minutes.

(Three-quarter-inch videocassette or other video formats on request.) See film listing above for description. For sale only ($260.00). Contact IEA Productions, Inc.

Multiple Couple Therapy: 60 minutes.

(Three-quarter-inch videocassette or other video formats on request.) An adult couples group in private practice, showing selection of couples for the group and excerpts from first and sixth group session. Produced by H. James Lurie, M.D. For sale only ($285.00). For professional audience. Contact IEA Productions, Inc.

Video Replay in Group Psychotherapy: 50 minutes.

(Available on three-quarter-inch Umatic Videocassette, half-inch Betamax cassette, half-inch VHS cassette, or half-inch reel-to-reel.) Expanded session of *The Use of Video Replay in Group Psychotherapy* (see above). Rental is $95.00. Purchase price is $295.00. Contact Health and Education Multimedia, Inc.

Making Videotapes Yourself

For a relatively small investment, most practitioners and institutions can make videotapes that are adequate for teaching or supervision. A skillful leader can use a videotape camera himself or have a group member manage the camera (Berger 1970). However, one fixed camera with a wide angle lens is adequate to film a group of five to seven persons, and spares the therapist the task of manipulating equipment while conducting the session. If the camera is located near the ceiling in one corner of the room, the backs of group members do not obstruct the view of others' faces. If the tape deck and monitor are in the group treatment room, the group leader needs only to be certain that all members of the group can be seen on the monitor. He can then turn off the monitor, start the tape, and conduct the group. Although a recording device undoubtedly affects the material dealt with in the group, the teaching advantages of videotaping and its availability for replay to the group far outweigh any inhibitions of the group process that may occur.

A more flexible setup includes two fixed cameras with wide angle lenses installed near the ceiling at opposite ends of the room. Using a split screen device, both cameras can record simultaneously.

The best setup is a studio-type arrangement with a producer, a console, and two or more camera operators in the therapy room with the group. The camera operators move the cameras to follow the action and the producer determines which camera records at any time.

One table model omnidirectional microphone or two overhead microphones are usually adequate for sound recording. Unfortunately, omnidirectional microphones pick up hall noises and other extraneous sounds, so the room and the outside hall need to be carpeted (carpeting the walls helps, too), and the room should be adequately insulated from street noises. Individual lavalier microphones are the best means to obtain audio input, but they are cumbersome and require multiple audio leads into the recording equipment.

Edited tapes are not necessary for supervision, but editing is important for producing good quality teaching tapes. For supervision, it is useful to focus on brief segments of videotape for short periods of time. Playing prolonged segments tends to dull the senses of supervisor and trainee alike.

References and Bibliography

Adler A: The Individual Psychology of Alfred Adler. New York, Harper and Row, 1956

Alcoholics Anonymous: Alcoholics Anonymous. New York, Alcoholics Anonymous World Services, 1955

American Psychiatric Association: The principles of medical ethics with annotations especially applicable to psychiatry. Am J Psychiatry 130:1058–1064, 1973

American Psychiatric Association: Diagnostic and Statistical Manual of Mental Disorders, 3rd ed. Washington, DC, American Psychiatric Association, 1980

American Psychological Association: Standards for Providers of Psychological Services. Washington, DC, American Psychological Association, 1975

Anderson BN, Pine I, Mee-Lee D: Resident training in cotherapy groups. Int J Group Psychother 22:192–198, 1972

Ansbacher H, Ansbacher R: The Individual Psychology of Alfred Adler. New York, Basic Books, 1956

Anthony EJ: The history of group psychotherapy, in Comprehensive Group Psychotherapy. Edited by Kaplan HI, Sadock BJ. Baltimore, Williams and Wilkins, 1971, pp 4–31

Aronson ML, Furst HB, Krasner JD, Liff ZA: The impact of the death of a leader on a group process. Am J Psychother 16:460–468, 1962

Asch SE: Opinions and social pressure. Sci Am 193:31–35, 1955

Bach GR: Discussion of Stoller FH: Accelerated interactions: a time-limited approach based on the brief intensive group. Int J Group Psychother 18:244–249, 1968

Baker v United States, 226 F. Supp. 129 (S.D. Iowa 1964)

Bandura A: Psychotherapy based on modeling principles, in Handbook of Psychotherapy and Behavior Change. Edited by Bergin AE, Garfield SL. New York, John Wiley and Sons, 1971, pp 653–708

Barron F, Leary TF: Changes in psychoneurotic patients with and without psychotherapy. Journal of Consulting Psychology 19:239–245, 1955

Bateson G, Jackson DD, Weakland J, Haley J: Toward a theory of schizophrenia. Behav Sci 1:251–264, 1956

Beavers WR: Psychotherapy and Growth. New York, Brunner/Mazel, 1977

Beck AT: Cognitive Therapy and the Emotional Disorders. New York, International Universities Press, 1976

Beck AT, Rush AJ, Shaw BF, Emery G: Cognitive Therapy and Depression. New York, The Guilford Press, 1979

Bednar RL, Lawlis GF: Empirical research in group psychotherapy, in Handbook of Psychotherapy and Behavior Change. Edited by Bergin AE, Garfield SL. New York, John Wiley and Sons, 1971, pp 812–838

Bell AP, Weinberg MS: Homosexualities: A Study of Diversity Among Men and Women. New York, Simon and Schuster, 1978

Benjamin SE Jr: Cotherapy: a growth experience for therapists. Int J Group Psychother 22:199–209, 1972

Benne KD: History of the T group in the laboratory setting, in T-Group Theory and Laboratory Method. Edited by Bradford LP, Gibb JR, Benne KD. New York, John Wiley and Sons, 1964, pp 80–135

Ben Yehudah N: Group therapy with methadone-maintained patients: structural problems and solutions. Int J Group Psychother 30:331–345, 1980

Berger LF, Berger MM: A holistic approach to psychogeriatric outpatients. Int J Group Psychother 23:432–444, 1973

Berger MM: Nonverbal communications in group psychotherapy. Int J Group Psychother 2:161–179, 1958

Berger MM: The use of videotape in the integrated treatment of individuals, couples, families, and groups in private practice, in Videotape Techniques in Psychiatric Training and Treatment. Edited by Berger MM. New York, Brunner/Mazel, 1970, pp 119–160

Bergin AE: The evaluation of therapeutic outcomes, in The Handbook of Psychotherapy and Behavior Change. Edited by Bergin AE, Garfield SL. New York, John Wiley and Sons, 1971, pp 217–270

Berland DI, Poggi R: Expressive group psychotherapy with the aging. Int J Group Psychother 29:87–108, 1979

Berne E: Transactional analysis: a new and effective method of group therapy. Am J Psychother 12:735–743, 1958

Berne E: Transactional Analysis in Psychotherapy. New York, Grove Press, 1961

Berne E: Games People Play. New York, Grove Press, 1964

Berne E: Principles of Group Treatment. New York, Oxford University Press, 1966

Betcher RW, Rice CA, Weir DM: The regressed inpatient in a graded group treatment program. Am J Psychother 36:229–239, 1982

Bieber TB: Group therapy with homosexuals, in Comprehensive Group Psychotherapy. Edited by Kaplan HI, Sadock BJ. Baltimore, Williams and Wilkins, 1971, pp 518–533

Bierer J: Group psychotherapy. Br Med J 1:214–217, 1942

Bilodeau CB, Hackett TP: Issues raised in a group setting by patients recovering from myocardial infarction. Am J Psychiatry 128:105–109, 1971

Bindrim P: A report on a nude marathon. Psychotherapy Theory, Research, and Practice 5:180–188, 1968

Bion WR: Experiences in Groups. New York, Basic Books, 1959

Blocker KH, Jones RT, Stone GC, Pfefferbaum D: Chronic users of LSD: the "acidheads." Am J Psychiatry 125:341–351, 1966

Borriello J: Group therapy with acting-out patients: specific problems and techniques. Am J Psychother 33:521–530, 1979

Bradford LP, Gibb JR, Benne KD: T-Group Theory and Laboratory Method. New York, John Wiley and Sons, 1964

Brende JO: Continued individual and group therapy for Vietnam veterans. Int J Group Psychother 31:367–378, 1981

Brenner C: An Elementary Textbook of Psychoanalysis, revised and expanded ed. New York, International Universities Press, 1973

Budman SH, Bennett MJ, Wisneski MJ: An adult developmental model of short-term group psychotherapy, in Forms of Brief Therapy. Edited by Budman SH. New York, The Guilford Press, 1981, pp 305–342

Budman SH, Demby A, Randall M: Short-term group psychotherapy: who succeeds and who fails? Group 4:3–16, 1980

Burnside IM: Loss: a constant theme in group work with the aged. Hosp Community Psychiatry 21:173–177, 1970

Burrow T: The group method of analysis. Psychoanal Rev 14:268–280, 1927

Busse EW, Blazer D: The theories and processes of aging, in Handbook of Geriatric Psychiatry. Edited by Busse EW, Blazer D. New York, Van Nostrand Reinhold, 1980, pp 3–45

Butler RN: Age-ism: another form of bigotry. Gerontologist 9:243–246, 1969

Butler RN: Why Survive? Being Old in America. New York, Harper and Row, 1975

Caldwell T, Weiner MF: Stresses and coping in ICU nursing, I: a review. Gen Hosp Psychiatry 3:119–127, 1981

Casriel D: A Scream Away from Happiness. New York, Grossett and Dunlap, 1972

Claghorn JL, Johnstone EE, Cook TH, Itschner L: Group therapy and maintenance treatment of schizophrenics. Arch Gen Psychiatry 31:361–365, 1974

Cobb S, Rose RM: Hypertension, peptic ulcer and diabetes in air traffic controllers. JAMA 224:489–492, 1973

Cohen AI: The impact of the death of a group member on a therapy group. Int J Group Psychother 26:203–212, 1976

Cohen RJ: Malpractice: A Guide for Mental Health Professionals. New York, The Free Press, 1979

Committee on History: A brief history of the American Group Psychotherapy Association. Int J Group Psychother 21:406–435, 1971

Cowden RC, Zax M, Hague JR, Finney RL: Chlorpromazine: alone and as an adjunct to group psychotherapy in the treatment of psychiatric patients. Am J Psychiatry 112:898–902, 1956

Dahlberg CC: Sexual contact between patient and therapist. Journal of Contemporary Psychoanalysis 6:107–124, 1969

Daley BS, Koppenaal GS: The treatment of women in short-term women's groups, in Forms of Brief Therapy. Edited by Budman SH. New York, The Guilford Press, 1981, pp 343–356

Davis FB, Lohr NE: Special problems with the use of cotherapists in group psychotherapy. Int J Group Psychother 21:143–149, 1971

Densen-Gerber J: We Mainline Dreams: The Odyssey House Story. New York, Doubleday, 1973

Dies RR: Bridging the gap between research and practice in group psychotherapy, in Advances in Group Psychotherapy. Edited by Dies RR, MacKenzie KR. New York, International Universities Press, 1983, pp 1–27

Dodds ER: The Greeks and the Irrational. Berkeley, Calif, University of California Press, 1971

Doe v. Roe, 345 N.Y.S. 2d 560 (Sup Ct 1973)

Donovan JM, Bennett MJ, McElroy CM: The crisis group: its rationale, format, and outcome, in Forms of Brief Therapy. Edited by Budman SH. New York, The Guilford Press, 1981, pp 283–304

Doroff DR: Group psychotherapy in alcoholism, in The Biology of Alcoholism, vol 5: Treatment and Rehabilitation of the Chronic Alcoholic. Edited by Kessin B, Begleiter H. New York, Plenum, 1977

Dreikurs R: Group psychotherapy from the point of view of Adlerian psychology. Int J Group Psychother 7:363–375, 1957

Dumont MD: The death of the leader in a therapy group of schizophrenics. Int J Group Psychother 16:209–216, 1966

Durkin H: The Group in Depth. New York, International Universities Press, 1964

Durkin H, Glatzer HT, Kadis AL, Wolf A, Hulse WC: Acting out in group psychotherapy: a panel discussion. Am J Psychother 12:87–105, 1958

Dusay JM: A crown of gold (a cure for a stiff neck). Transactional Analysis Journal 2:96–100, 1972

Dusay JM: Transactional analysis in groups, in Comprehensive Group Psychotherapy. Edited by Kaplan HI, Sadock BJ. Baltimore, Williams and Wilkins, 1983, pp 95–101

Eaves v. United States, 407 F. 2d 823 (4th Cir. 1969)

Edelstein EL, Noy P: Open groups within a changing psychiatric ward in Israel. Int J Group Psychother 22:379–383, 1972

Edelwich J: Burn-Out: Stages of Disillusionment in the Helping Professions. New York, Human Sciences Press, 1980

Ellenberger HF: The evolution of depth psychology, in Historic Derivations of Modern Psychiatry. Edited by Galdston I. New York, McGraw-Hill, 1967, pp 159–184

Ellenberger HF: The Discovery of the Unconscious. New York, Basic Books, 1970

Ellis A: Rational-emotive group therapy, in Basic Approaches to Group Psychotherapy and Group Counseling. Edited by Gazda GM. Springfield, Ill, Charles C Thomas, 1975, pp 287–316

Erickson RC: Inpatient Small Group Psychotherapy. Springfield, Ill, Charles C Thomas, 1984

Erikson EH: Young Man Luther. New York, W. W. Norton, 1958

Ezriel H: A psychoanalytic approach to group treatment. Br J Med Psychol 23:59–74, 1950

Fagan J, Shepherd IL (eds): Gestalt Therapy Now. Palo Alto, Calif, Science and Behavior Books, 1970

Federn P: Ego Psychology and the Psychoses. New York, Basic Books, 1952

Feld B: The psychiatrist's liability for malpractice. Psychiatric Opinion 8:6–8, 1971

Fenichel O: The Psychoanalytic Theory of Neurosis. New York, W. W. Norton, 1945

Fink N: Medical malpractice: the liability of psychiatrists. Notre Dame Lawyer 48:693–708, 1972

Flowers JV: The differential outcome effects of simple advice, alternatives, and instructions in group psychotherapy. Int J Group Psychother 29:305–316, 1979

Foulkes SH: Therapeutic Group Analysis. New York, International Universities Press, 1964

Foulkes SH: Interpretation in group analysis. Int J Group Psychother 18:432–445, 1968

Foulkes SH, Anthony EJ: Group Psychotherapy. London, Penguin, 1957

Frank JD: Group therapy in the mental hospital, in Group Psychotherapy and Group Function. Edited by Rosenbaum M, Berger MM. New York, Basic Books, 1963, pp 453–468

Frank JD, Gliedman LH, Imber SD, Stone AR, Nash EH: Patients' expectancies and relearning as factors determining improvement in psychotherapy. Am J Psychiatry 115:961–968, 1959

Freedman AM: Opiate dependence, in Comprehensive Textbook of Psychiatry/III, vol 2. Edited by Kaplan HI, Freedman AM, Sadock BJ. Baltimore, Williams and Wilkins, 1980, pp 1591–1614

Freud A: The Ego and the Mechanisms of Defense. New York, International Universities Press, 1946

Freud S (1900): The Interpretation of Dreams. New York, Basic Books, 1960

Freud S (1920): Beyond the pleasure principle, in The Standard Edition of the Complete Psychological Works of Sigmund Freud, vol 18. Translated and edited by James Strachey. London, Hogarth Press, 1955, pp 3–66

Freud S (1921): Group psychology and the analysis of the ego, in The Standard Edition of the Complete Psychological Works of Sigmund Freud, vol 18. Translated and edited by James Strachey. London, Hogarth Press, 1955, pp 67–134

Freud S (1923): The ego and the id, in The Standard Edition of the Complete Psychological Works of Sigmund Freud, vol 19. Translated and edited by James Strachey. London, Hogarth Press, 1961, pp 3–68

Furst W: Homogeneous versus heterogeneous groups. Topical Problems of Psychotherapy 2:170–173, 1960

Gendzel IB: Marathon group therapy and nonverbal methods. Am J Psychiatry 127:286–290, 1970

Givelber F, Simon B: A death in the life of a therapist and its impact on therapy. Psychiatry 44:141–149, 1981

Gladfelter JH: Videotape supervision of co-therapists, in Videotape Techniques in Psychiatric Training and Treatment. Edited by Berger MM. New York, Brunner/Mazel, 1970, pp 74–82

Gladfelter JH: The liabilities of individual psychotherapy. Group Process 6:21–25, 1974

Glasser W: Reality Therapy. New York, Harper and Row, 1963

Glatzer HT: The relative effectiveness of clinically homogeneous vs. heterogeneous psychotherapy groups. Int J Group Psychother 3:258–265, 1956

Golembiewski RT, Blumberg A: Sensitivity Training and the Laboratory Approach. Itasca, NY, F. E. Peacock, 1970

Goulding RL, Goulding NM (eds): The Power is in the Patient: A TA/Gestalt Approach to Psychotherapy. San Francisco, TA Press, 1978

Granvold DK, Welch GJ: Structured short-term treatment of post-divorce adjustment. Int J Group Psychother 29:347–358, 1979

Greenson RR: The struggle against identification. J Am Psychoanal Assoc 2:200–217, 1954

Greenson RR: The working alliance and the transference neurosis. Psychoanal Q 34:155–181, 1965

Greenson RR: The Technique and Practice of Psychoanalysis. New York, International Universities Press, 1967

Grinspoon L, Bakalar JB Jr: Drug dependence and non-narcotic agents, in Comprehensive Textbook of Psychiatry/III, vol 2. Edited by Kaplan HI, Freedman AM, Sadock BJ. Baltimore, Williams and Wilkins, 1980, pp 1614–1628

Grobman J: Group Psychotherapy for Students and Teachers: A Selected Bibliography, 1946–1979. New York, Garland, 1981

Groesbeck CJ, Taylor B: The psychiatrist as wounded physician. Am J Psychoanal 37:131–139, 1977

Grotjahn M: Growth experiences in the leader, in The Leader in the Group. Edited by Liff Z. New York, Jason Aronson, 1975, pp 146–150

Grunebaum H, Kates W: Whom to refer for group psychotherapy. Am J Psychiatry 134:130–133, 1977

Gulledge AD: The psychological aftermath of a myocardial infarction, in Psychological Aspects of Myocardial Infarctions and Coronary Care. Edited by Gentry AD, Williams RB Jr. St. Louis, C. V. Mosby, 1975, pp 107–123

Hadden SB: Treatment of male homosexuals in groups. Int J Group Psychother 16:13–22, 1966

Haley J: Uncommon Therapy: The Psychiatric Techniques of Milton H. Erickson. New York, Ballantine, 1973

Hammer v. Rosen, 198 N.Y.S. 2d 65 (Ct. App. 1960)

Hartmann EL: Sleep, in Comprehensive Textbook of Psychiatry/III, vol 1. Edited by Kaplan HI, Freedman AM, Sadock BJ. Baltimore, Williams and Wilkins, 1980, pp 165–177

Heath ES, Bacal HA: A method of group therapy at the Tavistock Clinic. Int J Group Psychother 18:21–30, 1968

Heilman R: Combined treatment for addicts and alcoholics, in Drug Dependent Patients. Edited by Craig RJ, Baker SL. Springfield, Ill, Charles C Thomas, 1982, pp 153–164

Henisz JE: Psychotherapeutic Management in the Day Program. Springfield, Ill, Charles C Thomas, 1984

Hochman JS, Brill NQ: Chronic marijuana use and psychosocial adaptation. Am J Psychiatry 130:132–140, 1973

Hollon SD, Shaw BF: Group cognitive therapy for depressed patients, in Cognitive Therapy of Depression. Edited by Beck AT, Rush AJ, Shaw BF, Emery G. New York, The Guilford Press, 1979, pp 328–353

Horowitz MJ, Weisberg PS: Techniques for the psychotherapy of acute psychoses. Int J Group Psychother 16:42–50, 1966

How to begin a psychotherapy group: six approaches [entire issue]. Group Process 7:1–138, 1976

Hunt AD, Gladieux JD: Guidelines for leading an adolescent therapy group, in Group and Family Therapy: 1980. Edited by Wolberg L, Aronson M. New York, Jason Aronson, 1980, pp 151–164

Jacobson E: Contributions to the metapsychology of psychotic identification. J Am Psychoanal Assoc 2:239–262, 1954

Jaffe SL, Scherl DJ: Acute psychosis precipitated by T-group experiences. Arch Gen Psychiatry 21:443–448, 1969

Janov A: The Primal Scream. New York, Putnam, 1970

Jenkins CD: Recent evidence supporting psychological and social risk factors for coronary disease. N Engl J Med 294:1033–1038, 1976

Johnson JA: Group Therapy. New York, McGraw-Hill, 1963

Jones M: The Therapeutic Community. New York, Basic Books, 1953

Jung CG: Man and His Symbols, New York, Doubleday, 1964

Kadis AL, Krasner JD, Weiner MF, Winick C: Practicum of Group Psychotherapy, 2nd ed. New York, Harper and Row, 1974

Kane FJ, Wallace CD, Lipton MA: Emotional disturbances related to T-group experience. Am J Psychiatry 127:954–957, 1971

Kaplan HI, Sadock BJ (eds): Comprehensive Group Psychotherapy, 2nd ed. Baltimore, Williams and Wilkins, 1983

Kaplan HS: The New Sex Therapy. New York, Brunner/Mazel, 1974

Kaplan S: The "group dream." Int J Group Psychother 23:421–431, 1973

Karasu TB: Psychotherapy of the medically ill. Am J Psychiatry 136:1–11, 1979

Kaufman E: Group therapy for substance abusers, in Handbook of Group Therapy. Edited by Grotjahn M, Kline FM, Freedman CTH. New York, Van Nostrand Reinhold, 1983, pp 163–191

Kelley C: Assertion Training: A Facilitative Guide. La Jolla, Calif, University Associates, 1979

Kernberg O: Borderline Conditions and Pathological Narcissism. New York, Jason Aronson, 1975a

Kernberg O: A systems approach to priority setting in groups. Int J Group Psychother 25:251–276, 1975b

Kernberg OF, Burstein ED, Coyne L, et al: Psychotherapy and psychoanalysis: the final report of the Menninger Foundation's psychotherapy research project. Bull Menninger Clin 36:1–275, 1972

Kety SS: Genetic and biochemical aspects of schizophrenia, in The Harvard Guide to Modern Psychiatry. Edited by Nicholi AM. Cambridge, Mass, Belknap Press, 1978, pp 93–102

Khantzian E, Kates W: Group treatment of unwilling addicted patients: pragmatic and clinical aspects. Int J Group Psychother 28:89–94, 1978

Kibel HD: A group member's suicide: treating collective trauma. Int J Group Psychother 22:42–53, 1973

Kibel HD: A conceptual model for short-term inpatient group psychotherapy. Am J Psychiatry 138:74–80, 1981

Klapman JW: Group Psychotherapy, Theory, and Practice. New York, Grune and Stratton, 1946

Klapman JW: Group psychotherapy as a catalyst in mental hospital treatment. Int J Group Psychother 6:80–85, 1956

Klein-Lipshutz E: Comparison of dreams in individual and group psychotherapy. Int J Group Psychother 2:143–149, 1953

Klerman G: Affective disorders, in The Harvard Guide to Modern Psychiatry. Edited by Nicholi AM. Cambridge, Mass, Belknap Press, 1978, pp 253–280

Knapp PH: Current theoretical concepts in psychosomatic medicine, in Comprehensive Textbook of Psychiatry/III, vol 2. Edited by Kaplan HI, Freedman AM, Sadock BJ. Baltimore, Williams and Wilkins, 1980, pp 1853–1862

Knobloch F, Knobloch J: Integrated Psychotherapy. New York, Jason Aronson, 1979

Kohut H: The Analysis of the Self. New York, International Universities Press, 1971

Kohut H: The Restoration of the Self. New York, International Universities Press, 1977

Korn ER, Johnson K: Visualization: The Uses of Imagery in the Health Professions. Homewood, Ill, Dow Jones-Irwin, 1983

Kosseff JW: The leader using object-relations theory, in The Leader in the Group. Edited by Liff Z. New York, Jason Aronson, 1975, pp 212–242

Kovan RA: Resistance of a marathon facilitator to becoming an intimate member of the group. Psychosomatics 9:286–288, 1968

Kraft IA: Group therapy with children, in Comprehensive Textbook of Psychiatry/III, vol 3. Edited by Kaplan HI, Freedman AM, Sadock BJ. Baltimore, Williams and Wilkins, 1980, pp 2667–2678

Krasner JD: Analytic group psychotherapy with the aged, in The Challenge for Group Psychotherapy: Present and Future. Edited by de Schill S. New

York, International Universities Press, 1974, pp 316–357
Krystal H: Trauma and affects. Psychoanal Study Child 33:81–116, 1978
Kübler-Ross E, Anderson JR: Psychotherapy with the least expected: modified group therapy with blind clients. Rehabil Lit 29:73–76, 1968
Lacoursiere R: The Life Cycle of Groups. New York, Human Sciences Press, 1980
Lahmeyer H: Methadone maintenance, in Drug Dependent Patients. Edited by Craig RS, Baker SL. Springfield, Ill, Charles C Thomas, 1982, pp 37–66
Lambert MJ, Bergin AE, Collins JL: Therapist-induced deterioration in psychotherapy, in Effective Psychotherapy: A Handbook of Research. Edited by Gurman AS, Razin AM. New York, Pergamon, 1977, pp 452–481
Langs RJ: The Technique of Psychoanalytic Psychotherapy, vol 1. New York, Jason Aronson, 1973
Lazarus AA: Group therapy of phobic disorders by systematic desensitization. Journal of Abnormal and Social Psychology 63:504–510, 1961
Lazarus AA: Multimodal behavior therapy in groups, in Basic Approaches to Group Psychotherapy and Group Counseling, 2nd ed. Edited by Gazda GM. Springfield, Ill, Charles C Thomas, 1975, pp 150–174
Lazell EW: The group treatment of dementia praecox. Psychoanal Rev 8:168–179, 1921
Leopold HS: Selective group approaches with psychotic patients in hospital settings. Am J Psychother 30:95–102, 1976
Lesser IM: A review of the alexithymia concept. Psychosom Med 43:531–543, 1981
Lester v. Aetna Casualty and Surety Co., 240 F 2d 676 (5th Cir. 1957)
Levene HI, Patterson V, Murphey BG, Overbeck AL, Veach TL: The aftercare of schizophrenics: an evaluation of group and individual approaches. Psychiatr Q 44:296–304, 1970
Levine B, Poston M: A modified group treatment for elderly narcissistic patients. Int J Group Psychother 30:153–167, 1980
Levine CA, Dang JC: The group within the group: the dilemma of cotherapy. Int J Group Psychother 29:175–184, 1979
Lewin K: Field theory, in Social Science: Selected Theoretical Papers. Edited by Cartwright D. New York, Harper and Row, 1951
Lewis JM, Beavers WR, Gossett JT, Phillips VA: No Single Thread: Psychological Health in Family Systems. New York, Brunner/Mazel, 1976
Lieberman MA, Yalom ID, Miles MB: Encounter Groups: First Facts. New York, Basic Books, 1973
Liff Z: Impasse: interpersonal, intergroup, and international. Group Process 3:7–30, 1970
Liff Z: The charismatic leader, in The Leader in the Group. Edited by Liff Z. New York, Jason Aronson, 1975, pp 114–122
Lion JR, Christopher R, Madden DJ: A group approach with violent outpatients. Int J Group Psychother 27:67–75, 1977
Lipschutz DM: Combined group and individual psychotherapy. Am J Psychother 11:336–344, 1957

Locke N: The use of dreams in group psychoanalysis. Am J Psychother 11:98–110, 1957

Lonergan EC: Group Interventions: How to Begin and Maintain Groups in Medical and Psychiatric Settings. New York, Jason Aronson, 1982

Lothstein LM: The group psychotherapy dropout phenomenon revisited. Am J Psychiatry 135:1492–1495, 1978

Low AA: Mental Health Through Will Training. Boston, Christopher Publishing, 1952

Lowenson J, Zwerling I: Group therapy with narcotic addicts, in Comprehensive Group Psychotherapy. Edited by Kaplan HI, Sadock BJ. Baltimore, Williams and Wilkins, 1971, pp 602–622

Luborsky L: Clinicians' judgments of mental health. Arch Gen Psychiatry 7:407–417, 1962

McCarty GJ: The leader using audiovisual methods, in The Leader in the Group. Edited by Liff Z. New York, Jason Aronson, 1975, pp 187–202

McCourt WF, Barnett RD, Brennan J, Becker A: We find each other: primary prevention for the widowed. Am J Psychiatry 133:98–100, 1976

McGee TF: Therapist termination in group psychotherapy. Int J Group Psychother 24:3–12, 1974

McGee TF, Schuman BN: The nature of the cotherapy relationship. Int J Group Psychother 20:25–36, 1970

MacKenzie KR, Dies RR: The CORE Battery. New York, American Group Psychotherapy Association, 1982

McLean P: Behavioral therapy theory and research, in Short-Term Psychotherapies for Depression. Edited by Rush AJ. New York, The Guilford Press, 1982, pp 19–49

Mahler MS: The Selected Papers of Margaret S. Mahler, M.D., vol 2: Separation-Individuation. New York, Jason Aronson, 1979

Malan DH, Balfour FHG, Hood VG, Shooter AMN: Group psychotherapy: a long-term follow-up study. Arch Gen Psychiatry 33:1303–1315, 1976

Mann J: Some theoretic concepts of the group process. Int J Group Psychother 5:235–241, 1955

Marrow AJ: The Practical Theorist: The Life and Work of Kurt Lewin. New York, Basic Books, 1969

Marsh LC: Group treatment of the psychoses by the psychological equivalent of the revival. Ment Hygiene 15:328–348, 1931

Masters WH, Johnson V: Human Sexual Inadequacy. Boston, Little, Brown, and Co., 1970

Maxmen JS: Group therapy as viewed by hospitalized patients. Arch Gen Psychiatry 28:404–408, 1973

Maxmen JS: An educative model for inpatient group therapy. Int J Group Psychother 28:321–338, 1978

Melson SJ, Rynearson ER, Dorzbach J, Clark RD Jr, Snyder AC: Short-term intensive group psychotherapy for patients with functional complaints. Psychosomatics 23:689–695, 1982

Meltzoff J, Kornreich M: Research in Psychotherapy. New York, Atherton, 1970

Mintz EE: Marathon Groups: Reality and Symbol. New York, Appleton-Century-Crofts, 1971

Mitchell KM, Bozarth JD, Krauft CC: A reappraisal of the therapeutic effectiveness of accurate empathy, nonpossessive warmth, and genuineness, in Effective Psychotherapy: A Handbook of Research. Edited by Gurman AS, Razin AM. New York, Pergamon, 1977, pp 482–502

Modzierz G, Machitelli F, Lisiecke J: The paradox in psychotherapy: an Adlerian perspective. J Individ Psychol 32:169–184, 1976

Mohl PC: Group process interpretation in liaison psychiatry nurse groups. Gen Hosp Psychiatry 2:104–111, 1980

Mora G: History of psychiatry, in Comprehensive Textbook of Psychiatry. Edited by Freedman AM, Kaplan HI. Baltimore, Williams and Wilkins, 1967, pp 2–34

Moreno JL: Psychodrama, in American Handbook of Psychiatry. vol 2. Edited by Arieti S. New York, Basic Books, 1959, pp 1375–1396

Moreno JL: Psychodrama, in Comprehensive Group Psychotherapy. Edited by Kaplan HI, Sadock BJ. Baltimore, Williams and Wilkins, 1971, pp 460–500

Mullan H, Sangiuliano J: Alcoholism: Group Psychotherapy and Rehabilitation. Springfield, Ill, Charles C Thomas, 1966

Naccarato v. Grob, 180 N.W. 2nd 788 (Sup. Ct. Mich. 1970)

Nobler H: A peer group for therapists: successful experience in sharing. Int J Group Psychother 30:51–61, 1980

O'Brien CP, Hamm KB, Ray BA, Pierce JF, Luborsky L, Mintz J: Group versus individual psychotherapy with schizophrenics. Arch Gen Psychiatry 27:474–478, 1972

Oehler-Giarratana J, Fitzgerald RG: Group therapy with blind diabetics. Arch Gen Psychiatry 37:463–467, 1980

Ormont L: Group resistance and the therapeutic contract. Int J Group Psychother 18:147–154, 1968

Ormont L: Acting in and the therapeutic contract in group psychotherapy. Int J Group Psychother 19:420–432, 1969

Parloff MB, Dies RR: Group therapy outcome research 1966–1975. Int J Group Psychother 27:281–320, 1977

Pattison EM, Brissenden A, Wohl T: Assessing specific effects of inpatient group psychotherapy. Int J Group Psychother 17:283–297, 1967

Peck RE: Comparison of adjunct group therapy with individual psychotherapy. Archives of Neurology and Psychiatry 62:173–177, 1949

Perls FS: Gestalt Therapy Verbatim. Lafayette, Calif, Real People Press, 1969

Perls FS, Hefferline RF, Goodman P: Gestalt Therapy. New York, Dell Books, 1951

Peters JJ, Pedigo JM, Steg J, McKenna JJ Jr: Group psychotherapy of the sex offender. Federal Probation 32:41–45, 1968

Pierce RA, Nichols MP, DuBrin JR: Emotional Expression in Psychotherapy. New York, Gardner Press, 1983

Polster E, Polster M: Gestalt Therapy Integrated. New York, Brunner/Mazel, 1973

Pope KS, Simpson NH, Weiner MF: Malpractice in outpatient psychotherapy. Am J Psychother 32:593–601, 1978

Powers HP, Acosta-Rua MV, Vornbrook RP: Terminating an open-ended therapy group. Group Process 6:115–123, 1974

Pratt JH: The principles of class treatment and their application to various chronic diseases. Hospital Social Service 6:404, 1922

Pratt JH (1917): The tuberculosis class: an experiment in home treatment, in Group Psychotherapy and Group Function. Edited by Rosenbaum M, Berger M. New York, Basic Books, 1963, pp 111–122

Rachman AW: Marathon group psychotherapy: its origins, significance, and direction. Journal of Group Psychoanalytic Process 2:57–74, 1969

Racker H: The meanings and uses of countertransference. Psychoanal Q 26:303–357, 1957

Rahe RH, Mahan JL Jr, Arthur RJ: Prediction of near-future health change from subjects' preceding life changes. J Psychosom Res 14:401–406, 1970

Rahe RH, Ward HW, Hayes V: Brief group therapy in myocardial infarction rehabilitation. Psychosom Med 41:229–242, 1979

Razin AM: The A-B variable: still promising after twenty years? in Effective Psychotherapy: A Handbook of Research. Edited by Gurman AS, Razin AM. New York, Pergamon, 1977, pp 291–324

Reiser MF: Changing theoretical concepts in psychosomatic medicine, in American Handbook of Psychiatry, 2nd ed, vol 4. Edited by Arieti S. New York, Basic Books, 1975, pp 477–500

Rhinehart L: The Book of EST. New York, Holt, Rinehart, and Winston, 1976

Richmond AH, Slagle S: Some notes on the inhibition of aggression in an inpatient psychotherapy group. Int J Group Psychother 21:333–338, 1971

Roback HB, Abramowitz SI, Strassberg DS: Group Psychotherapy Research: Commentaries and Selected Readings. Huntington, NY, Krieger, 1979

Rodman FR: Not Dying. New York, Random House, 1977

Rogers CR: The necessary and sufficient conditions of therapeutic personality change. Journal of Consulting Psychology 21:95–103, 1957

Rogers CR: On Becoming a Person. Boston, Houghton Mifflin, 1961

Rogers CR: The process of the basic encounter group, in Challenges of Humanistic Psychology. Edited by Bugental JFT. New York, McGraw-Hill, 1967

Rosen A, Spitz HI: The role of videotape in group psychotherapy with psychotic patient populations. Group 3:213–228, 1979

Rosenbaum M: Co-therapy, in Comprehensive Group Psychotherapy. Edited by Kaplan HI, Sadock BJ. Baltimore, Williams and Wilkins, 1971, pp 501–517

Rosenbaum M: The psychoanalytic group: formation and beginnings. Group Process 7:9–35, 1976

Rosenbaum M, Berger M: Group Psychotherapy and Group Function. New York, Basic Books, 1963

Rosenthal P: The death of the leader in group psychotherapy. Am J Orthopsychiatry 17:266–277, 1947

Roth P, Covi L: Cognitive group psychotherapy of depression: the open-ended group. Int J Group Psychother 34:67–82, 1984

Rothblatt HB, Leroy DH: Avoiding psychiatric malpractice. California Western Law Review 9:260–272, 1973

Rush AJ, Beck AT, Kovacs M, Hollon S: Comparative efficacy of cognitive therapy and imipramine in the treatment of depressed outpatients. Cognitive Therapy and Research 1:17–37, 1977

Rush AJ, Giles DE: Cognitive therapy: theory and research, in Short-Term Psychotherapies for Depression. Edited by Rush AJ. New York, The Guilford Press, 1982, pp 143–181

Sabin JE: Short-term group psychotherapy: historical antecedents, in Focus of Brief Therapy. Edited by Budman SH. New York, The Guilford Press, 1981, pp 271–281

Sadock BJ: Group psychotherapy, combined individual and group psychotherapy, and psychodrama, in Comprehensive Textbook of Psychiatry/III, vol 3. Edited by Kaplan HI, Freedman AM, Sadock BJ. Baltimore, Williams and Wilkins, 1980, pp 2178–2217

Sadock VA: Rape, in Comprehensive Textbook of Psychiatry/III, vol 2. Edited by Kaplan HI, Freedman AM, Sadock BJ. Baltimore, Williams and Wilkins, 1980, pp 1803–1805

Sadock VA: Group psychotherapy with rape victims and battered women, in Comprehensive Group Psychotherapy, 2nd ed. Edited by Kaplan HI, Sadock BJ. Baltimore, Williams and Wilkins, 1983, pp 282–285

Samuels AS: Use of group balance as a therapeutic technique. Arch Gen Psychiatry 11:411–420, 1964

Saretsky T: After the marathon: re-entry problems of patients returning to their ongoing therapy groups. Group Process 4:91–100, 1972

Saretsky T: The analyst's narcissistic vulnerability: its effect on the treatment situation. Contemporary Psychoanalysis 16:82–89, 1980

Saul SR, Saul S: Group psychotherapy in a proprietary nursing home. Gerontologist 14:446–450, 1974

Scheidlinger S: Psychoanalysis and Group Behavior. New York, W. W. Norton, 1952

Scher M: Observation in an aftercare group. Int J Group Psychother 23:322–337, 1973

Schilder P: Results and problems of group psychotherapy in severe neuroses. Mental Hygiene 23:87–98, 1939

Schimel JL: Some thoughts on the rise of wit and humor in the treatment of adolescents. New Directions for Mental Health Services 5:15–23, 1980

Schorr JE: Psychotherapy Through Imagery. New York, Intercontinental Medicinal Book Corp., 1974

Schutz W: Joy. New York, Grove Press, 1967

Schwitzgebel RK: Legal Aspects of the Enforced Treatment of Offenders. Rockville, Md, U.S. Department of Health, Education, and Welfare, 1979

Sealy v. Finkelstein, 206 N.Y.S. 2d 512 (Sup. Ct. 1960)

Shatton SP, DeCamp L, Fujii E, Fross GG, Wolff RJ: Group treatment of conditionally discharged patients in a mental health clinic. Am J Psychiatry 123:798–804, 1966

Sherif M: The Psychology of Social Norms. New York, Harper, 1936

Shuman DW, Weiner MF: The privilege study: an empirical examination of the psychotherapist-patient privilege. North Carolina Law Review 60:893–942, 1982

Sifneos PE: Problems of psychotherapy in patients with alexithymic characteristics and physical disease. Psychother Psychosom 26:65–70, 1975

Simon NM, Whiteley S: Psychiatric consultation with MICU nurses: the consultation conference as a working group. Heart and Lung 6:497–504, 1977

Singer E: The patient aids the analyst: some clinical and theoretical observations, in The Name of Life: Essays in Honor of Erich Fromm. Edited by Landis E, Tauber E. New York, Holt, Rinehart, and Winston, 1970, pp 56–68

Singer JL: Imagery and Daydream Methods in Psychotherapy and Behavior Modification. New York, Academic Press, 1974

Singer JL, Pope KS: The use of imagery and fantasy techniques in psychotherapy, in The Power of the Human Imagination. Edited by Singer JL, Pope KS. New York, Plenum, 1978, pp 3–34

Slavson SR: A Textbook in Analytic Group Psychotherapy. New York, International Universities Press, 1964

Snowden EL: Mass psychotherapy. Lancet 2:769–770, 1940

Spotnitz H: The borderline schizophrenic in group psychotherapy. Int J Group Psychother 7:155–174, 1957

Spotnitz H: The Couch and the Circle. New York, Knopf, 1961

Stampfl TG, Leaves DJ: Essentials of implosive therapy: a learning theory based on psychodynamic behavioral therapy. J Abnorm Psychol 72:496–503, 1967

Stanton M: Strategic approaches to family therapy, in Handbook of Family Therapy. Edited by Gurman AS, Kniskern DP. New York, Brunner/Mazel, 1981

Stein A, Hulse WC, Lulow WV, Kauffman MR: Group psychotherapy on the psychiatric ward of a general hospital. Journal of Mt. Sinai Hospital 22:104–111, 1955

Stieper DR, Wiener DN: The problem of interminability in outpatient psychotherapy. Journal of Consulting Psychology 23:237–242, 1959

Stoller FH: Accelerated interaction: a time-limited approach based on the brief intensive group. Int J Group Psychother 18:220–235, 1968

Stone WN, Whitman RM: Contributions of the psychology of the self to group process and group therapy. Int J Group Psychother 27:343–360, 1977

Stone WN, Rutan JS: Duration of treatment in group psychotherapy. Int J Group Psychother 34:93–110, 1984

Strupp HH: Toward a specification of teaching and learning in psychotherapy. Arch Gen Psychiatry 21:203–212, 1969

Strupp HH: Success and failure in time-limited psychotherapy. Arch Gen Psychiatry 37:595–603, 1980

Stunkard AJ: Obesity, in Comprehensive Textbook of Psychiatry/III, vol 2. Edited by Kaplan HI, Freedman AM, Sadock BJ. Baltimore, Williams and Wilkins, 1980, pp 1872–1882

Sullivan HS: The Interpersonal Theory of Psychiatry. New York, W. W. Norton, 1953

Tarasoff v. Regents of the University of California, 551 P. 2d 334 at 347 (Sup. Ct. Cal. 1976)

Thorley AS, Craske N: Comparison and estimate of group and individual methods of treatment. Br Med J 1:97–100, 1950

Tolpin M: Corrective emotional experience, in The Future of Psychoanalysis. Edited by Goldberg A. New York, International Universities Press, 1983, pp 363–379

Trent CL, Muhl WP: Professional liability insurance and the American psychiatrist. Am J Psychiatry 132:1312–1314, 1975

Truax CB, Carkhuff RR, Rodman F, Moles EA: Changes in self-concept during group psychotherapy as a function of alternate sessions and vicarious therapy pretraining in institutionalized mental patients and juvenile delinquents. Journal of Consulting Psychology 30:309–314, 1966

Truax CB, Mitchell KM: Research in certain therapist interpersonal skills in relation to process and outcome, in Handbook of Psychotherapy and Behavior Change: An Empirical Analysis. Edited by Bergin AE, Garfield SL. New York, John Wiley and Sons, 1971, pp 299–344

Vaccarino JM: Malpractice: the problem in perspective. JAMA 238:861–863, 1977

Vaillant GE: Adaptation to Life. Boston, Little, Brown, 1977

Vaillant GE: Dangers of psychotherapy in the treatment of alcoholism, in Dynamic Approaches to the Understanding and Treatment of Alcoholism. Edited by Bean MH, Zinberg NE. New York, The Free Press, 1981, pp 36–54

Wachtel AB: Videotape and group psychotherapy, in Comprehensive Group Psychotherapy, 2nd ed. Edited by Kaplan HI, Sadock BJ. Baltimore, Williams and Wilkins, 1983, pp 173–176

Walker JI, Nash JL: Group therapy in the treatment of Vietnam combat veterans. Int J Group Psychother 31:379–390, 1981

Watzlawick P, Weakland J, Fisch R: Change: Principles of Problem Formation and Problem Resolution. New York, W. W. Norton, 1974

Weeks GR, L'Abate L: Paradoxical Psychotherapy: Theory and Practice with Couples, Individuals, and Families. New York, Brunner/Mazel, 1982

Weiner MF: In defense of the therapist. Psychosomatics 10:156–158, 1969

Weiner MF: Levels of intervention in group psychotherapy. Group Process 3:67–81, 1970

Weiner MF: Levels of intervention in group psychotherapy. Journal of Group Process 3:67–81, 1971

Weiner MF: Termination of group psychotherapy. Group Process 5:85–96, 1973

Weiner MF: Genetic versus interpersonal insight. Int J Group Psychother 24:230–237, 1974a

Weiner MF: The psychotherapeutic impasse. Diseases of the Nervous System 35:259–261, 1974b

Weiner MF: Catharsis: a review. Group Process 7:173–184, 1977

Weiner MF: Healthy and pathological love, in On Love and Loving. Edited by Pope KS. San Francisco, Jossey-Bass, 1980, pp 114–132

Weiner MF: Contracts in psychotherapy. Journal of Psychiatric Treatment and Evaluation 3:127–131, 1981a

Weiner MF: Regression in group psychotherapy: a negative view. Unpublished paper presented at the 38th Annual Meeting of the American Group Psychotherapy Association, held in Houston on February 12, 1981b

Weiner MF: The Psychotherapeutic Impasse. New York, The Free Press, 1982a

Weiner MF: Identification in psychotherapy. Am J Psychother 36:109–116, 1982b

Weiner MF: Therapist Disclosure, 2nd ed. Baltimore, University Park Press, 1983a

Weiner MF: The assessment and resolution of impasse in group psychotherapy. Int J Group Psychother 33:317–336, 1983b

Weiner MF: The role of the leader, in Comprehensive Group Psychotherapy, 2nd ed. Edited by Kaplan HI, Sadock BJ. Baltimore, Williams and Wilkins, 1983c, pp 54–63

Weiner MF: Outcome of psychoanalytically oriented group psychotherapy. Group 8:3–12, 1984

Weiner MF, Caldwell T: Stresses and coping in ICU nursing, II: nurse support groups on intensive care units. Gen Hosp Psychiatry 3:129–134, 1981

Weiner MF, Caldwell T: The process and impact of an ICU nurse support group. Int J Psychiatry Med 13:47–55, 1983

Weiner MF, Caldwell T, Tyson J: Stresses and coping in ICU nursing: why support groups fail. Gen Hosp Psychiatry 5:179–183, 1983

Weinstock A: Group treatment of characterologically damaged, developmentally disabled adolescents in a residential treatment center. Int J Group Psychother 29:369–381, 1979

Wells CD: Dementia, 2nd ed. Philadelphia, F. A. Davis, 1977

Wender L: The dynamics of group psychotherapy and its application. J Nerv Ment Dis 84:54–60, 1936

Whitehorn JC, Betz BA: A study of psychotherapeutic relationships between physicians and schizophrenic patients. Am J Psychiatry 111:321–331, 1954

Whiteley JS, Gordon J: Group Approaches in Psychiatry, London, Routledge and Kegan Paul, 1979

Whitman RM: Dreams about the group: an approach to the problem of group psychology. Int J Group Psychother 23:408–420, 1973

Whitree v. State, 290 N.Y.S. 2nd 486 (Ct. Cl. 1968)

Williams W: The society of Alcoholics Anonymous. Am J Psychiatry 106:370–375, 1949

Wilmer HA: What do you say when a patient tells you a dream? Tex Med 78:46–48, 1982

Wolf A: The psychoanalysis of groups. Am J Psychother 3:525–558, 1949

Wolf A: Sexual acting out in the psychoanalysis of groups. Int J Group Psychother 4:368–380, 1954

Wolf A: Psychoanalysis in groups, in Comprehensive Group Psychotherapy, 2nd ed. Edited by Kaplan HI, Sadock BJ. Baltimore, Williams and Wilkins, 1983, pp 113–181

Wolf A, Schwartz EK: Psychoanalysis in groups: the role of values. Am J Psychoanal 19:38–51, 1959

Wolf A, Schwartz EK, McCarty G, Goldberg I: Beyond the Couch: Dialogues on Teaching and Learning Psychoanalysis in Groups. New York, Jason Aronson, 1970

Wong N: Combined group and individual treatment of borderline and narcissistic patients: heterogeneous versus homogeneous groups. Int J Group Psychother 30:389–404, 1980

Wong N: Combined individual and group psychotherapy, in Comprehensive Group Psychotherapy, 2nd ed. Edited by Kaplan HI, Sadock BJ. Baltimore, Williams and Wilkins, 1983, pp 73–82

Woods v. Brumlop, 377 P. 2d 520 (Sup. Ct. N.M. 1962)

Yablonsky L: Synanon: The Tunnel Back. New York, Penguin, 1967

Yalom ID: A study of group therapy dropouts. Arch Gen Psychiatry 14:393–414, 1966

Yalom ID: The Theory and Practice of Group Psychotherapy. New York, Basic Books, 1975

Yalom ID: Existential Psychotherapy. New York, Basic Books, 1980

Yalom ID: Inpatient Group Psychotherapy. New York, Basic Books, 1983

Yalom ID, Greaves C: Group therapy with the terminally ill. Am J Psychiatry 134:396–400, 1977

Yalom ID, Lieberman MA: A study of encounter group casualties. Arch Gen Psychiatry 25:16–30, 1971

Yalom ID, Rand K: Compatibility and cohesiveness in therapy groups. Arch Gen Psychiatry 13:267–276, 1966

Zarcone V Jr: Residential treatment for drug dependence, in Drug Dependent Patients. Edited by Craig RJ, Baker SL. Springfield, Ill, Charles C Thomas, 1981, pp 67–90

Zilboorg G: A History of Medical Psychology. New York, W. W. Norton, 1941

Zipkin v. Freeman, 436 S.W. 2d 753 (Miss. Ct. 1968)

Index

DATE DUE

FEB 20 '86			
NOV 05 '86			
MAR 14 1990			
MAY 10 1991			
DE 14 '99			